Lab Reports and Projects in Sport and Exercise Science

WITHDRAWN

2 5 MAR 2023

Most science degrees will have a practical or laboratory-based component which will require some sort of final report, whether this be a conventional laboratory report or a final-year dissertation. All of these formats require students to be able to analyse their data in an appropriate way and subsequently convey their key thoughts and information to a third party. Therefore, writing laboratory reports is an essential part of any science degree.

This new revised edition sees the expansion of statistical examples including initial data checks and assumptions, increased awareness of critical appraisal tools and resources, project planning and a range of 'Challenge yourself' activities to supplement understanding and provides a comprehensive overview of what should be contained within each section of a scientific report, and clearly explains how it should be presented. Written in a friendly and engaging style, it guides the reader through abstracts, literature reviews, methodology, reporting discussions and referencing and contains a wealth of examples and practical advice on how to improve and refine your own writing. From writing a first lab report to preparing a final-year dissertation or postgraduate thesis, sports and exercise science students at all levels will find this book a valuable resource in developing both skill and confidence in scientific communication.

Key features include:

- The layout of the book is designed to reflect that of a typical scientific report to help students plan their own projects.
- Each chapter includes numerous examples, exercises and activities to engage students and develop their skills in each aspect of report writing.
- The book includes discussion of critical appraisal techniques to help students refine their research questions.
- All data sets and illustrations used are drawn from the key disciplines in sport and exercise science, including physiology, psychology and biomechanics.

Mike Price, PhD, is Reader in Exercise Physiology at Coventry University. He has taught exercise physiology and research methods at undergraduate and postgraduate levels for o␣␣␣␣20 years and supervised␣␣␣␣␣rous postgraduate research students. He a␣␣␣␣␣␣an external examiner␣␣␣␣␣␣ught courses and PhD examinations and r␣␣␣␣␣␣␣␣␣␣␣␣␣␣␣␣sport and exercise science.

D1323493

WITHDRAWN

1 5 MAR 2023

Lab Reports and Projects in Sport and Exercise Science
A Guide for Students

Second Edition

Mike Price

YORK ST. JOHN
LIBRARY & INFORMATION
SERVICES

Routledge
Taylor & Francis Group

LONDON AND NEW YORK

Cover image: © SolStock / Getty images

Second edition published 2022
by Routledge
2 Park Square, Milton Park, Abingdon, Oxon, OX14 4RN

and by Routledge
605 Third Avenue, New York, NY 10158

Routledge is an imprint of the Taylor & Francis Group, an informa business

© 2022 Mike Price

The right of Mike Price to be identified as author of this work has been
asserted in accordance with sections 77 and 78 of the Copyright, Designs
and Patents Act 1988.

All rights reserved. No part of this book may be reprinted or reproduced
or utilised in any form or by any electronic, mechanical, or other
means, now known or hereafter invented, including photocopying and
recording, or in any information storage or retrieval system, without
permission in writing from the publishers.

Trademark notice: Product or corporate names may be trademarks
or registered trademarks and are used only for identification and
explanation without intent to infringe.

First edition published by Routledge 2013

Library of Congress Cataloging-in-Publication Data
Names: Price, Mike, 1971– author.
Title: Lab reports and projects in sport and exercise science : a guide for
  students / Mike Price.
Description: Second edition. | New York, NY : Routledge, 2022. |
  Includes bibliographical references and index.
Identifiers: LCCN 2021045865 (print) | LCCN 2021045866 (ebook) |
  ISBN 9780367631826 (hardback) | ISBN 9780367631819 (paperback) |
  ISBN 9781003112426 (ebook)
Subjects: LCSH: Sports sciences—Study and teaching. | Exercise—Study and
  teaching. | Educational reports—Study and teaching.
Classification: LCC GV558 .P75 2022 (print) | LCC GV558 (ebook) |
  DDC 613.71—dc23
LC record available at https://lccn.loc.gov/2021045865
LC ebook record available at https://lccn.loc.gov/2021045866

ISBN: 978-0-367-63182-6 (hbk)
ISBN: 978-0-367-63181-9 (pbk)
ISBN: 978-1-003-11242-6 (ebk)

DOI: 10.4324/9781003112426

Typeset in Times
by Apex CoVantage, LLC

For my girls Kerri and Lilly, and my boy Harry

Contents

Figures

Tables

Introduction

I.1 Background to second edition

After completing the first edition of 'Lab reports' I was just hopeful that readers would be receptive to my take on writing and experience of setting and assessing lab reports and projects over the years. At that time, I hadn't considered the possibility of a second edition (why would I?), very much a case of 'job done'. So, a few years later when I was approached to consider a second edition, I was delighted.

The new challenge was then what to change or add to the text.

As the text essentially covers key skills of scientific writing and data presentation and analysis, there were no specific developments regarding research theories as maybe expected for more subject or discipline specific texts such as those for exercise physiology, psychology, biomechanics or nutrition – statisticians forgive my naivety. Therefore, my take on developments for the new edition related more to general considerations of each stage of writing a lab report. For example, there has been a greater presence of undertaking systematic reviews in undergraduate and postgraduate study than in previous years – particularly due to the COVID-19 pandemic, which 'posed an enormous challenge for conducting student research' (Elmer and Durocher, 2020). Thus, a greater awareness of systematic (and other) reviews, their critical appraisal process and assessment of bias were timely. Indeed, reading around the area to determine updates for each chapter resulted in development of text for aspects I wouldn't have ordinarily considered. For example, the greater importance of key words and the development of search engine optimisation as a field in its own right was enlightening. However, the key point here is an awareness of such factors and their application so as not to detract from the books' philosophy and specific focus within sport and exercise science.

The main additions to the text have been within the 'Results' chapter. Having continued to teach a considerable number of research methods classes since the first edition, I felt that the general (and purposively so) approach in some areas needed expansion. Reflecting on the various undergraduate and postgraduate sessions I had taught suggested a review of underpinning

DOI: 10.4324/9781003112426-1

assumptions was required within the chapter to try and help truly understand each data set. In addition, the more sophisticated tests such as factorial ANOVA needed to reflect the wider range of research designs commonly undertaken in sport and exercise science along with addition of Bland–Altman analysis for repeatability – which is now firmly embedded within sport and exercise science practices. As with the first edition, care has been taken to ensure that this new edition is in no way a statistics text but maintains the focus on understanding, interpretating and reporting results. For those students who are confident and competent with the various components of report writing, there are suggestions to facilitate a greater level of understanding with 'Challenge yourself' activities.

Finally, there was an opportunity to update references – such as the International Committee of Medical Journal Editors guidance from 1997 to 2019 as well as a smaller number of more subject-specific sources and address those niggling typos that got through the original editing process that readers either didn't notice or were just too polite to tell me about!

So, thank you to everyone who at least opened the cover and at best found the first edition useful. You have afforded me my own critical appraisal opportunity and writing challenge. I hope you find the second edition of use.

I.2 Background to this book, the first edition

The idea for this book was born one academic year when I was marking a large pile of physiology lab reports. In amongst the range of marks awarded from first class down to those just warranting a pass, I found myself consistently commenting upon a range of points including errors of general report formatting, presentation of data and scientific wording. In addition, some students appeared unsure of what to include in each section of the report as well as how to adequately present and explain their results. This was also true for some students tackling their final-year project. Even though all of the students had been provided with the appropriate guidance as to what was required in writing laboratory reports, there was still a general underlying lack of report writing skills. Although writing is a skill that develops through practice and takes time to master, it was clear that having a recommended text relating specifically to writing lab reports would certainly be useful. This would certainly be useful for students if it could pre-empt a considerable amount of the generic comments I was writing. Consequently, as a result of developing various tutorials, practical exercises and coursework assessments to try and improve general laboratory writing skills it seemed reasonable to try and put them all together in one volume.

Initially, this book was intended to focus primarily upon undergraduate laboratory reports in exercise physiology. However, a logical extension of this concept was to focus upon sport and exercise science more widely and also to focus upon writing undergraduate project dissertations. Postgraduate students embarking upon their research journeys in the form of MSc and

PhD degrees may also find it useful. All of the expected outputs from such endeavours have similar underlying research processes requiring clear reporting and explanation of the data collected. This book is certainly not intended to be a replacement for any of the excellent statistics or research design textbooks currently used alongside undergraduate curricula but simply used to provide guidance towards writing up scientific findings.

Throughout this book, it is also not the author's intention to state what is right or wrong but to give guidance to the user in developing their own writing style rather than any prescribed one. It is also hoped that anyone using this book will gain an awareness of a range of aspects which may contribute to successful research and writing. Furthermore, it is noted regularly throughout the book that students should always seek the advice of their tutors for specific requirements with respect to their assignments. Similarly, postgraduate students should seek the advice of their research supervisors and research teams. Although postgraduate students often develop the writing style of their supervisors, due to the nature of feedback provided and their research relationship, they also should try to develop their own personal style and approach to writing.

I.3   Structure of this book

The structure of the book is designed to follow the sections of a typical laboratory report or dissertation, in other words; abstract, introduction/ literature review, methods, results discussion and references. As such students can dip in and out of the different sections as required. Furthermore, the requirements of each report are likely to differ with the level of study and the particular assessment. Both factors need to be considered by the user. For example, first-year undergraduate students may be required to simply describe a method used and compare their data to expected responses to demonstrate an understanding of the techniques used or key underlying principles. Final-year students will have more in-depth requirements relating to generating novel research questions and hypotheses, clear research design, undertaking of appropriate statistical tests and discussion of their results in relation to previous research studies. For postgraduate students the emphasis is certainly on development of and carrying out a novel research question. To this end, each chapter is designed to be used independently such as are the needs of the student. Chapters are also organised and numbered as they would be in a conventional report.

Each chapter of the book will also try to provide an awareness of certain concepts and procedures, some of which may not be the main concern of first- or second-year students. This instance refers to factors such as ethics applications and risk assessments for which each academic establishment will have their own specific guidelines and procedures. Other aspects such as more advanced statistical concepts including effects size and statistical power will be introduced. Each section will have student activities to provide a platform to practise various aspects of report writing. Examples will be given from key areas of sport and exercise science such as exercise physiology, psychology and biomechanics to illustrate various concepts. Where appropriate, each chapter will refer to three key examples of laboratory reports most students either will undertake during their studies or should at least be able to relate to, namely:

1 Measurement of maximal oxygen uptake
2 Ground reaction forces during walking and running
3 The effect of arousal on performance

Although these are not all encompassing, they do represent traditional laboratory classes undertaken by most sport and exercise scientists and may help to put each report aspect into context.

I.4 Undergraduate students

As alluded to earlier, the classic 'lab report' is used by many academic institutions to varying degrees and forms a significant component of your scientific training. As noted earlier, most lab reports are designed to assess the understanding and application of specific aspects of sport and exercise science and will differ depending on what the tutor is assessing. Some tutors may provide data for statistical analysis to be undertaken whereas others may use the data collected in a specific class. Your lab reports will therefore be specific to the module or unit taught and the stage you are at within your degree. Although most lab reports have the same component sections there is no substitution for following the advice and guidelines provided by your tutors as to what is required. You would be surprised at the number of times the answer to many questions from students are provided in the information given out by their tutors early on in the academic calendar and in good time for the report to be submitted.

I.5 Postgraduate students

The final report for your postgraduate degree is generally your thesis. For master's degrees the dissertation will reflect the nature of your studies. For example, some master's degrees will have an initial taught component in the first half of the course followed by a research study in the second half of the degree (i.e. a 'Taught MSc'). Others will be predominantly research based with significantly less time spent on taught units and the main emphasis focuses upon the research study undertaken (i.e. a 'Master's by Research'). For PhD studies, the format of the thesis will differ depending on both the nature and the area of your study. Generally, the PhD thesis presents a series of studies examining key components of a larger research question. Although the end result of a PhD is to forward knowledge in the research area in some way, it is more than just a thesis. A PhD is a research training, the thesis being just one – albeit large – component. Within postgraduate studies there is also a greater emphasis on publishing the results of each study as journal articles. Postgraduate students may therefore find this book useful for a number of endeavours.

Whichever way you use this book I hope that you find it useful and wish you well in your writing and your studies.

Dr Mike Price

1   Abstracts

In this chapter you will:

- learn what an abstract is

  (Section 1.1)

- be aware of different types of abstracts

  (Section 1.2)

- get used to using abstracts from literature searches

  (Section 1.3)

- practise writing an abstract

  (Section 1.4)

- critique an abstract and identify common errors

  (Section 1.5)

1.1   What is an abstract?

When you are first asked to search for or write an abstract as an undergraduate student, you may well not know what your tutor is asking for. Within the context of writing, the word 'Abstract' means 'a summary' or 'an abridgement' (Oxford English Dictionary, 2000). Therefore, an abstract is a short summary of your work. In the context of a journal article an abstract is the first section of an article that you will see. With this in mind an abstract should provide the reader with a good idea of the key aims, general methods undertaken, the key findings and the most important take-home message. Abstracts are therefore a helpful tool in informing readers about the work that has been undertaken.

As well as abstracts being the first section of any journal article you may read they are also most likely the first part of a journal article that you will come into contact with when undertaking a literature search. This is especially true as a result of the range of internet-based search engines with links

DOI: 10.4324/9781003112426-2

to electronic journals that are available to today's students. When *reading* an abstract, you should be able to obtain enough information to determine whether the study is related to your own research area and whether it is of use to you. The abstract may alternatively provide you with enough information to decide that the study is not appropriate for your needs or that it is not what you thought it would be about based on the title alone. Conversely, when *writing* an abstract, it is essential to be able to clearly communicate the key points of the study to the reader.

Following the abstract you will notice that there will usually be between three to ten key words (Peh and Ng, 2008), which are used to aid search engines in their searching patterns and are not usually contained within the title. Ideally, your key words should be standard terms contained within *Index Medicus* (International Committee of Medical Journal Editors; ICMJE, 2019), which is a comprehensive index of journal titles and conventional or accepted search terms for accessing information. As key words are used to aid search engines in their searching patterns, they should also reflect those used by potential readers (Green, 2018). If writing a journal article, these key words are important as they help potential readers find your work and subsequently cite it. In recent years, search engine optimisation – initially developed for web sites – has become a common procedure and an important marketing tool (Cushman, 2018; Bhandari and Bansal, 2018). Indeed, academic search engine optimisation has become a research area in its own right (Beel et al., 2010) and may also be used to aid researchers in becoming more discoverable (Taylor and Francis, 09/01/2021).

1.2 Types of abstracts

When searching and reading the literature during your studies, you will come across a range of abstract types. The format of each type will depend upon whether you are writing a dissertation, a journal article or submitting your work for a conference. For undergraduate laboratory reports an abstract is not usually required whereas for final-year projects this is an important component of the dissertation. The following sections provide an overview of the types of abstracts you are most likely to read or be asked to write.

1.2.1 Abstracts in journal articles

Within the journals you are most likely to consult there are a range of abstract formats. These formats differ depending on the journal's specific requirements. Some journals require a brief abstract of 100–150 words (e.g. *Journal of Sport and Exercise Psychology*) or up to 200 words (e.g. *Journal of Sports Sciences*) whereas others allow slightly longer abstracts of up to 250 (e.g. *Journal of Biomechanics*) or 275 words (e.g. *Journal of Strength and Conditioning Research*). Some journals require what is termed a 'structured abstract' with specific headings within them relating to the 'Introduction',

Methods', Results' and Conclusions' sections of a study (e.g. *Medicine and Science in Sports and Exercise*). There may also be more specific aspects that are required such as 'Purpose', 'Study Design' (e.g. the *British Journal of Sports Medicine*) or 'Outcome Measures'. Theoretically, the structured abstract approach ensures certain aspects of the study design and main outcomes are clearly and consistently reported, thus aiding literature reviews and extraction of information (Squires, 1990).

The required type of abstract usually depends upon the choice of journal you plan to submit your work to or any specific guidelines provided for your project. Either way, a well-written abstract should provide all the information you need to appreciate what was done and the key findings as well as to determine whether you should read the rest of the article. Both structured and non-structured abstracts should therefore contain similar types of information. As noted earlier, abstracts usually follow the general structure of a scientific report itself, that is, Introduction, Method, Results and Discussion, often termed the 'IMRaD' principle (Alexandrov and Hennerici, 2007; Pamir, 2002, Hartley, 2000). However, no one type of abstract is better than another if they provide the key points of the work done. Structured abstracts simply provide more specific prompts for content and, when reading them, they may be easier to glean key information from.

1.2.2   *Abstracts in dissertations*

Abstracts for dissertations are essentially the same as those for journal articles in that they too inform the reader of what was done and the key findings. As noted earlier, abstracts are not usually presented within laboratory reports; however, you should consult your coursework guidelines as to what your tutor expects. Just as abstracts will differ between journals, the requirements of universities and colleges for dissertation abstracts also differ. In general, abstracts for dissertations either will have a specific word length (e.g. 500 words) or should fit comfortably onto one page (approximately 300 words for Times Roman script, font size 12 and double-spaced text).

1.2.3   *Abstracts for conferences*

A further form of abstract is that of abstracts submitted to conferences. The majority of researchers will endeavour to present their research findings at a conference or other scientific meetings to disseminate their work. Such presentations provide a whole range of networking and feedback opportunities and is often one of the initial goals for postgraduate students prior to submitting their work as a journal article for publication. For a researcher's work to be accepted for presentation at a conference, whether as an oral presentation or as a scientific poster, authors will have to submit an abstract. As for journal articles the submitted abstract undergoes a peer review process. Peer review involves a number of reviewers assessing the content of the abstract and, if it is of the desired standard and relevant to the theme of the conference, it may be accepted for presentation.

As with journal articles there are a range of abstract formats specific to each conference with guidelines usually provided through the conference website. This is an important point of reference for all potential presenters regarding abstract format, length and specific requirements. In addition to requiring some form of abstract, conferences may also provide the opportunity for extended abstracts or short articles to be submitted. These are usually published separately within special issues or supplements of appropriate journals. Either way, presenting an abstract is usually a precursor to the authors writing the full journal article after having gained valuable feedback from the conference delegates.

1.3   Using abstracts

As alluded to at the start of this chapter, many first-year university students are unlikely to have come into contact with abstracts prior to their degree studies. Indeed, Hartley (2004) notes that undergraduate students simply do not have the same experience of reading journal articles that researchers, academics and postgraduate students have acquired. Therefore, it will likely take much longer to appreciate key information presented within an abstract whether reading or writing one. Consequently, before getting to grips with writing abstracts, it is important to become accustomed to both searching for and reading abstracts and assessing the information contained within them. This approach will hopefully get you accustomed to the level of information presented in an abstract prior to writing one.

1.3.1   Searching for literature and extracting information

The tutors on your research methods modules have probably told you about different ways to search for literature. Search engines, such as Medline, Sports Discuss and Google Scholar to name but a few, are all useful for finding out academic information and journal articles. For the first exercise in this chapter log on to your recommended or preferred, academic search engine. Search for journal articles in an area of your choice or the area of interest for the specific laboratory report that you are working on. At this stage you may want to refer to Chapter 2 'Introductions and Literature Reviews' where literature searching is covered in greater detail (Section 2.3). If you have already undertaken this process, please move on to Exercise 1.1.

Many academic and non-academic search engines will readily provide the abstract of your chosen articles. Indeed, in many instances this may be all the information that is required. For example, you may just want to give an example of an athletes' maximal oxygen uptake ($\dot{V}O_{2max}$), an example of how personality has been measured or the differences in performance time after a nutritional intervention. This is fine but remember that after reading the abstract you should always read the full article (Foote, 2006a, 2009a) to ensure that you fully appreciate the design and content of the research undertaken. Reading the full article will mean you are likely to gain more information about the study and your particular area of research. When referencing your sources, some universities request that you specifically state when only the abstract has been used.

Exercise 1.1   Extracting information from an abstract

For one of the abstracts you have found in your literature searching, use the IMRaD principle to determine the key aspects of the study. Read the abstract you have obtained and complete the following table (Table 1.1). As each abstract should include information relating to each of the headings provided, you should be able to pick out the key points of the study quite easily. If you have obtained a structured abstract, this process should be more straightforward.

Table 1.1 Key points derived from each section of an abstract

Abstract component	Key point
Introduction/aims	
Participants	
Method	
Results	
Discussion/conclusion	

1.4   Writing an abstract

Although abstracts are generally a short summary of your project, don't be mistaken into thinking that they will not take you a significant amount of time to write. Writing an abstract can be difficult, especially if you have a lot that you want to say but not many words to say it in. Writing concisely and informatively within a constrained word limit is often much more difficult than using a large number of words. It is therefore good practice to learn to write concisely. Unfortunately, this is not a skill that many researches or students initially hold and it does take practice. However, writing does improve with experience. For many undergraduate students the abstract is written quickly as an afterthought, usually just before binding and submitting the final version of their dissertation. When writing your abstract bear in mind how informative *you* expect abstracts to be when searching the literature and that this is the first section seen by your assessor or reviewer!

1.4.1   *Background to writing an abstract*

Writing an abstract means to extract and summarise (Alexandrov and Hennerici, 2007). A number of researchers concerned with educational and scientific writing have examined the effectiveness of (structured) abstracts for the reader as well as providing advice and guidance for writing them (Squires, 1990; Hartley, 2000, 2004). However, these points are just as important for non-structured abstracts as well as for writing in general, and so are worthy of note here. You may also want to refer to the section on 'General writing tips' later in this book (Section 6.4).

Hartley (2000) noted that there are three important aspects to consider when assessing the clarity of structured abstracts. These aspects include: the language or readability of the abstract, the sequence of information or structure of the abstract and the typography or presentation (Figure 2.1). When considering the first point, avoid the use of complex terminology or jargon for key concepts to be understood by readers who are not subject experts (Hartley, 2000). You should also write in the past tense. The second point relates to providing a logical flow of information within the text and is consistent with the IMRaD principle (Alexandrov and Hennerici, 2007; Pamir, 2002; Hartley, 2000). The third point is concerned with formatting your abstract and therefore of most interest to journal editors. Table 1.2 considers the content that may be expected to be contained within each part of an abstract in more detail. After consulting Table 1.2, complete the accompanying exercise to help you to appreciate how to get the key points of your study across succinctly. As abstracts are not usually expected in a laboratory report, this exercise is more suited towards students writing their final-year projects and who have a sizeable data set to analyse and report.

Table 1.2 Key components of abstracts and what should be contained in each one

---

Title – clear and concise, but not too short as to leave the reader uninformed.

The opening statement – there does not have to be a lengthy introduction or justification for the study, often the aims will suffice.

Participants – give as many details as you can regarding your participants. This information is usually presented in one or two sentences and is often accompanied by a statement regarding ethics committee approval – although this is more likely reserved for the methods section within the report.

Method – the reader must get a good idea of what you have done. For the specific points regarding exercise protocols or measurements, for example, the reader can refer to the methods section in the full article. If the research was concerned with a validation or a new exercise protocol, there may be a bias towards this aspect in the abstract.

Results – this may be considered as one of the most important aspects of the abstract as readers will want to know what has been found. Pick out the most important findings which relate to your research question or hypothesis. If the word limit allows add appropriate values. Any abbreviations used should be defined in the previous methods section.

Conclusions – you will note that we haven't considered a discussion component. This is mainly because there are not enough words available to provide a full discussion of the results; therefore, the conclusion is used to present the key findings. You need to ensure that your conclusion is consistent with the key results reported earlier and the aims of your study.

Exercise 1.2   Writing an abstract

For the data you have collected in your project or one of the data sets provided in Appendix 1 try the following exercises.

> **Exercise 1.2a** With reference to Tables 1.1 and 1.2 write a summary of your research in approximately 400 words. You may find it useful to consult Table 1.2 first and then complete Table 1.1 that we used for determining the key information in a given abstract, but this time you are writing *your* abstract and need to ensure that you provide what *you* think is important.
>
> **Exercise 1.2b** Once you have completed Exercise 1a., then try to reduce the length of your abstract to approximately 200 words.

To help you, an example of a longer abstract such as for a dissertation and a shorter abstract such as for a journal article have been provided (see Example abstracts 1 and 2).

Example abstract 1: Maximal oxygen uptake lab, approximately 400 words

Assessment of maximal oxygen uptake during running, cycling and arm cranking

The aim of this study was to determine the maximal oxygen uptake during running, cycling and arm cranking. Ten healthy non-specifically trained males (age 19 (2.6) years; height, 1.79 (6.7) m, body mass, 71.2 (7.1) kg) volunteered to participate in this study which had received the University Ethics Committee approval. Participants undertook three incremental exercise tests to volitional exhaustion in order to determine maximal oxygen uptake ($\dot{V}O_{2max}$). The protocols were undertaken using during treadmill running (TR; Powerjog), cycle ergometry (CE; Monark 813E) and arm crank ergometry (ACE; Lode). The TR protocol involved an initial speed of 8 km·h^{-1} with increases in 2 km·h^{-1} every three minutes at a gradient of 1%. The CE protocol involved an initial power output of 70 W with further increases in power output of 35 W every three minutes whereas the ACE protocol involved an initial power output of 50 W and increases of 20 W every 2 minutes. Both CE and ACE were undertaken at 70 rev·min^{-1}. Expired gas samples were taken during the final minute of exercise. Heart rate was continually monitored throughout all tests. Ratings of perceived exertion (RPE) for cardiovascular strain were recorded in the last 15 s of each exercise stage. One-way analysis of variance (ANOVA) demonstrated a significant difference between protocols (P<0.05). Tukey post hoc analysis indicated that the $\dot{V}O_{2max}$ during TR (58.5 ±6.1 ml·kg^{-1}·min^{-1}) was similar to that achieved during CE (53.4 ±5.4 ml·kg^{-1}·min^{-1}; P>0.05). During the ACE protocol participants obtained peak rather than maximal oxygen uptake ($\dot{V}O_{2peak}$) values with the mean $\dot{V}O_{2peak}$ being lowest during this mode of exercise than for TR and CE (38.7 ±6.4 ml·kg^{-1}·min^{-1}; P>0.05). Maximal heart rates were similar during TR and CE (194 ±5, 186 ±5 beats·min^{-1}, respectively) but not different between exercise modes (P>0.05). Peak heart rate during ACE was lower than for both TR and CE (179 ±6 beats·min^{-1}; P<0.05). RPE at volitional exhaustion followed a similar pattern to heart rate with lower values during ACE than for TR and CE (17.6 ±2.3, 20.0 ±1.2 and 18.8 ±2.7, respectively; P<0.05). The results of this study demonstrate that arm crank ergometry elicits lower peak oxygen uptake, heart rate and RPE than for treadmill running and cycle ergometry. The lower values for ACE are likely due to development of peripheral fatigue rather than to cardiorespiratory fatigue.

Example abstract 2: Maximal oxygen uptake lab, approximately 200 words

Assessment of maximal oxygen uptake during running, cycling and arm cranking

The aim of this study was to determine maximal oxygen uptake during treadmill running (TR), cycle ergometry (CE) and arm crank ergometry (ACE). Ten healthy, none specifically, trained males volunteered to participate in this study which had received University Ethics Committee approval. Participants undertook three incremental exercise tests to volitional exhaustion in order to determine maximal oxygen uptake ($\dot{V}O_{2max}$). Expired gas samples were taken during the final exercise stage of each protocol. Heart rate and ratings of perceived exertion (RPE) were recorded in the last 15 s of each exercise stage. The $\dot{V}O_{2max}$ during TR (58.5 ± 6.1 ml·kg^{-1}·min^{-1}) was similar to that achieved during CE (53.4 ± 5.4 ml·kg^{-1}·min^{-1}; $P>0.05$) with both being greater than for ACE (38.7 ± 6.4 ml·kg^{-1}·min^{-1}; $P>0.05$). Maximal heart rates were also similar during TR and CE (194 ± 5, 186 ± 5 beats·min^{-1}, respectively) with both being greater than for ACE ($P<0.05$). RPE was lowest during ACE ($P<0.05$). The results of this study demonstrate that arm crank ergometry elicits lower peak oxygen uptake, heart rate and RPE than for treadmill running and cycle ergometry. The lower values for ACE are likely due to development of peripheral fatigue rather than due to cardiorespiratory fatigue.

You can see from the example abstracts provided that there is a considerable amount of information presented in fewer than 400 words. Consider each aspect of Table 1.1 in conjunction with the example abstracts and use them to guide your writing and assess whether there is enough information contained in your own abstracts. Can you get a good idea of what was done in the study and what was found? Figures 1.1 and 1.2 may help you decide.

Although many dissertation abstracts are not required to be as short as the 200 words suggested in Exercise 1.2b, some journal articles are. The exercise just completed will help you to appreciate writing concisely and reduce your word use. If you have found this difficult, consider what your research question or research hypotheses were and your main findings. This is essentially what was in Table 1.1. These are the questions you were trying to answer and the information you were trying to find out. You may also find it helpful to try the exercise in reverse by first writing out your key findings in around 100 words and then increasing your word count gradually up to 200 or 400 words as required. Ensure that you include the pertinent aspects suggested in Table 1.1.

Example abstract 1: Maximal oxygen uptake lab, approximately 400 words

---

Assessment of maximal oxygen uptake during running, cycling and arm cranking.

Aim →

The aim of this study was to determine the maximal oxygen uptake during running, cycling and arm cranking. Ten healthy none specifically trained males (age 19 (2.6) years; height, 1.79 (6.7) m, body mass, 71.2 (7.1) kg) volunteered to participate in this study which had received University Ethics Committee approval. ← Participants Participants undertook three incremental exercise tests to volitional exhaustion in order to determine maximal oxygen uptake (VO_{2max}). The protocols were undertaken using either during treadmill running (TR; Powerjog), cycle ergometry (CE; Monark 813E) and arm crank ergometry (ACE; Lode). The TR protocol involved an initial speed of 8 km.h^{-1} with increases in 2 km.h^{-1} every three minutes at a gradient of 1%. The CE

Methods →

protocol involved an initial power output of 70 W with further increases in power output of 35 W every three minutes whereas the ACE protocol involved an initial power output of 50W and increases of 20 W every 2 min. Both CE and ACE were undertaken at 70 rev.min^{-1}. Expired gas samples were taken during the final minute of exercise. Heart rate was continually monitored throughout all tests. Ratings of perceived exertion (RPE) for cardiovascular strain were recorded in the last 15 s of each exercise stage. One way analysis of variance (ANOVA) demonstrated a significant difference between protocols (P<0.05). Tukey post hoc analysis ← Results indicated that the VO_{2max} during TR (58.5 ±6.1 ml.kg.$^{-1}$min^{-1}) was similar to that achieved during CE (53.4 ±5.4 ml.kg.$^{-1}$min^{-1}; P>0.05). During the ACE protocol participants obtained peak rather than maximal oxygen uptake (VO_{2peak}) values with the mean VO_{2peak} being lowest during this mode of exercise than for TR and CE (38.7 ±6.4 ml.kg.$^{-1}$min^{-1}; P>0.05). Maximal heart rates were similar during TR and CE (194 ±5, 186 ±5 beats .min^{-1}, respectively) but not different between exercise modes (P>0.05). Peak heart rate during ACE was lower than for both TR and CE (179 ±6 beats.min^{-1}; P<0.05). RPE at volitional exhaustion followed a similar pattern to heart rate with lowers values during ACE than for TR and CE (17.6 ±2.3, 20.0 ±1.2 and 18.8 ±2.7, respectively; P<0.05). The results of this study demonstrate that arm crank ergometry elicits lower peak oxygen uptake, heart ← Conclusions rate and RPE than for treadmill running and cycle ergometry. The lower values for ACE are likely due to development of peripheral fatigue rather than to cardiorespiratory fatigue.

Word count: 386

Figure 1.1 Annotated abstract for Exercise 1.2a

Example abstract 2: Maximal oxygen uptake lab, approximately 200 words

Assessment of maximal oxygen uptake during running, cycling and arm cranking.

Aim →

The aim of this study was to determine maximal oxygen uptake during treadmill running (TR), cycle ergometry (CE) and arm crank ergometry (ACE). Ten healthy none specifically trained males volunteered to participate in this study which had received University Eth Participants Committee approval. Participants undertook three incremental exercise tests to volitional exhaustion in order to determine maximal oxygen uptake (VO_{2max}). Expired gas samples were taken during the final exercise stage of each protocol. Heart rate and ratings of

Methods →

perceived exertion (RPE) were recorded in the last 15 s of each exercise stage. The VO_{2max} during TR (58.5 ±6.1 ml.kg.$^{-1}$min^{-1}) was similar to that achieved during CE (53.4 ±5.4 ml.kg.$^{-1}$min^{-1}; P>0.05) with both being greater than for ACE (38.7 ±6.4 ml.kg.$^{-1}$min^{-1}; P>0.05). Maximal heart rates were also similar during TR and CE (194 ±5, 186 ±5 beats .min^{-1}, ← Results respectively) with both being greater than for ACE (P<0.05). RPE was lowest during ACE (P<0.05). The results of this study demonstrate that arm crank ergometry elicits lower peak oxygen uptake, heart rate and RPE than for treadmill running and cycle ergometry. The lower values for ACE are likely due to development of peripheral fatigue rather than to cardiorespiratory fatigue.

Word count: 195

Conclusions

Figure 1.2 Annotated abstract for Exercise 1.2b

1.5 Critiquing an abstract and common errors

When asked to undertake a critique of a piece of work or a scientific study, most students focus upon negative aspects. Indeed, from an assessor's perspective these are often the key points that are immediately obvious and likely to be noted so they can be improved upon. However, noting positive aspects, which may not be explicitly obvious, are just as important (see Chapter 2, Section 2.8). To demonstrate some common errors that students regularly exhibit when writing abstracts and to make you aware of some key aspects to avoid an example of a poorly written abstract (Example abstract 3) is provided here.

Exercise 1.3 Critiquing an abstract

Read the abstract and complete Table 1.3 to note how many errors you can spot or improvements that could be made. Try to find ten, however, there are at least 15 more immediate points to consider (Table 1.4), but there may be more! Within your critique you should always consider the required word length and information required from each section of the study.

Example abstract 3

Title – Lab report

$\dot{V}O_{2max}$ is really important. It is the most important factor to show fitness levels in different people. We tested ten students to see if there was a difference in their values. Treadmill testing gave the largest values (58.417) and arm exercise the lowest. Exercise on the bike was a greater value than arm cranking. The $\dot{V}O_{2max}$ values for the three tests were different (58.417, 53, 38.7 ±6.4 ml·kg^{-1}·min^{-1}). Heart rate (194.12 bpm, 186, 178.7) was recorded in the last seconds of the exercise stage whereas Douglas bags were recorded at the end of each test. Our results show that treadmill testing is best.

Table 1.3 Points to improve/abstract errors

1 ....

2 ....

3 ....

4 ....

5 ....

6 ....

7 ....

8 ....

9 ....

10 ....

Table 1.4 Potential errors within Example Abstract 3

1 Title does not inform the reader of what was done. Each lab that you undertake will have aims or a specific title
2 VO_{2max} is not defined and there is no subscript used
3 Third person past tense not used
4 No participant characteristics provided
5 No indication of the protocols used prior to results
6 No units for values provided
7 Too many decimal places for variables presented
8 Inconsistent decimal places given
9 Terminology of 'bike' incorrect, should read 'cycle ergometer'
10 Timing of heart rate measures and Douglas bag collections (method) given after some results already stated
11 Decimal values for heart rates, units wrong and not reported correctly
12 States values were different but not indication of tests used or P values or the direction of any differences
13 Awkward wording throughout
14 Abstract very short and not informative
15 Concluding statement – why is treadmill testing best, what is meant by this?

1.6   Chapter summary and reflection

This chapter has provided an overview of different types of abstracts and how you may extract information from them. We also considered how to plan and write an abstract using the same tools as for extracting information from them. This means that when you are writing your abstract you will hopefully include what you consider to be important for the reader to know. You will also find the other chapters of this book relating to the methods and results sections of dissertations helpful in reporting the key aspects required for your abstract. To assess your understanding of abstracts, consider the following summary questions.

* What is an abstract?
* What different types of abstracts are there?
* What information is contained within an abstract?
* How should you approach writing an abstract?
* What are common errors when writing abstracts?

1.7   Further activities

Browse the websites of journals that you regularly read or are aware of. Direct yourself to the author guidelines and consider the advice given for writing and presenting abstracts.

Consult the methods and results chapters of this book to provide guidance in reporting key aspects of these sections of a dissertation within your abstract.

If you are submitting a conference abstract, consult the conference website for example abstracts or journals where special editions have published previous abstracts for that conference.

2 Introductions and literature reviews

In this chapter you will be able to:

*   appreciate the role of an introduction

    (Section 2.1)

*   differentiate between an introduction and a literature review

    (Section 2.2)

*   undertake a literature search

    (Section 2.3)

*   extract and use information from literature sources

    (Section 2.4)

*   practise writing an introduction

    (Section 2.5)

*   critique an introduction

    (Section 2.6)

*   plan and write a literature review

    (Section 2.7)

*   critique a journal article

    (Section 2.8)

*   develop your aims, objectives and hypotheses

    (Section 2.9)

*   identify common problems when writing introductions

    (Section 2.10)

DOI: 10.4324/9781003112426-3

2.1   An introduction to introductions

All types of scientific report will have some form of introductory section. Although the structure and length of these may differ the function of introductions is essentially the same; to move the reader from what is known about an area to what is unknown or; to move the reader from general to specific information (Foote, 2006b). For a dissertation or scientific journal articles the introduction will end with the research question and hypothesis whereas for an undergraduate lab report it will likely end with the aims and objectives of the specific lab class.

Foote (2006a) considers a scientific article's introduction to be as important as the need to make a good impression in a job application. Indeed, imagine reading an introduction to a journal article or lab report where the author does not clearly present the information or effectively develop their experimental aims and objectives. Would you continue reading or give the report many marks? The following sections will consider how an introduction may differ between lab reports and dissertations as well as how your introduction may be integrated within a literature review.

2.1.1   *Introductions in lab reports and journal articles*

Depending on your level of study the introduction to your lab report will serve a number of purposes. However, all introductions will require you to have read widely and to have reviewed the literature to some extent. The accompanying exercise to this section will help you determine the type of information usually included within an introduction. At the simplest level the introduction, as the name of the section implies, should *introduce* any key terms or concepts. For example, consider a first-year lab report relating the measurement of energy expenditure at rest and during exercise, most likely using techniques for the first time. Here the reader, and most likely the assessor, will be expecting to see evidence of understanding and background reading rather than development of a rationale for a Nobel Prize winning research study. The reason for this is due to undergraduate lab classes generally being designed to learn the skills and processes required for both your final-year project and professional career. It is your final-year project which will most likely have a novel research aspect to it.

Introductions usually start with a more general or 'introductory' paragraph and become more specific as the introduction develops, culminating in the aims of your study (Figure 2.1). Continuing with the energy expenditure example the introduction could take the form of that outlined in Figure 2.2. (NB: it is important to note that the content of your introduction will clearly depend upon the contents and aims of the specific lab class. The following example is used purely to demonstrate a point.) Depending on the specific content required the flow chart in Figure 2.2 could demonstrate a general understanding of what energy expenditure is, how it can be measured (reflecting the methods used in the lab class) and what you would expect to

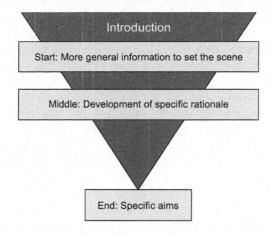

Figure 2.1 General format of introduction

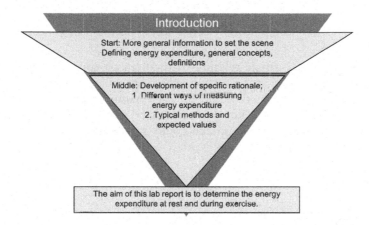

Figure 2.2 Example introduction for a hypothetical lab report examining energy expenditure

find. From this the reader will hopefully be aware of whether the student understands the key concepts required. As the introduction progresses, more specific details emerge relating to the specific activities undertaken within the lab class. These activities will be reflected in your aims and objectives (see Section 2.9). It is important to note that you should always follow the assessment guidelines provided by your tutor regarding the required content. Also consider the specific word count if provided. Whether you have specific guidelines provided or not, you need to spend time planning the content of your introduction to reflect the aims of the class. If you are struggling to come up with key aspects of your lab report to include in your introduction, you should consider key words contained within the title of your lab report, the aims or objectives and key procedures undertaken in the methods.

As your lab classes become more complex throughout your degree studies, and certainly when writing journal articles, the introduction is used to serve the purpose of justification (Hopkins et al., 2009). This is generally to justify your research question or what is often termed generating the 'rationale' for your study. For example, you may need to justify the use of a particular group of participants or research design (Hopkins et al., 2009). The information you present should convince the reader that you have a sound reason for the study being undertaken. Whether you are writing an undergraduate lab report or writing up your fiftieth research paper all introductions must reflect the scientific question being asked and therefore what has been done within the study. A common error in lab report introductions is going 'off topic' or presenting what may be correct but irrelevant information. Although Exercise 2.1 focuses on journal articles and the introductions to these differ from those of lab reports the exercise is designed to consider the flow of information presented.

Exercise 2.1   What is in an introduction?

Choose a journal article relating to the area of your lab report or project. Make sure that it is a study which has collected some original data. Read the introduction and for each paragraph make a note in one or two words of the key point that is being made or what aspect is being described. This approach could also be used when you are planning or proofreading your work.

Paragraph 1: . . . .

. . . .

Paragraph 2: . . . .

. . . .

Paragraph 3: . . . .

. . . .

Paragraph 4: . . . .

. . . .

Ask yourself the following questions:

1   Is there a logical flow of information?
2   How do the key points you have noted earlier compare to the title of the article and the aims?

Also consider the point made earlier regarding development of the rationale:

1 Why is it important to have done this study?
2 What is known beforehand?
3 What is the new aspect to be investigated?

2.2 Introduction versus literature review

One important question that is often asked by final-year project students is 'what is the difference between an introduction and a literature review?'. The answer really relates to the type of report you are writing. For shorter reports, such as undergraduate lab reports and scientific research studies, the introduction is as considered earlier – a short informative introduction to the area to establish your area of study or research question. If you look at any published journal articles you should be able to see this (i.e. Exercise 2.1). Although your introduction will contain references to previous research and briefly review the area, a 'literature review' per se is generally a much longer chapter within a thesis such as those written by final-year undergraduate and postgraduate students. Here, the examiner is looking to establish that the student has both a greater breadth and depth of knowledge, that a clear understanding exists regarding the chosen topic area and that the current, pertinent literature has been surveyed. For this reason, undergraduate and postgraduate dissertations generally have both an introduction and a literature review whereas lab reports have only an introduction. In final-year or postgraduate dissertations the introduction would give an overview of the main topic of the thesis in two or three pages to set the scene for the study. The introduction would then be followed by the main literature review to provide a broader and in-depth review of pertinent literature. Figure 2.1 can now be expanded to demonstrate these differences (Figure 2.3).

2.2.1 Types of literature review

Within your literature search you will come across both original research articles and review articles. The latter are an ideal way to introduce yourself to a topic and also to see how literature reviews are structured. Literature reviews consist of a detailed and comprehensive narrative analysis of recent or evolving developments in specific topics (Ng and Peh, 2010b). Literature reviews may also help to consolidate data or opinions within a specific area or re-evaluate current knowledge in light of new findings or concepts. In this respect, literature reviews are often more up to date than textbooks (Green et al., 2001). Although review articles may synthesize information from previous studies, they generally do not present new data. This is the

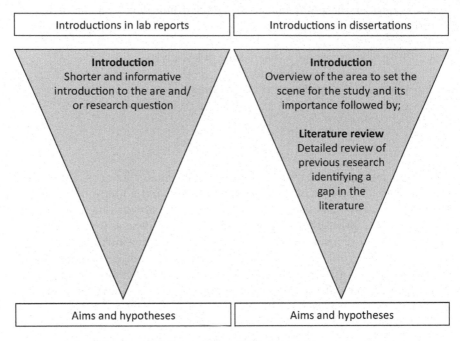

| Introductions in lab reports | Introductions in dissertations |

Introduction
Shorter and informative introduction to the are and/ or research question

Introduction
Overview of the area to set the scene for the study and its importance followed by;

Literature review
Detailed review of previous research identifying a gap in the literature

| Aims and hypotheses | Aims and hypotheses |

Figure 2.3 Introductions in lab reports and dissertations

main difference between 'original' journal articles and literature reviews. The former has methods and results sections whereas the latter does not. For undergraduate and postgraduate students your literature review needs to demonstrate that you understand the area and present current theories and underlying processes or mechanisms. Furthermore, and importantly, you need to also identify a gap or gaps in the literature which can then be developed into your research question and subsequently your aims and hypotheses.

Literature reviews can generally be further separated into 'systematic' or 'narrative' reviews. The latter are sometimes termed 'non-systematic reviews'; however, this does not mean that a systematic approach has not been undertaken and they are certainly not less worthy (Sandelowski, 2008). Within both the scientific and educational literature there are a range of articles providing guidance on how to approach writing both narrative (Green et al., 2001; Peh and Ng, 2010) and systematic (Ng and Peh, 2010a; Sandelowski, 2008; Wieseler and McGauran, 2010) reviews of literature and searching scientific literature (Foote, 2009a). The purpose of this section is to provide an awareness of different types of literature review and reviewing processes. As noted earlier, whether writing an introduction for a lab report or a journal article a review of literature is essential.

Systematic literature reviews are often found in medical or clinical areas of research and are considered to be the cornerstone of evidence-based practice (Sandelowski, 2008). Indeed, the use of specific systematic reviews in sport and exercise science has certainly increased in recent years. Systematic reviews are considered to help clinicians keep up to date with medical research findings and aid in the development of practical guidelines and policy decision-making (Wieseler and McGauran, 2010) – outcomes that are also of importance in both sport and exercise science and sports therapy. As the approach undertaken when writing systematic reviews is explicitly structured, this process is considered to be the least biased and most rational way to search and report literature (Ng and Peh, 2010b). So how does a systematic review differ from other reviews? The key factor is the way in which the research studies are searched and subsequently included within or excluded from the review. For example, systematic reviews often relate to clinical trials where patient populations, age ranges, types of drugs or interventions employed, randomised control trials, double-blind studies, etc. may all differ and significantly affect any clinical outcome. Ng and Peh (2010a) give the example of a literature search where 121 articles were retrieved from a given database. Fifty-one of these articles were excluded after reading the abstract. Of the seventy remaining articles, forty-two were excluded as they did not fit given criteria for the review leaving twenty eight articles to be included. Note here that the more stringent your inclusion criteria the fewer articles you will end up with for review. If the aim of your review is to develop practical guidelines you will need enough articles to enable a consensus to be reached.

Owing to the importance of systematic reviews given to shaping clinical practice and to provide consistency in systematic reviewing the 'Preferred Reporting Items for Systematic Reviews and Meta-Analyses' (PRISMA) statement was originally developed in 2009 and recently update (Page et al., 2021). The PRISMA statement provides a twenty-seven-item checklist for systematic reviews and is available online (www.prisma-statement.org) as well as being published through a number of journals. Many of the key components to be included in systematic reviews represent the range of possible subheadings included within structured abstracts (see Chapter 1, Section 1.2.1). Although this structured approach requires (and hopefully ensures) all key aspects of importance to clinicians and specific clinical outcomes are included, many of these factors are not key components for sport and exercise science generally involving 'healthy' or non-clinical participants. However, the underlying principles for searching literature are essentially the same as for narrative reviews, and it is certainly worth perusing the components of the PRISMA statement. A summary of the items presented in the PRISMA statement is shown in Figure 2.4. These will be considered later in this chapter (see Section 2.3 Literature searching). For details regarding the specific content of the PRISMA statement, please consult the full document.

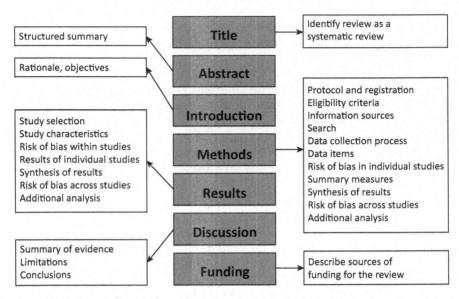

Figure 2.4 Summary of PRISMA checklist for systematic reviews and meta-analyses
Source: (adapted from Moher et al., 2009).

2.2.1.ii   *Narrative literature reviews*

Similar to systematic reviews, narrative reviews will still require a statement regarding the search terms used and any inclusion or exclusion criteria applied to the various research studies obtained. In contrast to systematic reviews, no relevant report is excluded (Sandelowski, 2008), and authors must be careful not to be biased in their opinions and remain objective in their information extraction (Green et al., 2001). Narrative reviews therefore have the potential to be more wider reaching and inclusive than systematic reviews.

2.2.1iii   *Other types of literature review*

As well as systematic and narrative reviews you may come across other types of review. Grant and Booth (2009) noted how the development of evidence-based practice had resulted in a large range of review types. Indeed, the authors presented fourteen different types of review with their associated methodologies, descriptions and perceived strengths and weaknesses. Differences between review types were best summarised in relation to the search strategy (i.e. comprehensive or systematised, constrained by time or scope), appraisal of the resultant articles (i.e. whether study quality assessment was considered), synthesis (i.e. narrative, graphical or tabular) and analysis (e.g. conceptual, numerical, chronological, thematic, quantity/quality of literature). However, whether writing a systematic, narrative, scoping or rapid review or meta-analysis you will first have to acquire your literature sources. Therefore, it is important to address the basics of literature searching here.

2.3 Literature searching

Your initial literature search will depend upon how familiar or experienced you are with a topic (Thomas and Nelson, 2001) and your current level of understanding of the area. Students who are not well grounded in a topic may benefit from reading appropriate chapters in textbooks and general information sources (Thomas and Nelson, 2001). Such an approach is most likely the starting point for most undergraduate students, especially in their first year of study. For those students who are more confident in their understanding of their topic area reading a review article is a good first step. Not only will review articles provide up-to-date information at the time of publication, but they will also give an overview of the area and recommendations for future research. In addition, there will likely be a long list of references to consult.

Throughout your research methods modules most students will have been made aware of a range of literature search engines and how to use them. Tutorials relating to this will often be available through your university or college library or through education sections of medical journals, for example, Greenhalgh (1997). Scientific search engines are a great way to get an idea of what literature is available on your chosen topic but also, depending on your university or college library subscriptions, this is a good way of obtaining electronic copies of journals. When you first obtain an article in a literature search it is likely that you will be able to access the abstract. This will give you an overview of the study and the key findings (see Chapter 1). Although it is always best to read the full article, the abstract may give you some important and useable information. However, your search doesn't have to be limited to electronic or web-based searches. Also, don't forget that browsing through hard copies of journals on the library shelves and their reference lists is also a good way of finding information.

When considering the process of searching the literature a number of important factors should be considered (Foote, 2009a; Figure 2.5). First, consider the basics of undertaking literature searches, including determining the search terms to be used, databases to be searched, range of dates to search, type of articles to consider, etc. Second, the output of the search should then be reviewed. Your resultant output may require refinement of your search terms to enable a more helpful search output or manageable number of sources to be obtained. The third consideration is then the 'explication', or analysing and explaining the literature in order to construct the review (Foote, 2009a). Thomas and Nelson (2001) suggest six steps to ensure a thorough and productive literature review. When combining these steps

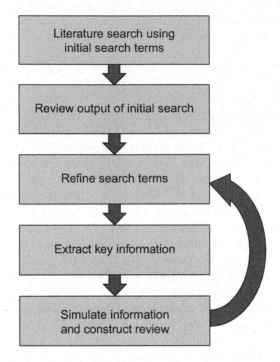

Figure 2.5 Schematic representation of literature searching and writing
Source: (based on Foote, 2009a).

with Foote's considerations, you can see that experienced and less experienced researchers may have different starting points for their searches but
still undertake essentially the same processes (Figure 2.6). Updating your
searches as you progress through your project is also very important as new
and pertinent literature may well be published while you are writing up your
project. As noted already, always read the full text of any article of interest
and do not dismiss those articles that you can't get free online. Most universities have excellent inter-library loan systems and many also allow students
of other universities to access their resources. This aspect is certainly worth
checking out.

Exercise 2.2   Literature searching

When searching for literature, please note that if your search terms
are quite general, such as 'anxiety', 'performance' or 'carbohydrate
ingestion', you will have many thousands of results. You may find it
easier to include more specific search terms such as the specific aspect

of performance or sport you are interested in. Refining your search terms will provide a more specific and useable search output. Indeed, this is essentially how systematic reviews result in manageable numbers of articles to review. The inclusion criteria for systematic reviews are based on search terms reflecting the specific nature of the intervention, treatment or population of interest and focusing solely on those. For example, Table 2.1 shows how the search results can be initially over-whelming but then constrained and reduced to those more appropriate for your needs. Searching for literature and getting to grips with appro-priate search terms is a skill in itself. However, the more you search for information and the more you read around an area the more likely you are going to be able to refine and undertake your searches successfully.

Within Table 2.1 are spaces for you to add your own search terms. Try different combinations of terms to obtain a useable output of potential articles. Once you have done this, please move on to the next section.

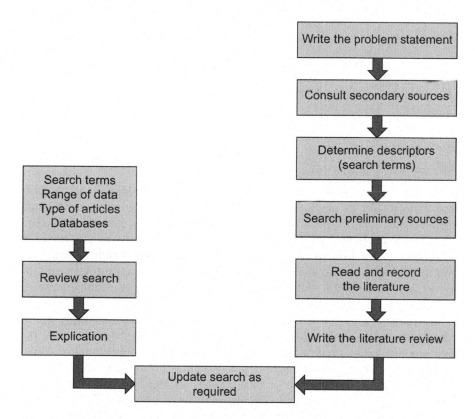

Figure 2.6 Schematic representation of literature searching
Source: (based on Foote, 2009a [left panel] and Thomas and Nelson, 2001 [right panel]).

Table 2.1 Likely outputs from one search engine for three topics in sport and exercise science

General search

Area of interest	Search terms	Number of articles found*
Anxiety	Anxiety	256,351
Performance	Performance	3,518,093
Carbohydrate ingestion	Carbohydrate ingestion	30,620
Your area of interest	. . . .	. . . .

Specific search

Area of interest	Search terms	Number of articles found
Anxiety	Anxiety	256,352
Performance	AND Tennis	265
Carbohydrate ingestion	Performance	3,518,093
Your area of interest	AND Running	22,834
	AND Elite	1,671
	Carbohydrate ingestion	30,620
	AND Marathon running	51
	. . . .	. . . .
	. . . .	. . . .
	. . . .	. . . .

*From a typical scientific or academic search engine.

2.4 Extracting information and using literature sources

Now that you have undertaken a literature search and obtained a range of information sources what do you do with them? When you are using your various sources of information it is important to be able to extract exactly what you want from them. This may seem obvious, but when you haven't used this type of information before it may not be as straightforward as you think. Furthermore, it is likely that within your literature review or lab report introduction you will be explicitly required to use scientific literature to back up your statements.

So, what information is important? This will depend quite simply upon what you require. Your needs may be quite broad such as an example of how anxiety is measured or an example of a personality questionnaire. Conversely, your needs may be more detailed such as an in-depth explanation of the mechanisms of fatigue or how anxiety differs between performers. Within review articles you will often see a table summarising key research studies. This is a very useful way to consolidate your thoughts on the available literature and consistently assess the same key points from each article you have read. Indeed, when you are reading journal articles, certain aspects may continually come to mind that may affect the results of a given study. For example, the participants studied, the protocol or method used and the design of the experiment as well as specific measures taken can all affect the results obtained. With this in mind, summary tables will likely include information regarding participants and methodological aspects. Consider these aspects with respect to the key components of a structured abstract noted in Chapter 1 and for systematic reviews. When using a summary table, the reader can quickly assess different approaches taken within the area and how diverse these may be, which may be why there are differing viewpoints within a topic.

Whether or not you include a summary table in your thesis is down to personal choice and supervisory guidance. However, as a way of summarising what may be quite a daunting pile of research papers a summary table can very useful. A simple approach to summarising data will relate to your research question. For example, if your research question relates to the effects of a nutritional supplement, such as sodium bicarbonate or creatine phosphate ingestion, on performance what is the general consensus? Here you would simply need to note down for each research study that you read whether performance was improved, negatively affected or not affected at all. You may then want to find out if there was a consistent aspect in those studies which observed enhanced performance. Examining the participant characteristics, exercise protocols, administration of the supplement, etc. may help pinpoint specific important factors. Similarly, you may be interested in the effects of anxiety on performance. You could again determine from your research articles those which have shown performance to be affected by anxiety and those which have not. From here you may be able to determine a certain level of anxiety where performance is affected or whether certain groups of participants or certain types of skill are most affected by anxiety. You could, of course, obtain all this information from simply reading the research articles and remembering the facts, but you may find that summarising your data in such a way is helpful.

Exercise 2.3 will help you to assess how well you extract information and also give you some practice in determining what may be important in a given source of information. When recording information from literature sources, Thomas and Nelson (2001) suggest considering, amongst other factors, the characteristics of the participants, instruments and tests (including reliability and validity), testing procedures, treatments applied, study design and statistical analysis and key findings. The list of factors that you may be interested in will be similar to those usually considered when critiquing studies (see Section 2.8). Indeed, there are a range of guidelines for critiquing scientific studies such as a checklist sheet from Thomas and Nelson, the PRISMA statement, a peer review checklist developed by Seals and Tanaka (2000) and an assessment checklist sheet for narrative reviews (Green et al., 2001). However, as many of these are designed for the peer review of journal articles they are possibly more complicated and consider more factors than you require at present. Consider what it is you really want to find out from a particular source. You may not need all that detail.

Abstract 1

Svedenhag J, Sjödin B (1985). Maximal and submaximal oxygen uptakes and blood lactate levels in elite male middle- and long-distance runners. *International Journal of Sports Medicine*, 5(5): 255–61.

Physiological characteristics of elite runners from different racing events were studied. Twenty-seven middle- and long-distance runners and two 400-m runners belonging to the Swedish national team in track and field were divided, according to their distance preferences, into six groups from 400 m up to the marathon. The maximal oxygen uptake ($\dot{V}O_{2\,max}$, ml·kg^{-1}·min^{-1}) on the treadmill was higher the longer the main distance except for the marathon runners (e.g., 800–1500-m group, 72.1; 5000–10,000-m group, 78.7 ml·kg^{-1}·min^{-1}). Running economy evaluated from oxygen uptake measurements at 15 km/h ($\dot{V}O_2$ 15) and 20 km/h ($\dot{V}O_2$ 20) did not differ significantly between the groups even though $\dot{V}O_2$ 15 tended to be lower in the long-distance runners. The running velocity corresponding to a blood lactate concentration of 4 mmol/l (vHla 4.0) differed markedly between the groups with the highest value (5.61 m/s) in the 5000–10,000-m group. The oxygen uptake ($\dot{V}O_2$) at vHla 4.0 in percentage of $\dot{V}O_2$ max did not differ significantly between the groups. The blood lactate concentration after exhaustion ($\dot{V}O_2$ max test) was lower in the long-distance runners. In summary, the current study demonstrates differences in physiological characteristics of elite runners specialising in different racing events. The two single (but certainly inter-related) variables in which this was most clearly seen were the maximal oxygen uptake (ml·kg^{-1}·min^{-1}) and the running velocity corresponding to a blood lactate concentration of 4 mmol/l.

Abstract 2

O'Toole ML, Hiller DB, Crosby LO, Douglas PS (1987). The ultraendurance triathlete: A physiological profile. *Medicine and Science in Sports and Exercise*, 19(1): 45–50.

To better characterise the athletes who participate in ultraendurance triathlons, 14 triathletes in training for the Hawaii IRONMAN triathlon were studied. A physical and physiological profile was developed from anthropometric measurements and oxygen uptake during maximal exercise on a treadmill, cycle ergometer and arm ergometer. A comparison of the maximal values among exercise modes and between males and females was made. A comparison of height, weight and percent body fat of these triathletes with elite athletes from the sports of swimming, cycling and running showed the physique of triathletes to be most similar to that of cyclists. Oxygen uptake at maximal exercise was, for males and females, respectively: 68.8 ml·kg^{-1}·min^{-1}, 65.9 ml·kg^{-1}·min^{-1} on the treadmill; 66.7 ml·kg^{-1}·min^{-1}, 61.6 ml·kg^{-1}·min^{-1} on the cycle ergometer; and 49.1 ml·kg^{-1}·min^{-1}, 39.7 ml·kg^{-1}·min^{-1} on the arm ergometer. When comparing the highest oxygen uptake attained at maximal exercise in any one of the three exercise modes, the male triathletes are comparable to swimmers, but they have a lower aerobic capacity than cyclists or distance runners. The female triathletes studied were able to attain oxygen uptake values greater than those previously reported for female athletes.

Abstract 3

Astorino TA, Tam PA, Rietschel JC, Johnson SM, Freedman TP (2004). Changes in physical fitness parameters during a competitive field hockey season. *Journal of Strength and Conditioning Research*, 18(4): 850–4.

Competitive field hockey requires a substantial amount of muscular strength, speed and cardiovascular endurance. It is unknown how these parameters of physical fitness change between pre-season conditioning to post-season recovery. Therefore, Division III female field hockey athletes (n = 13) completed tests of muscular strength, body composition and maximal oxygen uptake ($\dot{V}O_{2max}$) during each phase of their season. Muscular strength was assessed using one repetition maximum (RM) leg and bench press tests. Body composition was assessed by anthropometry (skinfolds [SKF]), circumferences ([CC]) and bioelectrical impedance analysis (BIA). Incremental treadmill testing was administered to assess $\dot{V}O_{2max}$. $\dot{V}O_{2max}$ was unchanged during the season, although a trend ($p >$ 0.05) was shown for a higher $\dot{V}O_{2max}$ during and after the season versus before the season. Upper- (10%) and lower-body strength (14%) decreased ($p > 0.05$) during the season. Per cent body fat (%BF) from BIA, fat mass (FM) from CC and body mass index (BMI) were significantly lower in ($p < 0.05$) in-season and post-season versus pre-season. In conclusion, pre-season training was effective in decreasing %BF and increasing $\dot{V}O_{2max}$, yet muscular strength was lost. Coaches should incorporate more rigorous in-season resistance training to prevent strength decrements. Moreover, these data support the superior levels of muscular strength and leanness in these athletes compared with age-matched peers.

Abstract 4

Price MJ, Campbell IG (1999). Thermoregulatory responses of spinal cord injured and able-bodied athletes to prolonged upper body exercise and recovery. *Spinal Cord*, 37(11): 772–9.

STUDY DESIGN: Single trial, two-factor repeated-measures design. SETTING: England, Cheshire. OBJECTIVES: To examine the thermoregulatory responses of able-bodied (AB) athletes, paraplegic (PA) athletes and a tetraplegic (TP) athlete at rest, during prolonged upper body exercise and recovery. METHODS: Exercise was performed on a Monark cycle ergometer (Ergomedic 814E) adapted for arm exercise at 60% $\dot{V}O_2$ peak for 60 minutes in cool conditions ('normal' lab temperature; 21.5+/–1.7 °C and 47+/–7.8% relative humidity). Aural and skin temperatures were continually monitored. RESULTS: Mean (+/–SD) peak oxygen uptake values were greater (P<0. 05) for the AB when compared to the PA (3.45+/–0.45 l min^{-1} and 2. 00+/–0.46 l min^{-1}, respectively). Peak oxygen uptake for the TP was 0.91 l min^{-1}. At rest, aural temperature was similar between groups (36.2+/–0.3 °C, 36.3+/–0.3 °C and 36.3 °C for AB, PA and TP athletes, respectively). During exercise, aural temperature demonstrated relatively steady state values increasing by 0.6+/–0.4 °C and 0.6+/–0.3 °C for the AB and PA athletes, respectively. The TP athlete demonstrated a gradual rise in aural temperature throughout the exercise period of 0.9 °C. Thigh skin temperature increased by 1.3+/–2.5 °C for the AB athletes (P<0.05) whereas the PA athletes demonstrated little change in temperature (0.1+/–3.4 °C and –0.7 °C, respectively). Calf temperature increased for the PA athletes by 1.0+/–3.6 °C (P<0.05), whereas a decrease was observed for the AB athletes of –1.0+/–2.0 °C (P<0.05) during the exercise period. During 30 minutes of passive recovery, the AB athletes demonstrated greater decreases in aural temperatures than the PA athletes (P<0. 05). Aural temperature for the TP increased peaking at 5 minutes of recovery remaining elevated until the end of the recovery period. Fluid consumption and weight losses were similar for the AB and PA athletes (598+/–433 ml and 403+/–368 ml; 0.38+/–0.39 kg and 0.38+/–0. 31 kg, respectively), whereas changes in plasma volume were greater for the AB athletes (–9.8+/–5.8% and 4.36+/–4.9%, respectively; P<0. 05). CONCLUSION: The results of this study suggest that under the experimental conditions PA athletes are at no greater thermal risk than AB athletes. A relationship between the available muscle mass for heat production and sweating capacity appears evident for the maintenance of thermal balance. During recovery from exercise, decreases in aural temperature, skin temperature and heat storage were greatest for the AB athletes with the greatest capacity for heat loss and lowest for the TP athlete with the smallest capacity for heat loss. Initial observations on one TP athlete suggest substantial thermoregulatory differences when compared to AB and PA athletes.

Table 2.2 demonstrates some of the key information that could be taken from the abstract provided. Please note that the importance of each key point will differ depending on what you are interested in reporting or stating. The following examples demonstrate some potential combinations of information. How you use the information will be determined by what you want to say in your introduction and what the specific question is that you are asking.

1 **A general comment regarding measurement of maximal oxygen uptake**

Maximal oxygen uptake values for a range of athletes have been determined (Astorino et al., 2004; Price and Campbell, 1997; O'Toole et al., 1987; Svedenhag and Sjödin, 1985).

2 **Describing $\dot{V}O_2$max within a specific athlete group**

Svedenhag and Sjödin (1985) determined the maximal oxygen uptake of a range of elite runners. Athletes ranged from those competing at distances of 400 m up to the marathon. The greatest values were seen for 5000–10,000-m runners (78.7 ml·kg^{-1}·min^{-1}).

3 **Describing $\dot{V}O_2$max across sports**

Maximal oxygen uptake values are greatest in distance runners when compared to cyclists and wheelchair athletes (Price and Campbell, 1997; O'Toole et al., 1987; Svedenhag and Sjödin, 1985).
OR

Elite distance runners demonstrate $\dot{V}O_{2max}$ values of over 70 ml·kg^{-1}·min^{-1} (Svedenhag and Sjödin, 1985). Triathletes have demonstrated lower $\dot{V}O_{2max}$ values than this during cycling (68.8 ml·kg^{-1}·min^{-1}) and lower values still during arm exercise (49.1 ml·kg·min^{-1}; O'Toole et al., 1987).
OR

$\dot{V}O_{2max}$ is generally greatest during treadmill running and cycling with lower values observed for arm exercise (Price and Campbell, 1997; O'Toole et al., 1987; Svedenhag and Sjödin, 1985). Values may also change over a competitive season (Astorino et al., 2004).

Now that you have practised extracting and linking information from difference sources, it is time to put your introduction together. The following section will help you do this.

2.5   Writing an introduction

Whether you are writing a lab report, a dissertation or embarking upon writing a research paper or a review article you need to have a good grasp of what has been previously reported in the literature. Most authors addressing the different stages of a research project (Eston and Rowlands, 2000) or manuscript preparation (Altinörs, 2002) highlight the importance of undertaking an initial 'detailed survey' of the literature. Indeed, being well read in your area is an important first step of the writing process (Hall, 2011). Having read a wide range of pertinent literature, you will then need to synthesise the information to develop and finalise your research question. For lab reports this will be more directed based upon what you have done in your classes; however, it is still important to read widely.

When writing an introduction a number of authors suggest a 'three paragraph approach' (Alexandrov, 2004; Foote, 2006a). This follows the 'general to specific' nature of introductions noted earlier with the information presented leading clearly on to the aims and hypotheses. Consider the first exercise in this chapter where you described each paragraph of an introduction using one or two words. We will use this principle in writing an introduction.

Exercise 2.4   Writing an introduction

For the key aspects of your introduction plan out three paragraphs (you can, of course, use more). Start by considering the key aspects you need to cover based on your title, aims and the methods undertaken in your class.

Paragraph 1: ....

....

Paragraph 2: ....

....

Paragraph 3: ....

....

Once done, expand each aspect with information from the literature which helps to introduce each term or shows how a term may be used or providing example values.

2.6   Critiquing an introduction

We noted earlier in the text (see Chapter 1) that when asked to critique a piece of writing it is important to note positive aspects as well as those you consider could be improved. Being able to critique previous work is an important aspect of your research methods and scientific training and is considered in greater detail later in this chapter (Section 2.8). The skill of being able to critique your own work is also of great importance and may help you achieve better marks. Exercise 2.5 is designed to start critiquing introductions, but you can try it for your own work once you have your first draft ready.

Exercise 2.5 Critiquing an introduction

In conjunction with Section 2.10 ('Common problems in writing introductions and literature reviews'), read the introduction and determine whether you think it would achieve many marks for a lab report assessment. Using the same skills that you used for critiquing abstracts in the previous chapter (Section 1.5, Exercise 1.3) note any good aspects or those that could be improved as you can. Some comments are provided in Table 2.3.

Example introduction for ground reaction force lab report

Damavandi et al. looked at ground reaction forces in exercise (2012). Ground reaction forces are forces that the body produces during exercise. Biomechanics is therefore very important for sport and exercise science. In this lab class we will look at different ground reaction forces. We looked at different running speeds and measured the ground reaction forces with a force plate. The data was analysed.

Lipfert et al. (2012) examined ground reaction forces and developed a model of ground reaction forces in running and walking. This is useful for assessing values when you can't measure them. Hall (2018) defines ground reaction forces in relation to Newton's third law of motion. These forces differ between people who are rearfoot and midfoot strikers. It is therefore important to measure these forces for footwear and injury concerns.

The aim of this lab class was to measure ground reaction forces in walking and running. We hypothesised that they would differ between conditions.

Table 2.3 Points of critique for the example introduction

Overall, the introduction is very short and does not provide information in a coherent way. There are also wording and referencing errors.

Paragraph 1

1. The paragraph does refer to a previous study (Damavandi et al., 2012) but incorrectly referenced and provided little if any information. It would be better to provide appropriate definitions of ground reaction forces and background information to start with.
2. The ground reaction force definitions are vague and incorrect and are also not referenced.

(Continued)

Table 2.3 (Continued)

3. Third sentence is very general. It would be useful to start the introduction if it contained more information.
4. From the fourth sentence the introduction begins to provide methods information.

Paragraph 2

1. Some more background information is provided, but it lacks specific details. The reader will be unable to determine specific facts from what is reported or why it is important to cite this study in relation to the lab report.
2. More definitions of ground reaction forces but these should really be in the first paragraph.
3. It is good that some applications of measuring ground reaction forces have been attempted. However, these are not referenced and the specific details relating to what measurements would be useful and how the results could be specifically used is missing.

Paragraph 3

1. Both the aim and hypothesis are provided. However, the aim itself does not relate to what is covered in the introduction. It would be expected that if your aim relates to ground reaction forces in walking and running then these are described and explained in the introduction. Provide examples of expected values.
2. Likewise, the hypothesis does not provide an indication of which forces may be greatest.

2.7   Planning and writing a literature review

There are a range of texts about how to write literature reviews across a number of disciplines (Ridley, 2008; Hart, 1998). There are also some general texts within the area of sport and exercise science regarding undertaking final-year projects (Lynch, 2010) and research methods (Thomas and Nelson, 2001) which contain useful information regarding literature searches and report writing. However, as writing a literature review is not the sole purpose of this book the aim of the following section is simply to provide some basic guidance.

As we noted earlier, a literature review is a much more in-depth approach to demonstrating your understanding of an area when compared to a lab report introduction. In addition, it must form a solid basis for your research study and the rationale or justification for your study. By this we mean that you have to show that there is a gap in the literature which has not been examined and that this is what you intend to study. You need to make it clear why your study is different from those that have been reported previously. Just because something has not been done before it is not a good reason to study it! Thomas and Nelson (2001) consider Type III and Type IV errors. The former relates to asking the wrong research question and the latter relates to solving a problem that is not worth solving. A thorough literature review should hopefully prevent these errors occurring and indeed a potential fifth error of researching something that has already been reported. For example, there have been many studies assessing differences in personality on exercise behaviours or whether carbohydrate ingestion improves performance, but why is your research study different from all the others? Ask yourself whether someone could read your literature review and, without reading your aims, have a good idea of what your research question is likely to be. If the answer is yes, then you have done a good job. If it is likely that someone could read your literature review and be left struggling to see what you wish to examine, then the review is not clear. Furthermore, if your aims do not relate to what you have reviewed, then you are again off topic and you will need to refocus your review. By carefully planning your review in the same way as planning an introduction (Exercises 2.3 to 2.5), each section of the review should be related to your research question.

Don't underestimate how difficult it may be to clearly justify your study. If you are struggling to get your ideas written down clearly, try and explain your ideas to someone. Verbalising your thoughts may help focus your explanation. When my PhD supervisor was confronted with various unclear paragraphs of text he would ask me to simply tell him what I meant. When I did, in one or two sentences, he would then ask, 'Why didn't you just write that?' It may not be as quite easy as that all the time and of course you will need to add your references and underlying theories or responses to explain your ideas, but it is certainly one method of clarifying your ideas. Many undergraduate and postgraduate supervisors, myself included, often repeatedly write questions or comments on students' work, such as 'Why?' or 'How?' to get them to try and clarify and rationalise their research questions.

2.7.1   Planning a literature review

Before putting pen to paper, you need to know the literature relating to your research questions – you also need to know your research question! Many students (especially undergraduate students) know this well before they may understand the specifics of the area being studied. Don't try and plan too much prior to reading the literature; you may find that your review plan may change dramatically as the story behind the underlying literature unfolds. Furthermore, literature reviews evolve as you undertake and write other sections of your project. This is also true when you are writing your discussion where important components may come to light which you had not originally considered. You may then decide to add these areas to your review.

So, how do you start to plan your review? Consider the summary table you developed for your literature sources suggested earlier in the chapter. From this there may be a pattern of responses or specific themes that you can use as subheadings (Hardy and Ramjeet, 2005). You will also need to critique the literature you have obtained and always have your research question in mind. Ensure that you have read and summarised your research papers before attempting Exercise 2.5.

Do you remember the 'three-paragraph' approach to writing introductions? You may find it helpful to consider a similar approach to your literature review but this time, instead of three paragraphs, consider three sections (Figure 2.7). The first section should relate to introducing the research area. Here you may want to state what areas the review will cover, if you undertake a systematic review you can note what your search terms and criteria were (see Section 2.2.1.i), include why the area of study is important, what the applications for the results of such a study may be. It may also be useful to note the areas that you will be covering to give an overview of the reviews structure and content (Bem, 1995). If you always have your research hypotheses in mind, this can give you significant direction in your planning.

A second section of the review would be the main body of the review. Unfortunately, there is no easy answer as to how to plan this section of the review as all reviews differ depending upon what you are studying and what you intend to develop for your rationale. An important tip is not to be too inclusive and try to cover everything but also not to be too exclusive by using only one or two key references (especially if you obtained only recent electronic sources). In this section of your review a literature summary table can become very useful. Each factor that has emerged may help you devise the main headings and subheadings within the text. Here subheadings are essential, so the reader knows exactly what they are supposed to be reading about. However, a common error here is when the text does not relate to what the subheading suggests it should. An error such as this can be overcome by proof reading and using the 'one word descriptors' for each of your paragraphs, as in Exercise 2.1, to ensure the content is relevant to the heading. An important point here is to note that for some research areas there may not be many articles relating to your research question. Students often struggle if there are no studies asking

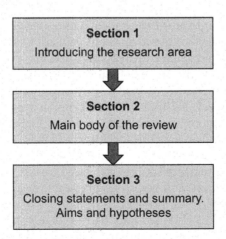

Figure 2.7 Three potential sections for a literature review

exactly the same research question that they have developed. This is not a problem; if there were similar studies, why is yours original? There will certainly always be a range of related studies from which you can develop your hypotheses. In addition, there will likely be a number of key or opposing viewpoints on the subject area, it is important to demonstrate that you know these and that you can back up and explain your decision.

The third and final section of the review should bring the review to a close, ending in a summary and your subsequent aims and hypotheses. Bem (1995) considers that you should end a literature review with a bang rather than a whimper. What research has not been reported so far and which studies should be undertaken to bridge the gap in knowledge? Hopefully, one of these suggestions will be related to your research hypothesis.

Exercise 2.5   Planning a literature review

Hopefully by now you will be happy with your research question and will be well read in the supporting literature. Consider the key themes within the literature and what factors have emerged as being important to the area. The suggestions in Sections 1 and 3 are simply to get you started in formatting and planning your review. For Section 2 revisit your literature summary table for key themes. Using these key themes is one approach you may find useful. However, the content will vary with the area studied and the research question. Therefore, it is worth trying this approach even though you may use other methods to plan your literature review. You should always discuss the content with your supervisor.

Section 1:

> What areas will the review cover?
> For systematic reviews, what search terms and criteria were considered?
> Why is the area of study important?
> What applications are there for the results of such studies?

Section 2:

> Consider the key themes as subheadings

Section 3:

> What research has not been reported so far?
> Which studies should be undertaken to bridge the gap in knowledge?
> Aims and objectives
> Hypotheses

> If you are struggling trying to plan your review, you may find it help-
> ful to work backwards from your research question considering what
> would be useful to discuss from specific to general points.

2.7.2   Writing a literature review

Once the key planning of your review has been done you can begin writing
in earnest. At this stage you will have ideally read the literature, critiqued
the studies and written or at least be happy with your research hypothesis.
Essentially, you will be adding the detail to each of your subheadings. Please
note that your headings may well evolve as your writing does and your focus
becomes clearer. Some headings may disappear whereas other new ones may
appear. Much of your writing will relate to the reporting and critiquing of
research studies (Section 2.8) and developing your research question; so, it
is important that you are happy with extracting information from your literature sources (Exercise 2.2). You must also ensure that you produce a clear
overview. Many reviews at undergraduate level can become either catalogues
of information involving long lists of studies which lack integration of key
points or summaries of information with few links made between them. Try
to avoid such an approach and integrate your key studies together clearly
and logically (Exercise 2.3). Moreover, if no one has reported an aspect of the
area you are interested in, it is perfectly acceptable to state that. However, in
this instance you may have to think a little more laterally to try and develop
aspects of your rationale.

   Bem (1995) provides a helpful overview of scientific writing when considering literature reviews submitted to the journal *Psychological Bulletin*.
Although literature review articles may differ from undergraduate and postgraduate dissertations, the key aspects of scientific writing are essentially
the same. Bem notes that a key factor differentiating between those articles
accepted and rejected for publications is that of good writing and further
notes the primary criteria for good scientific writing are accuracy and clarity.
For accuracy, ensure that any information provided is correct. Your supervisor will likely know the details of the studies you are citing, and may well
have written the articles themselves, so they will know specific results and
explanations. For clarity, make sure you state enough information to give
an idea of the direction or magnitude or any previous results. For example,
stating that 'ground reaction forces were different' is not very enlightening.
Stating that 'ground reaction forces were greater during running than walking' or adding an idea of the magnitude of such changes or absolute values
provides a much clearer message to the reader. General writing tips are covered later in this text, and it is recommended that you read that chapter while
writing your review (see Section 6.4). The critique aspect of using literature
is considered in the following section.

2.8 Critiquing journal articles

The ability to think independently and critically is a key aspect of higher education (Ryall, 2010) and is particularly important in the final year of degree-level study. However, students often find critical analysis difficult. How do you go about beginning your critique of an article? How can you critique something that is already published? This section will hopefully provide some answers to those common questions and some ideas of how to approach the critical appraisal of a journal article or any other information source. Postgraduate students may find journal clubs or research seminar series quite useful for the discussion or critique of various journal articles or research studies, including their own.

So, what is critical analysis? Ryall (2010) notes that a critical thinker is able to make judgements based on sound reasoning. These judgements will depend on what is important to you and the sound reasoning will likely relate to previous research findings and your interpretation of them. Young and Solomon (2009) state that critical analysis is a systematic approach applied to determine the strengths and weaknesses of a journal article to assess both its usefulness and the validity of the reported findings. Greenhalgh (1997) states that critical analysis is the assessment of methodological quality. Importantly, Coughlan et al. (2007) note that critical analysis is not a criticism but an objective and balanced scrutiny of a piece of work not only highlighting strengths and weaknesses but also help ascertain whether the source is trustworthy and unbiased.

The majority of definitions of critical appraisal, such as those mentioned earlier, note that both the strengths and weaknesses of a source are to be considered. Critique is not just negative or 'bad' points, it is also a consideration of what is new, novel and 'good'. Students can often be quite negative in critiquing work but remember that if the research studies you read were truly 'bad' it is unlikely that they would be published. Just because a study has not measured a variable that you are particularly interested in does not mean that it is bad, it probably just wasn't of key importance or interest to the authors. Furthermore, any criticism of other authors' work should be expressed in an objective manner (Wieseler and McGauran, 2010). Your critique should not be a demolition or 'trashing' of someone else's work (Ridley, 2008; Young and Solomon, 2009). Consider how you would react if similar comments were passed on your piece of work.

So how do you go about critiquing a journal article? You have already done this at a basic level in extracting what you thought was important from the abstracts in the earlier exercise (Exercise 2.4) and in establishing where gaps in the literature exist for your project area. Exercise 2.4 also noted that what you think is important may differ from what someone else considers to be important. Part of a critique is taking this one step further. Some authors suggest focusing upon the methods section (Greenhalgh, 1997) and a lot of critique does indeed focus on the 'what did they do aspects'. As Greenhalgh (1997) notes, most journal articles conform to the IMRaD principle covering not only methods but also the 'why did they do it?' (Introduction), 'What did they find?' (Results) and 'What do the results mean?' (Discussion) aspects. These other sections are also worthy of your critique.

2.8.1   Critical appraisal tools

There are a range of critical appraisal tools available in the literature which may help develop your critiquing skills. More seasoned academics are unlikely to use a structured profoma when critiquing or reviewing journal articles; instead, they rely predominantly upon their research and publishing experience. However, for those less experienced researchers published guidelines will be of much more value. Guidelines and advice have been produced for the critical appraisal of journal articles in both quantitative and qualitative research in nursing (Coughlan et al., 2007; Ryan et al., 2007), physiology (Seals and Tanaka, 2000), psychology (Hyman, 1995), medicine, (Greenhalgh, 1997; Young and Solomon, 2009), general practice (MacAuley, 1994), public health (Heller et al., 2008) and physical therapy (Domholdt et al., 1994; Maher et al., 2004) and many other areas. Although these guides are all very useful and developed for specific research disciplines there is no 'gold standard' procedure and whatever process is undertaken must evolve with advances in methodological and non-methodological factors (Greenhalgh, 1997). To illustrate this point, when you read older journal articles or 'classic' studies and critique them for not using a particular technique, bear in mind that many techniques commonly employed today may not have been widely available at the time of writing. Differences also exist between quantitative and qualitative research processes and in the way in which the critique process should be approached (Ryan et al., 2007).

More general models of critical appraisal provide general concepts for the appraiser to consider. For example, Deane (2010) considers seven points for the general critique of information sources including whether the evidence presented is convincing and what level of subjectivity or bias exists within the work (Table 2.4). Similarly, Young and Solomon (2009) provide ten questions to ask from a clinical perspective including whether the study is relevant and adds anything new and if any conflicts of interest exist, an important aspect for clinical drug trials (Table 2.5). Other more detailed models provide a greater number of specific questions to be asked within each section of the article (Heller et al., 2008; Seals and Tanaka, 2000).

2.8.1.i   Critiquing and changing your professional practice

As noted earlier, there are a large number of critical appraisal tools in the literature. Crowe and Sheppard (2011) compared 44 critical appraisal tools

Table 2.4 Seven questions to ask when critiquing an information source (Deane, 2010)

1 Does the source use primary evidence?
2 Does the source use secondary evidence?
3 Is the evidence convincing?
4 What are the author's credentials?
5 What assumptions does the author make?
6 What subjectivity or bias is evident in the source?
7 Is the language emotive?

Table 2.5 Young and Solomon's ten questions to ask when critically appraising a research article (Young and Solomon, 2009)

1 Is the study question relevant?
2 Does the study add anything new?
3 What type of research question is being asked?
4 Was the study design appropriate for the research question?
5 Did the study methods address the most important potential sources of bias?
6 Was the study performed according to the original protocol?
7 Does the study test a stated hypothesis?
8 Were the statistical analyses performed correctly?
9 Do the data justify the conclusions?
10 Are there any conflicts of interest?

concluding that users need to be careful about which tool they use and how they use it. The authors later developed their own critical appraisal tool (Crowe et al., 2011, 2012). With this in mind, an important aspect of critical appraisal is whether you wish to assess the scientific rigour of an article (i.e. its quality or internal reliability) or how applicable the work is to your own practices (i.e. its value or external validity) (MacAuley, 1994; Maher et al., 2004). The majority of undergraduate and postgraduate students in sport and exercise science are probably critiquing with respect to scientific rigour as they are generally, but not exclusively, writing an academic piece of work. Conversely, those students in areas such as sports therapy and certainly those professionals currently in practice may be more likely to be interested in how a piece of research may affect their treatments or clinical practices. The choice of critical appraisal tool would therefore be extremely important. The following paragraphs will consider some aspects of both these forms of critical appraisal.

To help assess whether the scientific evidence considered will affect your clinical behaviour or the practical approach to treatment, MacAuley (1994) developed the 'READER' aid to critical appraisal. This aid was initially developed for general practitioners with limited time to undertake extensive reviews of the literature (MacAuley, 1994). The 'READER' acronym stands for Relevance, Education, Applicability, Discrimination, Evaluation and Reaction, the main tenets of which are shown in Table 2.6. Each component

Table 2.6 MacAuley's READER aid to critical appraisal of research articles (MacAuley, 1994)

Component	Main factor/s and scoring system
Relevance	The article is assessed within the readers context 1 Not relevant to general practice 2 Allied to general practice 3 Only relevant to specialised general practice 4 Broadly relevant to all general practice 5 Relevant to me
Education	Context of behaviour modification Could it change your behaviour? 1 Would certainly not influence behaviour 2 Could possibly influence behaviour 3 Would cause reconsideration of behaviour 4 Would probably alter behaviour 5 Would definitely change behaviour
Applicability	Can the research be done in the reader's own practice? Can you identify with the practice or circumstances? 1 Impossible in my practice 2 Fundamental changes needed 3 Perhaps possible 4 Could be done with reorganisation 5 I could do that tomorrow
Discrimination	Is the message valid? 1 Poor, descriptive study 2 Moderately good, descriptive study 3 Good descriptive study but methods not reproducible 4 Good descriptive study with sound methodology 5 Single-blind study with attempts to control 6 Controlled single-blind study 7 Double-blind, controlled single-blind study with method problem 8 Double-blind, controlled single-blind study with statistical deficiency 9 Sound scientific paper with minor faults 10 Scientifically excellent paper
Evaluation	If epidemiologically sound paper should be considered seriously Score based on READ elements
Reaction	Scoring category (NB: the research is not necessarily 'bad', just not for your current needs) 24+ Classic paper which should make an immediate impact on practice 20–23 Paper is of value and filed for immediate access 15–19 Paper may be of interest <15 Paper had failed to fulfil the criteria

has a score with the usefulness of the information being graded according to the total score. This scale has been shown to be valid and reliable and has been used in a range of educational scenarios for general practitioners (Bleakley and MacAuley, 2002; MacAuley, 1996; MacAuley and McCrum, 1999; MacAuley and Sweeney, 1997; MacAuley et al., 1998).

The main reason for introducing this scale here relates to the 'Relevance' component. A key factor of the component stresses that the article is assessed within the readers' own context, highlighting that what is useful for one reader may not be useful for another and is thus an individual process. Also, your needs may differ over time and in different situations. This is especially true if it has the potential to change your behaviour. Similar tools and appraisal advice have been provided for public health (Heller et al., 2008) and physical therapy (Maher et al., 2004; Domholdt et al., 1994). Students may find these useful for the practical aspects of their courses. Even though the focus of these appraisal tools is towards that of potentially altering professional practice, they still involve assessing the appropriateness of research questions and hypotheses, study design and interpretation of results (Heller et al., 2008) and the scientific or clinical basis of the work. Don't forget that changing professional practice is not just limited to those people working in clinical areas or with patients. Professional practice of sport and exercise scientists includes why you use certain exercise protocols or questionnaires and data collection and analysis techniques, all of which may be affected by what you read in the literature and thus your evidence-based practice.

2.8.1.ii   Critiquing scientific rigour

Most students writing dissertations and compiling literature reviews are probably concerned with the scientific rigour of journal articles. Here, experience in research and writing is invaluable. Most students though will not have developed these skills to a large extent as they are in the early stages of their subject-specific research training. Many of the suggested critique questions within the various published critical appraisal guidelines parallel the advice given for writing literature reviews and the other sections of lab reports, dissertations and research studies. Seals and Tanaka (2000) developed a guide for critiquing scientific articles based upon the forum of postgraduate research seminars. The contents of the guide (Table 2.7) relate to most areas of sport and exercise science whether examined from physiological, psychological or biomechanical perspectives. If we compare this to the general model of critical appraisal the underlying themes are identical, it is the specific terminology that changes with respect to subject discipline.

To help researchers develop their critical appraisal skills, there a number of resources available, some of which your supervisors may well direct you to. These include, but are by no means limited to, the Critical Appraisal Skills Programme (or CASP), The Centre for Evidence-Based Medicine, the Joanna Briggs Institute and The Cochrane Collaboration. Some of the most used

Table 2.7 Critiquing a journal article (Seals and Tanaka, 2000)

Section	
Title	Does the title accurately reflect the purpose, design, results and conclusions of the study?
Abstract	Succinct, clear, comprehensive summary of the main text of the paper? Content consistent with that presented in the main text? Data or other key information presented here but not in the main text (or vice versa)
Introduction	Succinctly state what is known and unknown about the topic? Functional, biological and/or clinical significance established Specific experimental question, goal or aim to be addressed stated? Are previous studies' strengths and limitations described? Is it clear how experimental approach will provide unique insight?
Methods	Participants adequately described? Population appropriate for the research question? Participant number sufficient? Population used allow extensive or limited generalisability? Assignment of participants to conditions randomised? Ethical issues and consent described? Does the design allow hypothesis to be rigorously tested scientifically? Are proper control groups/conditions included? Are confounding factors controlled? Has the method been described in sufficient detail to be repeated? Are measurement techniques reliable, precise and valid? Rationale for measures explained? Appropriate data calculation and analysis? Statistics appropriate for the study design? Statistical assumptions tested/violated? Alpha level clearly stated?
Results	Data reported in a clear, concise and well-organised manner? Where necessary are standard deviations and standard errors reported (any excess variability)? All data presented? Any data presented on any measurement not described in the methods? Are all the figures and tables needed? Tables and figures properly labelled with correct units and scaled appropriately? Any repetition of data in figure and tables? Is the data within the expected range? How do group differences compare to measurement variability?
Discussion	Major new findings clearly described and properly emphasised? Key conclusions adequately supported by the experimental data? Is there any alternative way to interpret the data? Significance of the results described? How do results extend previous knowledge? Observations for previous studies described in the context of present results? Statements supported by appropriate references? Data discussed with insight beyond previously? Unique aspects and other experimental strengths properly highlighted? Experimental limitations described so as to interpret the results appropriately? Suggestions for future work?

critical appraisal tools within health sciences have been developed by these centres. Although appraisal tools developed for randomised controlled trials appear to be the most abundant (Zeng et al., 2015), they are also available for a range of other designs such as appraising systematic reviews, qualitative studies, cohort studies, case control studies, case series and case reports, etc. (See Table 3.1 for a description of typical research designs.) Worksheets or checklists for these reviews are available for download from these sites. As well as these established tools, new appraisal tools are always being developed as well as existing tools being adapted. For example, Long et al. (2020) developed an additional question to the CASP qualitative study appraisal tool as well as providing guidance on its application.

It is important to remember that although critical appraisal is often a personal, albeit evidence-based view, you should consider the different components of quality rather than a study simply being evaluated as just good or poor (Long et al., 2020). Where the different components of quality are evaluated individually critical appraisal tools are considered as 'domain-based'. It is though possible to generate an overall score for methodological quality of a study to aid in the overall rating. For example, Downs and Black (1998) developed a checklist for use with both randomised and non-randomised control trials to alert reviewers of the strengths and weaknesses of the study's methodological quality. More specifically, a profile of scores for quality of reporting, internal validity (bias and confounding factors), power and external validity is generated (Appendix 2a). Originally, a total of 27 items were presented with 25 of these scored as either one point for 'yes' and zero for 'no' or 'unable to determine'. One item relating to whether specific 'confounders' within each participant group were stated was scored as two, one and zero for 'yes', 'partially' and 'no', respectively, and another item relating to the power of the study was rated out of five. The latter scoring system has since been adapted by a number of users to be in line with the majority of items (i.e. a maximal score of 28 rather than 32 for randomised studies and 25 for non-randomised studies). The consideration of 'confounders' within the assessment has allowed authors within sport and exercise science to include specific methodological factors relating to the review question (e.g. Baumgart et al., 2020). For example, a review of peak oxygen uptake obtained from the use of different modes of upper body exercise utilised confounders of age, sex, body mass, type of disability, physical activity and test protocol. A score of '2' was achieved if all were noted, and '1' if five of the six were noted (Baumgart et al., 2020). The overall Downs and Black score has subsequently been used to categorise studies into those of excellent (26–28), good (20–25), fair (15–19) or poor quality (≤14) (Hooper et al., 2008). If assessed items are not relevant to the study, these can be omitted and the maximal score adjusted accordingly and expressed as a percentage.

Similar to the Downs and Black tool, Kmet et al. (2004) developed the 'QualSyst' tool for scoring qualitative and quantitative studies. In addition to 'yes' and 'no' scoring the fourteen-item quantitative tool (Appendix 2b) allows for 'not applicable' options in the ratings and, with these items omitted, an adjusted overall maximal score is produced. Within the ten-item qualitative tool (Appendix 2c) a 'not appliable' response is not permitted. In discussing the agreement between reviewers using these tools Kmet et al. also considered the use of a minimal threshold for quality scores for the inclusion of potential studies within a systematic review. For both qualitative and quantitative tools as the threshold score for inclusion increased from 55% to 75% the number of excluded studies also increased (i.e. more stringent criteria for inclusion). However, the use of threshold summary scores to identify studies that are of high quality for inclusion in reviews does introduce bias to that review (Kmet et al., 2004), particularly a form of selection bias (Stone et al., 2019). The use of such quality ratings (numerical or otherwise) by undergraduate students is most likely in their inclusion within any summary table of studies reviewed and subsequent integration within the discussion. For example, if you identify twenty studies within your search criteria and all are rated as excellent, this is likely to put a different perspective on your discussion than if a number (or all) are rated as poor. Within discussions, it is important to consider what contributes to your lower ratings and studies consequently being considered as poor. You may see a pattern emerge which is excellent for demonstrating higher-level appreciation and use of whatever tool has been implemented. Are lower ratings due to simply a lack of reporting specific points required within the appraisal tool or poor design and discussion?

The use of a single overall score for the purposes of quality evaluation is not without its limitations or critics. O'Connor et al. (2015) note how the inclusion of factors such as ethics and statistical analysis within the assessment that are not directly related to quality or potential bias per se could be misleading to the evaluation. Indeed, the authors further note how a well-reported study but with methodological bias could still present a high-quality rating. Conversely, although many aspects of critique are indeed general, important components relating to bias are not universal and depend upon the particular research area (O'Connor et al., 2015). As with all aspects of sport and exercise science – and likely research in general – there are many protocols and procedures available to reach the required end goal, all with their pros and cons, and critical appraisal is no exception. So, no matter whether you use a domain-based or an overall numerical scoring tool, all quality assessment tools require each study to be read thoroughly, critiqued and understood to provide your overall opinion. The more this process is undertaken and reflected upon the more critical appraisal will hopefully become second nature in conjunction with your reading – and that is what is important. Just as 'all roads lead to Rome' hopefully all critical appraisal tools will lead to development of critical appraisal skills which, as a developing researcher, is the key goal.

Even with detailed checklists and scoring, critical appraisal tools remain subjective, and bias should be avoided. To help with assessing bias, the Cochrane Risk-of-Bias tool was developed – and has been considered the best tool for this purpose (Zeng et al., 2015). A full explanation of the Cochrane risk-of-bias tool can be seen on the Cochrane website (https://

training.cochrane.org/handbook/current/chapter-08). In brief, the tool considers five domains of bias that are known to affect randomised controlled trials. These being the risk of bias arising from the randomisation process; bias due to deviations from the intended intervention; bias due to missing outcome data; bias in the measurement of the outcome and bias in the selection of the reported result. A number of 'signalling questions' are then completed for each domain to elicit information relevant to the risk of bias. These questions are answered as either 'yes', 'probably yes', 'probably no', 'no' and 'no information'. Each domain can then be given a risk-of-bias judgement of low risk, some concerns or high risk resulting in an overall risk-of-bias judgement using the same descriptors. The existence, or otherwise, of bias, like quality ratings can then be integrated into your review.

In conclusion, critical appraisal can take many forms and is specific to the needs of the reader at that time and the task they are set. All of the examples and guidelines given are essentially the same but focus upon different aspects of critique. For example, Deane's (2010) questions are more general and assess the type of information source reviewed and its validity whereas Young and Solomon's (2009) questions cover more discipline-specific considerations. Although MacAuley's (1994) critique is focused mainly with the applicability of research to practise and the potential to change professional behaviour, as with Young and Solomon, the methodological aspects have a large emphasis on the overall score. In this context, many reviewers would have considered the specific points raised by Seals and Tanaka (2000) in evaluating methodological components. Similarly, any scientist assessing the rigour of an experimental design may well subsequently decide to use that method. With these guidelines and comments in mind your critical appraisal skills will develop as you read and assess more information sources. Consider the aspects of each model presented here (please note that there are many more available) in relation to the stage of research you are at and put them into practice with the next article you read. Your critique and application of knowledge will then soon develop.

Exercise 2.7

For a journal article obtained from your literature search use the different methods provided for appraising journal articles to:

1   Determine whether the article is useful for your literature review
2   Critique the article using the specific criteria of Seals and Tanaka (2000)
3   Determine whether the article will affect what you do with respect to your research design.

2.9   Aims, objectives and hypotheses

At the end of the introduction or literature review you will need to state the aim/s of your experiment. Your aims should follow on smoothly from your literature review and be based on logical reasoning (Thomas and Nelson, 2001). If you have written a clear and informative literature review, the reader should have a good idea of what you intend to study or at least where the gaps in the literature exist. Your aim may further be considered to be something that is achievable or a 'resolvable question' (Hopkins et al., 2009). The aim is often expected to be followed by your scientific hypotheses, this is especially true for undergraduate and post-graduate theses. In many cases, the aim will be very similar to your title as this reflects what you are investigating. The objectives of a study are often required for final-year projects and essentially relate to what you will do to achieve your aims.

The hypothesis relates to what you think will happen in your study. This should be based upon the information present in your introduction or literature review and therefore previous knowledge. There are two key hypotheses usually presented; the null hypothesis, which states there is no difference between conditions, and the alternative or experimental hypothesis, which states the change in direction or magnitudes of change you expect to find. The null hypothesis is what we are testing statistically. Hence, you may read that researchers have 'rejected their null hypothesis' when a statistically significant result is obtained. A common error is to state that there will be a difference between your conditions but not stating the direction in which you think it may occur. Another common error is stating hypotheses which are not consistent with or that contradict what you have stated in the introduction or literature review.

Many students will write their aim and hypotheses of their study quite quickly without giving much thought to their importance. However, don't underestimate how important they are as they underpin everything that you are doing. As such each section of your dissertation has an important link to your aims and hypotheses. For your methods, consider what you are actually testing. Does your study design reflect the question you are actually trying to answer? Do the variables measured reflect the responses in question? For your results, does your analysis examine the appropriate differences or relationships postulated? Within your discussion, are you actually explaining your results with your aims in mind? If not, then you may be off topic. It seems obvious that you would discuss your data in relation to your key research question, but this is seldom the case in many first drafts of theses. Table 2.8 shows examples for aims, objectives and hypotheses for the three lab class examples used throughout this book.

Table 2.8 Examples aims, objectives and hypotheses for the three lab class examples used throughout this book

Lab class	Aim	Objectives	Null hypothesis	Alternative hypothesis
Maximal oxygen uptake	To determine maximal oxygen uptake in running, cycling an arm ergometry	To measure maximal oxygen uptake during treadmill running, cycling and arm ergometry To measure maximal heart rate during treadmill running, cycling and arm ergometry To measure peak running speeds or power output during treadmill running, cycling and arm ergometry	There will be no differences in maximal oxygen uptake between exercise modes	Maximal oxygen uptake will be greatest during treadmill running and lowest during arm ergometry
Ground reaction forces	To determine ground reaction forces during walking and running	To measure ground reaction forces using a force plate To measure walking and running speed using timing gates	There will be no differences between ground reaction forces between walking and running	Ground reaction forces during running will be greater than those during walking
Anxiety on performance	To determine the effects of anxiety on basketball shooting performance	To measure basketball shooting performance To produce high and low anxiety conditions To measure heart rate in low and high anxiety conditions	There will be no differences in basketball shooting performance in high and low anxiety conditions	Basketball shooting performance will be worse in high anxiety conditions.

Exercise 2.8   Writing aims and hypotheses

Based on the earlier examples, write the aims and hypotheses for your lab report or dissertation. Are they consistent with the title of your report?

Title:. . . . .

. . . .

. . . .

. . . .

Aims:. . . . .

. . . .

. . . .

. . . .

Objectives:. . . . .

. . . .

. . . .

. . . .

Null Hypothesis:. . . . .

. . . .

. . . .

. . . .

Alternative Hypothesis:. . . . .

. . . .

. . . .

. . . .

2.9.1   A note on titles

Having considered the introduction, literature review, aims and hypothesis, it would be remiss of us not to consider the actual title of your report! For a lab report this will most likely be provided in the lab schedule and should describe what has been done within the class – don't just title it as 'Lab report'. However, for a final-year project your title will most likely be determined by you and should reflect your study aims. Most journal guidelines state that a short informative title should be provided with some authors suggesting that the title should be between 10 and 15 words (Coughlan et al., 2007). However, as Thomas and Nelson (2001) note, a title that is too short may not be very helpful, particularly if it contains 'waste' words such as 'An investigation of' or 'A study of'. Conversely, a title that is too long can become cumbersome and awkward. Consider one of our example lab reports measuring ground reaction forces. A title of 'An examination of ground reaction forces measured from a force plate during walking and running at different speeds on a treadmill in Sports Science students' is too long. A better attempt may be 'Ground reaction forces during treadmill walking and running'. The latter title cuts out extraneous information regarding how the ground reaction forces were measured and who the participants were. However, if the participant population studied was key to the research question, then it should be contained in the title, such as '. . . . in men and boys'. You should make sure that your key research question is addressed in a clear way.

Your title should not be ambiguous or lead the reader into thinking that you are measuring something different to what you actually are. For example, Seals and Tanaka (2000) give an example of a hypothetical cross-sectional study of blood pressure in two groups of people, those with low or high sodium intake. A title such as 'Effects of sodium intake on blood pressure' would be misleading as the study did not involve participants consuming sodium prior to blood pressure being measured. However, for such a study with a cross-sectional design the authors consider 'Blood pressure in humans with low and high sodium intake' as a much more appropriate title.

2.10   Common problems in writing introductions and literature reviews

If you follow the guidance provided throughout this chapter, you will hopefully have fewer errors in your work. However, there are some common mistakes related to the advice which are worth emphasising. The following points should be read in conjunction with the 'Referencing and general writing tips' chapter later in this book (Chapter 6).

2.10.1   *No clear rationale developed*

A lack of focus in your introduction or literature review can be a key problem (Foote, 2006a). Here, students often do not clearly identify their research question or the rationale for their study; instead, they provide a general account of facts relating to the general area of the subject. Indeed, Greenhalgh (1997) notes that, amongst other reasons, journal articles are rejected by reviewers as the studies do not address an important scientific issue, the study was not original or that they were just badly written. Similarly, Peh and Ng (2010) note the common problems with [invited] literature reviews include a lack of critical evaluation, problems or unresolved areas not being highlighted – which may even be reason for your own study – and no clear take-home message. All of these points are related to developing and clearly communicating the reason for your study. Constructing a clear rationale is therefore not just a problem for undergraduate and postgraduate students.

2.10.2   *Writing 'off topic'*

This particular error is often linked to no specific rationale being developed and is a common error in lab report introductions. If your writing is going 'off topic', you may be presenting correct information but it is not relevant to your report area or what was done. In order to counteract this, always have your research question or aims in mind and ask yourself 'is this section related to my report?'. Students often include statements relating to the methods that are to be undertaken or the tests used. Unless your study is specifically focusing on protocol or procedure development save this information for the methods section. A similar problem exists in writing literature reviews. Here it is most likely that you will initially have various sections that do not help explain your research question or relate to the topic in hand. Don't be concerned about deleting large portions of text or sections you have written if they do not relate to your key aims. You can always save it in a different file, so your work is not lost. This work may come in useful for another assignment and will certainly be useful for background knowledge.

2.10.3   Aims, objectives and hypotheses

A key problem with stating the aims of a study or lab report is that they don't relate to what you have presented in the literature review or introduction. If you consider that these statements are setting the scene for your work and providing the scientific reason for the study, the aims must be consistent with these. Even when the aims relate to your rationale, a common error is that they have no direction. By this, it is meant that based on what you have stated happens in the introduction or literature review you should have an idea of how your treatment will affect the variables measured. Based on your logical reasoning, would you have expected a value to increase, decrease or have specific effects?

2.10.4   Under or over referencing

Most students know, or are at least taught, that you should always reference the information sources that you use in your work. However, a common problem, and not just in lab reports or projects, is the underuse and overuse of references. With respect to under referencing, although most lecturers will know which sources the key information you present has come from, it is still of paramount importance to acknowledge who has done the work. Stating where your information has come from is of key importance in avoiding plagiarism (Chapter 7). You should also note that your lecturers will know the sources they used within their lectures; so don't just cite these, it shows that you haven't looked for other sources yourself. An account with few or no references rings alarm bells that students do not know how to reference or have not used previous literature to develop their research questions or describe their aims.

The opposite of the underuse of references is the overuse of references. This is also a common problem (Foote, 2006a). Although it is essential to reference all your statements and the facts presented, you do not need to cite every study that has investigated or noted your given point. Depending on what you are reporting, choose one or two references which are the most recent, those which are considered influential studies or those which have utilised a similar protocol or technique. Similar to using over wordy or 'flowery' language, don't try and impress by using a large number of references. The person marking your work will see how many sources you have used by looking at your reference list. Just as writing a large number of words is not always better than a shorter concise passage, using a large number of references is not always worth more marks. The appropriateness, interpretation and use of your references are what is important. In addition, consider how the readability is affected by excessive referencing. Too many references in each sentence will certainly affect the flow of your writing.

2.10.5 Over reliance on one or two studies

You may find that one key reference, most likely a textbook or review article, will cover all your needs for the range of factors you wish to write about in your introduction. In this case, even though you have referenced appropriately the same authors will be cited in every sentence, or in a large number of sentences, within a paragraph. Here you appear over reliant on just these one or two sources. This is usually more of a problem in the earlier years of your study before you get to grips with using journal articles. However, learning to paraphrase and extract the information you need should reduce this problem. Use original journal articles whenever you can.

2.10.6 Text and subheadings

As mentioned earlier, it is a good idea to use subheadings in your literature review. Subheadings are not required within introductions of lab reports as this section is limited to a few paragraphs, and in a thesis it is just a few pages. A common error here is when the text does not match up with what the subheading suggests it should. This can be easily checked when proofreading your work and writing in the margin just one key word that the paragraph covers. If this word does not match the heading, then you should either change the heading or the content.

2.11 Chapter summary and reflections

In this chapter we have considered how to access and extract information to develop a scientific rationale for your introduction or literature review. The focus and content of your introduction or review will depend upon the level of study and the requirements of your report. For undergraduate lab reports you will be demonstrating an understanding of key principles and techniques rather than developing a rationale for a novel research study.

Undergraduate and postgraduate dissertations generally have both an introduction and a literature review whereas lab reports have only an introduction. For final-year projects, you need to consider what the gap in the literature is that has led to your research question or more simply, what your area of interest is and what hasn't been reported previously. Your rationale should therefore be based upon your critical appraisal of the literature. Once you have identified your gap or gaps in the literature these can be developed into your research question and subsequently your aims and hypotheses. To assess your understanding of introductions and literature reviews, consider the following summary questions.

- What is an introduction?
- How does an introduction differ from a literature review?
- What is critical appraisal or critiquing an article?
- What is systematic review?
- How do you generate your research question?
- What are the common errors in introductions and literature reviews?

2.12   Further activities

Browse the websites of a journal that you regularly read or are aware of. Direct yourself to the author guidelines and consider the advice given for writing and presenting introductions. See how these differ for review articles in the same journal or for journals specialising in reviews.

Use the critical appraisal tools to evaluate or critique journal articles as you undertake your background reading.

3 Methods

In this chapter you will:

• understand the importance of the methods section

(Section 3.1)

• appreciate the key components usually reported in the methods

(Section 3.2)

• write a section of your methods

(Sections 3.3 & 3.7)

• critique part of a methods section

(Section 3.8)

• identify common problems when writing methods sections

(Section 3.9)

3.1 The importance of a methods section

The methods section (not a methodology, which is a study of methods) is an integral part of your lab report or dissertation and most likely more important than many students realise. Although the results are obtained within the study, the associated conclusions and take-home message may be of primary importance to the researcher in answering their research question, the process by which they were arrived at is just as important (Ng and Peh, 2010a). The methods section should provide full details of how you intend to answer your research question (Foote, 2008; Kallet, 2004) to enable someone to replicate your study. As such it also provides a medium against which the validity of the study will be judged (Foote, 2008; Kallet, 2004; Azevedo et al., 2011; Huwiler-Müntener et al., 2002). Consider the emphasis placed on the methods section in the critical appraisal section of Chapter 2 (Section 2.8) and also the recommendation from Kyrgidis and Triaridis (2010) that if

DOI: 10.4324/9781003112426-4

the required information is not present within the methods section journal reviewers should read no further.

This chapter will outline the key components usually expected to be contained within a methods section. It is likely that if you are writing a lab report you will not require all the aspects and details noted here. However, as you progress through your studies to your final-year project and possibly on to postgraduate studies all aspects will require your consideration. Depending upon your study and research design, some methodological components may require greater description than others. As such, some components covered here have much more to them in terms of the underlying physiology, biomechanics, psychology or research methods detail than is simply reported here. If these aspects affect your study more than others, you should research them further or consult the literature for greater understanding. As with other chapters the examples provided will, where possible, reflect the main areas of sport and exercise science and the theme of the three lab reports throughout this text. However, as most undergraduates will likely have a core of exercise physiology modules to their degree studies, the content is (unintentionally) biased towards this area.

3.2   Key components of the methods section

Within the methods section there are a number of specific aspects which should be considered. In general, these follow the order in which your experiment takes. For example, you would first determine your research design based on your research question, gather participant consent and characteristics. You would then, most likely for a dissertation rather than a lab report, undertake some preliminary testing prior to your main experimental trials. Your data would then be collected in a predetermined and systematic order subsequently being analysed or processed by known procedures or techniques. Finally, you would analyse your data statistically. Therefore, in a methods section you would normally find subheadings relating to 'Study design' and 'Participants' including procedures such as ethics, informed consent and health screening. These sections are then usually followed by 'Preliminary trials', including familiarisation, and 'Experimental trials', which is probably the largest aspect including all your data collection procedures and sample analysis. The final aspect is 'Statistical analysis'. Exercise 3.1 will make you think about potential subheadings for your methods and the order of reporting your methods.

Exercise 3.1   Components of a methods section

Obtain a journal article relating to your project area or, if you are writing your final-year project, a previous dissertation from your tutor. A project that achieved a good grade will be useful; however, one that was not so successful may help too for the purposes of critique. Postgraduate students can generally obtain past dissertations from your supervisor or your university library. For your chosen report, read the methods section and consider the order of information. What are the key headings presented?

Key headings:

1 ....

2 ....

3 ....

4 ....

5 ....

Now consider the key areas of your own methods and note down your own potential subheadings.

Potential headings:

1 ....

2 ....

3 ....

4 ....

5 ....

The following subsections do not necessarily reflect the exact subheadings you would use in all lab reports and dissertations but rather reflect a number of important aspects to consider and those which need to be included in the methods wherever possible. Again, it is important to emphasise that not all of these suggestions will be required for a lab report where the research design is not necessarily an issue, and you may have only one or two participants rather than larger experimental and control groups.

3.2.1 Study design

The design of your research study is the backbone of good research and is much more than simply directing the statistics that are to be used (Knight, 2010). As such the study design reflects the strategy undertaken to control and manipulate variables to help answer your research question (Kallet, 2004). Subsequently, a great deal of importance should be placed upon the design used (Ng and Peh, 2010a). Azevedo et al. (2011) suggest starting with a general paragraph to set the scene for the study design and main characteristics of the study. Just as was suggested in the introduction and literature review chapter (Chapter 2), you should keep your research question in mind at all times. Consider all the factors taught in your research methods classes with respect to study design. What kind of study do you have? Do your participants act as their own controls in a repeated-measures design, that is, do they complete a control trial and a treatment trial in a crossover format? Are there two separate groups being compared in different conditions? If so, how are they matched? Where possible have you blinded or double-blinded your experimental groups? All of these aspects – and potentially many more – are of key importance in assessing the strength of your research design. If you are unsure as to the type of design you have, a summary of common research design descriptors is shown in Table 3.1 (Hertel, 2010).

Table 3.1 Typical research designs (Hertel, 2010)

Type of study	Description of study design
Meta-analysis	A systematic overview of studies that pools the results of two or more studies to obtain an overall answer to a question or interest. Summarises quantitatively the evidence regarding a treatment, procedure or association.
Systematic review	An article that examines published material on a clearly described subject in a systematic way. There must be a description of how the evidence on this topic was tracked down, from what sources and with what inclusion and exclusion criteria.
Randomised controlled clinical trial	A group of patients is randomised into an experimental group and a control group. These groups are followed up for the variables/outcomes of interest.
Crossover study	The administration of two or more experimental therapies, one after the other in a specified or random order to the same group of patients.
Cohort study	Involves identification of two groups (cohorts) of patients, one that received the exposure of interest and one that did not and follows these cohorts forward for the outcome of interest.
Case-control study	A study that involves identifying patients who have the outcome of interest (cases) and patients without the same outcome (controls) and looks back to see if they had the exposure of interest.
Cross-sectional study	The observation of a defined population at a single point in time or time interval. Exposure and outcome are determined simultaneously.

Case series	Describes characteristics of a group of patients with a particular disease or who have undergone a particular procedure. Design may be prospective or retrospective. No control group is used in the study, although the discussion may compare the results with others published in the literature.
Case report	Similar to the case series, except that only one case or a small group of cases is reported.
Controlled laboratory study	An in vitro or in vivo investigation in which one group receiving an experimental treatment is compared with one or more.
Descriptive epidemiology study	Observational study describing the injuries occurring in a particular sport.
Descriptive laboratory study	An in vivo or in vitro study that describes characteristics such as anatomy, physiology or kinesiology of a broad range of subjects or a specific group of interest.
Qualitative study	A study that uses qualitative methods such as grounded theory, phenomenology, ethnography or the case-study approach to understand a phenomenon. Data collection methods may include participants describing their experiences orally or in writing or researcher observation of participants' behaviour.

Stating the number of trials or conditions undertaken by your participants early on in the methods is also informative for the reader, thus providing an insight into the design of your study from the start. You can then also abbreviate your trials to aid the flow of text for the reader. For example, consider the three laboratory classes referred to throughout this book. The following statements could be used to provide the reader with initial information regarding the design of those studies.

Lab 1: Maximal oxygen uptake lab

Each participant visited the laboratory on three separate occasions. Each visit involved an incremental exercise test to exhaustion on either the treadmill (TM), cycle ergometer (CE) or arm crank ergometer (ACE).

Lab 2: Ground reaction forces lab

Each participant undertook a range of exercise trials to assess ground reaction forces during walking (WLK) and running (RUN). Due to the short exercise durations and low exercise intensities undertaken all trials were performed on the same day with each trial separated by 10 minutes of seated rest.

Lab 3: Anxiety and performance lab

Following familiarisation each participant undertook two testing sessions. One involved a low anxiety condition (LOW) and the other a high anxiety condition (HIGH).

Both statements for lab class 1 and lab class 3 inform the reader that each trial was undertaken on a separate visit to the laboratory. For lab class 2 the reader is aware from the start that all trials were performed on the same visit. In these statements, it is also useful to note that the participants were familiarised or accustomed to the exercise tests.

3.2.2 Participants or subjects?

Recently, there has been a move towards reporting the experimental groups as 'participants' rather than 'subjects'. This essentially relates to individuals participating of their own free will rather than being subjected to procedures against their will or without consent. A number of journal articles now state within their author guidelines that the term participants is their preferred description.

3.2.2.i Participant characteristics

Along with the study design, the characteristics of your participants are one of the first aspects of the method to be covered. For lab reports you may have only data for one person to report instead a group data set. In case study reports you will most certainly have only specific individuals to consider. Either way, reporting the characteristics of your participant is still important. The standard characteristics usually reported are age, height and body mass. However, you can also report characteristics such as body fat percentage or maximal oxygen uptake ($\dot{V}O_{2max}$) if these are not the main outcome measure to be reported in the results'. It is also useful, especially for final-year projects, to note the background of the population tested. It is recommended that you describe the participants in the context of the research question (Kallet, 2004). Were they trained or untrained? What training did they do at the time of the study? Has the standard of training been consistent for the six or twelve months preceding the study? Were they all from a team sport background or endurance athletes, untrained but otherwise healthy? The benefit of reporting the participant characteristics is that the reader then knows exactly what may be expected of the population in terms of exercise capacity or performance. For example, if you state 'healthy but otherwise untrained', the informed reader will have a good idea as to what, for example, their maximum oxygen uptake ($\dot{V}O_{2max}$) may be. This is when functional characteristics such as these are useful, so the reader can decide for themselves how well trained the athletes were. If your participant characteristics include more than age, height and weight, or if there are more than one group of participants resulting in laborious or confusing sentences for the reader, these data can easily be displayed in a table.

3.2.2.ii Matching groups

Stating the participant characteristics is also important when you have a matched group for comparison. Matching groups means that as many characteristics as possible, except for those distinguishing each specific group, are the same for all participants. For example, you may match groups based on age, body mass, body fat percentage, training backgrounds or characteristics, competitive standard or sex. Closely matching groups reinforces your research question and aids the effectiveness of your experimental groups. It is also important to consider the range of values with each characteristic for the groups tested and whether there is an overlap between groups, especially when fitness or competitive experience are considered.

3.2.2.iii Inclusion and exclusion criteria

Along with the number and selection of participants Ng and Peh (2010a) also consider the population and sampling methods, inclusion and exclusion criteria and how the control group (if appropriate) was selected. When it comes to data collection for many undergraduate projects the sample used is often a convenience sample of fellow students or participants from a range of university sports teams. However, inclusion and exclusion criteria should still be set. Inclusion criteria relate to any specific factors which are required to be able to participate in the study. For example, do the participants have to play specific sports, play at a given competitive standard or train a certain number of times per week? In the case of sports therapy projects do participants have to have suffered a certain injury? These factors are important for the application of your results and can increase the validity of your study considerably. Exclusion criteria are not just the opposite of inclusion criteria and relate to factors which mean not all of your potential participants are able to take part. Examples here may be having certain medical conditions. For example, would asthmatics or diabetics be able to take part in your study or would these conditions affect the results in a different way to other participants? Conversely, these conditions may also be used to define the specific population that you are interested in studying.

3.2.3 Ethics, informed consent and health screening

3.2.3.i Ethics

As you read more journal articles you will see that after the participant information has been provided there should be a statement about ethics approval and informed consent. All research studies must have received some form of ethics committee approval to allow data collection to proceed. Reporting ethics considerations is mandatory for published studies (Azevedo et al., 2011) with a number of journals requiring reference to specific statements or guidelines (e.g. Harriss and Atkinson, 2009).

Ethical approval can be obtained through an institutional ethics committee, as in the case of many universities or through other avenues such as the local health authority or clinically related ethics committees (e.g. the Integrated Research Application System or 'IRAS'; www.myresearchproject.

org.uk/). You may have read some published studies noting ethics approval through the 'Institutional Review board' which is the route taken for ethics application in the United States. You may also see reference to work being 'in accordance with the Helsinki declaration' which ensures that all research is undertaken with, amongst other factors, patient [participant] safety in mind (BMJ, 1996). When considering your ethics application, you will also likely come into contact with General Data Protection Regulations (GDPR; https://www.gov.uk/government/publications/guide-to-the-general-data-protection-regulation), which essentially replaced the Data Protection Act (www.legislation.gov.uk/ukpga/1998/29/contents) and, if using human tissues in any way, the human tissues act (www.legislation.gov.uk/uksi/2008/3067/contents/mad). Your tutors can give you further guidance on these important aspects.

Ethical approval is of key importance for undergraduate and postgraduate projects and all aspects of research undertaken. However, for the laboratory classes you undertake within your taught courses all procedures will likely be standard or established protocols with an associated risk assessment already undertaken to reduce any potential harm to the participants or experimenter. In this instance, you personally will not have had to apply for ethics approval. Consequently, the general procedure for laboratory classes is for participants to complete a health screening questionnaire and to provide written informed consent.

3.2.3.ii   *Informed consent, health screening and risk assessment*

Once a research study's ethics application has been approved data collection can proceed. Each participant will be given a participant information sheet in which all procedures are clearly outlined using terminology non-experts can understand. Terminology is very important here as not all of your participants will be studying the same degree that you are or will have the same specific knowledge. Consequently, participants may not understand the tests to be done and the language that you are used to using. Once the consent form has been read and the participant is happy to proceed they must sign the informed consent form to state that all aspects of the study have been understood and understand that they are able to withdraw at any time without question or consequence. This process is usually summarised as 'participants gave written informed consent' and is provided once at the start of the study prior to any experimental testing occurring.

In contrast to informed consent, a health screening form should be completed before every testing session. The health screening form is a declaration of the participant's health at that time and does not usually contain any details regarding the study itself, other than a statement regarding the specific tests or protocols planned for that specific testing session. The health screening form used will likely be written specifically by your university or research institution based on nationally or internationally recognised guidelines and procedures (e.g. British Association of Sport and Exercise Sciences, American College of Sports Medicine). In your laboratory reports it is important to be specific as to which forms have been completed. The forms used are often confused by undergraduate students and incorrectly reported. A health screening form is completed by every participant prior to any testing session, be it a lab class or project testing session. However, for final-year projects participants complete *one* informed consent form at the start of the study and a health screening from at the start of *every* testing session.

As part of your project ethics application, you will most likely have to complete a risk assessment form for the tests and procedures proposed. Here, the term risk refers to all aspects of health and safety and any potential injuries or unexpected events which could occur. As with health screening forms this is usually institution specific and not completed by students for lab classes. This will have been done previously by staff. However, as undergraduate students submit ethics applications for their final-year projects, completing a risk assessment form is an important component. There is always potential risk when exercising, it is the measures undertaken to reduce this risk which are important.

3.2.4 Pre-testing considerations

In every methods section you read there will be, or should be, a range of factors considered to try and reduce the amount of variation and error within the data collected. Some general factors are described here, but there are likely to be other factors specific to your own study which may potentially contribute to error in your data.

3.2.4.i Circadian rhythms

In most research studies which examine performance in some way you will no doubt read that testing occurred at the same time of day but on different days. This former aspect, time of day, is due to the effects of the body's endogenous circadian rhythms on human physiology. Circadian rhythms essentially reflect our body clock with many physiological responses co-varying with changes in body temperature over a 24-hour cycle (Reilly, 2007; Atkinson and Reilly, 1996). There are numerous studies and reviews evaluating the effects of circadian rhythms on performance (e.g. Thun et al., 2015; Teo et al., 2011), and you should try and find out whether your protocols and performance measures are affected. Determining any circadian rhythm effect is particularly important if circumstances beyond your control mean that you are unable to test participants at the same time of day on each day. Furthermore, you should always state the duration of rest between testing sessions such as 'Testing occurred at the same time of day with at least three days between trials'.

3.2.4.ii   Diet and physical activity

You will most likely be aware of studies of glycogen depletion resulting in various performance measures being affected (Suriano et al., 2010) as well as acute or chronic changes in diet (Pitsiladis and Maughan, 1999; Maughan et al., 1997). As a result of potential changes in performance due to diet and eating behaviour, it is important to ensure that your participants maintain both a consistent diet and physical activity pattern during the period of your testing and, importantly, prior to each day of testing. Similarly, when reporting the time of day at which testing occurred you will often read a statement to the effect that normal diet was maintained, and physical activity was avoided in the 24 hours prior to testing. However, the latter point may be difficult to uphold when working with athletes, so it may be phrased as 'intense physical activity was avoided'. You can check these potential confounding factors quite simply by using diet and activity questionnaires. However, if you state this has been done, you need to note whether the data was specifically analysed or checked visually or verbally.

3.2.4.iii   Menstrual cycle

The majority of physiology textbooks will likely describe the menstrual cycle with respect to the cyclical changes in sex hormones and body temperature. The range of known physiological responses which occur during the respective phases of the cycle may have subsequent effects on exercise performance. Therefore, the phase of the menstrual cycle in which female participants are in at the time of testing needs to be considered and ideally kept consistent. Such an approach will help ensure that any performance changes are a result of the treatment or intervention rather than varying concentrations of hormones (Burrows, 2007). This is particularly important for your final-year project data collection where testing can be timetabled appropriately, unlike your lab classes. There are a number of recent review articles summarising the physiology of the female athlete (Burrows and Bird, 2000; Charkoudian and Joyner, 2004), the effect of the menstrual cycle on various performance measures (Constantini et al., 2005; Janse de Jong, 2003; Lebrun, 1994) and testing considerations for the female athlete (Burrows, 2007). As with circadian rhythms, these should be consulted with respect to your own laboratory tests.

3.2.4.iv   Familiarisation to testing procedures

When you are about to begin your data collection, it is important to realise the majority of your participants are unlikely to have experienced the exact test procedures before. This is true unless of course they are on your specific degree course and have actively experienced the same lab classes or have been involved in previous research studies, Therefore, it is essential to familiarise, or accustom (Winter, 2005), your participants to the protocols and techniques required. Consider exercising for the first time wearing a face mask or using a mouthpiece and nose clip for analysis of expired gas or undertaking a test of maximal exertion. How would this feel, especially for less fit participants? For psychological or motor skill studies involving tests of reaction time or some form of cognitive function test it is likely that participants will improve their performance over the first few attempts. If participants are not given time to practise the tests and an improvement in performance is observed in your results, this could simply be due to a learning effect rather than a true experimental affect. Many authors will therefore state that 'participants were fully familiarised with all procedures prior to testing'. It is important here to give as much detail as you can with respect to how this was done.

Exercise 3.2   Has a learning effect occurred?

To determine whether a learning effect has occurred is relatively straightforward. If you have two performance trials, such as for ingestion of a supplement and a placebo these would ordinarily be undertaken in a counterbalanced, crossover design (i.e. half your participants undertake the placebo first and half undertake the treatment first [counterbalanced], conditions are then swapped on the participants second trial [crossover]). You then analyse your performance data with respect to the order in which the trials were undertaken, that is, the first trial completed compared to the second trial completed irrespective of treatment. If there is an improvement from the first to the second trial it is likely a learning effect has occurred. If there is no difference from trial one to trial two but there is when considering the treatment, then you can be confident that the improvement is a result of the treatment.

When you have collected your performance data, undertake the aforementioned analysis to determine whether a learning effect has occurred.

Although it is considered good lab practice to ensure participants are accustomed to all procedures the specific effects of this process are not widely reported. However, the effects of familiarisation have been considered for a range of performance tests including canoeing and cycling time trials (Hibbert et al., 2017; Sealey et al., 2010; Corbett et al., 2009; Laursen et al., 2003), repeated sprints (Spencer et al., 2006; McGawley and Bishop, 2006) and prolonged exercise containing performance components (Tyler and Sunderland, 2009; Marino et al., 2002). Improvements in performance following one (Sewell and MaGregor, 2008; Laursen et al., 2003), two (Higgins et al.,

2014), three (Vrbik et al., 2016; Tyler and Sunderland, 2009; Marino et al., 2002) or four trials (Sealey et al., 2010) have been noted along with or alterations in pacing strategy (Tyler and Sunderland, 2009; Corbett et al., 2009). The best performance results have also been noted to occur following a full familiarisation (i.e. all instrumentation and the exercise protocol) rather than a 'half' familiarisation or an equipment-only familiarisation (Hibbert et al., 2017). Therefore, not providing your participants with an opportunity to become accustomed to your study procedures could have a significant effect on your results.

Exercise 3.3   Your methodological considerations

For each of the factors noted earlier consider how you have overcome any of the potential limitations or how you have controlled for them. Not all of these factors will be of importance to your study, especially for lab reports, but it is worth considering how many are and how they could affect your data or comparisons.

	How important?	Key information required
Participant characteristics	....	....
Circadian rhythms	....	....
Diet and physical activity	....	....
Menstrual cycle	....	....
Familiarisation	....	....

3.3   General reporting of procedures

As noted earlier, the method should provide all the information required to allow a researcher to repeat the experiment. Although the methods can be likened to a recipe (Foote, 2008), the method is not a step-by-step tutorial (such as in a lab schedule) but a systematic and complete description of the work done (Azevedo et al., 2011). A common error is to include extraneous information that does not aid the description of your procedures. Kyrgidis and Triaridis (2010) suggest that there are four levels of reporting methods: 1) those known to everyone, 2) those which are less common but well documented, 3) those which are relatively uncommon and 4) those which are developed by the researchers and should be described in detail (Figure 3.1). If a novel method is being introduced this will require full description and discussion (Kallet, 2004). Indeed, the whole purpose of your study may be developing a new exercise protocol, questionnaire or method and assessing its validity and reliability. In this instance, a clear description of what was

Four levels of reporting methods

1) those known to everyone

2) those which are less common but well documented

3) those which are relatively uncommon

4) those which are developed by the researchers and should be described in detail

Figure 3.1 Four levels of reporting methods (Kyrgidis and Triaridis, 2010)

done is of paramount importance. For most undergraduate lab reports the methods used are likely to be well established and your report should consider reporting all the important elements to illustrate your knowledge of the techniques used. Details should be provided of all exercise protocols undertaken, measurements made and at what time points they were recorded. For dissertations a schematic diagram (Section 3.6) is often useful here especially where a large number of measures are taken, and a large number of time points are involved with the written description being potentially lengthy.

An important consideration of the methods is where procedures are based on any assumptions or rationales. This is particularly true when variables can be approached only indirectly (Kallet, 2004). A good example of is indirect calorimetry to determine oxygen uptake and/or energy expenditure values. Most description of these procedures will consider what is actually measured by the researcher rather than any underlying assumptions. Students will also be assumed to have a level of knowledge commensurate with their level of study. For example, it is important to show an understanding of cardiorespiratory variables in first-year degree studies by defining stroke volume and cardiac output or how to calculate respiratory exchange ratio. However, in your final-year of study, providing information such as this is generally not required as it is expected knowledge. You would most likely be expected to comment on more complex adaptations to variables such as end diastolic volume, pre-load, left ventricular diameter, etc. It is always best to check with your tutor if you are unsure. A rule of thumb is to use any definitions provided in your lectures. If definitions are not given there, you can assume you should know it!

3.3.1 Describing exercise protocols

Within the sport and exercise sciences most projects will involve some form of exercise or movement. This section is therefore biased towards some of the most commonly used exercise protocols you will encounter. Nevertheless, the principles are the same whether you are reporting physiology, biomechanics or psychology-based studies.

3.3.1.i *Typical exercise protocols*

When reporting your exercise protocols, it is important to appreciate the different terminology used to describe them. For example, the typical test for maximal oxygen uptake ($\dot{V}O_{2max}$) is incremental exercise (meaning increasing in intensity) to volitional exhaustion. The protocol may be continuous or discontinuous and is usually straightforward to describe. You will need to consider the initial power output or treadmill velocity, the magnitude of increases in power output or velocity with each stage, the duration of each stage and any rest periods undertaken between stages. For cycling and arm cranking studies you will also need to report the cadence or crank rate used (i.e. rev·min^{-1}). If you are using a protocol from a previous study you can reference this, but it is still useful to provide a description of what was undertaken or key factors in the protocol design. For example,

> Participants undertook an incremental test to volitional exhaustion to determine maximal oxygen uptake (Price and Halabi, 2005). This protocol involved an initial velocity of 8 km.h^{-1} for 5 minutes followed by increment of one km.h^{-1} every minute, or
> Maximal oxygen uptake was determined from an incremental treadmill test (Price and Halabi, 2005).

Other aspects of protocols can also be referenced. A common aspect of treadmill protocols is to set the gradient at 1% in order to elicit the same energy cost as running outdoors (Jones and Doust, 1996).

When considering multiple sprints or intermittent exercise definitions can get a little more confusing. For example, 'multiple sprints' usually refers to short duration, maximal sprints similar to that of the Wingate Anaerobic Test (participants sprinting as fast as possible for 30 seconds against a resistive load of 7.5% body mass) but of shorter duration and with a set recovery between sprints. The model of 10 × 6 seconds repeated sprints has commonly been used to examine multiple sprint responses during cycling, (Gaitanos et al., 1991) running (Hamilton et al., 1991) and arm cranking (Artioli et al., 2007).

A number of exercise protocols use the term 'intermittent exercise'. This term refers to exercise with rest periods in between exercise bouts or a range of exercise intensities simulating team sports. The exercise could be of high intensity such as that undertaken by athletes during interval training (Helgerud et al., 2007; Rozenek et al., 2007; Seiler and Hetlelid, 2005), of low intensity such as used in more clinical scenarios (Campbell et al., 2011; Bougault et al., 2005) or a mixture of intensities to simulate team sport activities (Drust et al., 2000; Nicholas et al., 2000). Describing the specific exercise undertaken with an indication of the exercise intensity is useful here. For example, a large number of studies have examined responses to 'high intensity shuttle running' (Morris et al., 2000; Sunderland and Nevill, 2003, 2005). Specific exercise definitions favoured by your tutors will no doubt be provided in lectures or laboratory manuals, so it is always best to go with those.

3.3.1.ii Ergometers

A range of ergometers are available for exercise testing. The word 'ergometer' comes from 'ergo' meaning 'work' and 'meter' meaning 'to measure'. In my years of marking laboratory reports, I have come across a range of descriptions and spellings, for example, ergo meter, ergonometer and cycling machine. The most common mistake relates to the term cycle ergometer. The standard cycle ergometer has one wheel and should not be termed bicycle ergometer. Bicycles have two wheels. A confounding factor to describing ergometers, and one that probably adds to the confusion is that the word 'ergometer' is not generally recognised by spell checkers, so will likely always be highlighted in your word processing document as incorrect. This doesn't mean that it is spelled incorrectly, just that is it not in standard use.

3.3.1.iii Describing techniques and procedures

EXPIRED GAS ANALYSIS

Using the correct descriptors for your various processes is important to demonstrate understanding of the technique. For example, one of the most common techniques used in undergraduate Sport and Exercise Science is that of collecting and analysing expired gas. First, note that the samples collected are termed expired gas rather than expired air. It may seem pedantic, but air is a known concentration of components (20.9% oxygen and 79.0% nitrogen, and small quantities of carbon dioxide and inert gasses) whereas the gas breathed out is of unknown concentrations, although admittedly within a known or expected range, hence it is measured and not assumed.

Many published studies have well-described sections pertaining to the collection and analysis of expired gas samples, and it is not the purpose of this chapter to overview the procedure but rather to ensure that what is written within your method makes sense to the reader. Key errors of description are usually centred around the process itself which involves collecting samples, analysing them and calculating the desired values (i.e. minute ventilation, oxygen consumption, carbon dioxide production, and respiratory exchange ratio). When analysing the gas samples this is done using gas analysers which provide measures of the fraction of expired gas that is oxygen (F_EO_2) or carbon dioxide (F_ECO_2). The analysers themselves do not directly provide measures of oxygen consumption and carbon dioxide production. Values for these latter variables are obtained from subsequent calculations often using in-house software. Therefore, descriptions will often state that 'expired gas was analysed for fractions of oxygen and carbon dioxide with oxygen consumption, carbon dioxide and respiratory exchange ratio being subsequently calculated'. Students also often state that 'gas volume and temperature were measured using a dry gas meter'. Dry gas meters do not measure temperature, they measure gas volume. Gas temperature is measured using a thermistor or other device within the system. Using the correct wording for a given process will certainly improve the clarity of your descriptions.

FORCE PLATE AND MOTION ANALYSIS

Biomechanics reports often require some quite technical descriptions. When force plates or cameras for motion analysis are used it is important to note the number and type of cameras, how the data was collected and how it was processed. Reporting how data was treated is also important for data such as electromyography (EMG) recordings, particularly when a range of methods may be available and used by different authors. For example, if collecting force plate data, consider the following:

> Ground reaction forces were measured by means of a force plate (Kistler Force Plate 9281B, Kistler Instruments, Switzerland). The three force components (X, Y and Z) were amplified and converted from analogue to digital signals. Data was recorded on a personal computer at a sampling frequency of 1000 Hz. The changes in the resultant force vector as measured by the centre of pressure (COP) and corresponding area, path, velocity, frequency and amplitudes were calculated. Data acquisition and processing was undertaken using Vicon Workstation® (Vicon Peak Workstation®, Oxford Metrics, UK).
>
> (Hill et al., unpublished data)

When collecting motion camera data, you may consider the following:

> Six Vicon infrared motion capture video cameras were positioned around the participants. Cameras were set on tripods and operated at a frequency of 50 Hz. Prior to testing the system was calibrated in order to allow the software to calculate the relative location and orientation of the cameras and to define the 3-dimensional coordinate system. Eight light reflective caption markers (Vicon, Oxford Metrics, UK) were placed on selected bony landmarks on the right hand side of the body (greater tuberosity, olecranon process, ulnar styloid, spinous tubercles, anterior superior iliac spine, mid femur, lateral condyle and lateral malleolus) for analysis of the kinematic responses. The distance between each marker and the markers position relative to the bony landmark was measured and recorded for subsequent trials. All reflective markers captured were

subsequently identified and labelled. Data were exported into an Excel file for further analysis of joint movements.

(Hill et al., unpublished data)

METABOLITES

Various methods for the analysis of metabolites can also be referenced by author as the full procedures may be quite lengthy. Blood glucose and lactate concentrations, if not analysed from handheld portable monitors or bench-based instruments, can be analysed spectrophotometrically using commercially available assays or standard procedures, respectively. However, if you were writing an analytical style paper based around an analysis method, then specific biochemical assays or formulae are of greater importance. If writing a thesis such specific aspects should be added to the appendices.

3.3.1.iv *Questionnaires and scales*

Where questionnaires are involved it is imperative to state who it was developed by, the version used and any comments regarding its validation. For example, there are a large number of scales for assessing anxiety or personality. Just stating that 'personality was assessed using a questionnaire' or 'anxiety was assessed by standard procedures' is not enough.

Besides questionnaires, there are also a range of perceptual scales used within sport and exercise science. Here, verbal descriptors are attached to a number on a finite scale. The best-known scale of this type is for ratings of perceived exertion (RPE) as measured by the Borg Scale (Borg, 1973). When considering RPE, there are different scales for different types of RPE (overall or differentiated) or versions developed for specific clinical populations (Noble and Robertson, 1996). Other scales include 'Readiness to Exercise' (Nurmekivi et al., 2001) and 'Ratings of Perceived Thermal Strain' (Young et al., 1987). As with questionnaires, it is important to note who developed the scale to be used and whether it has been validated.

3.3.1.v *Stating formulae*

As with exercise protocols, there are a range of techniques that are used which have standard components. For example, when assessing body composition using the skinfold method, it is frequently cited that body fat was calculated using the formula of Durnin and Womersley (1974) or through densitometry techniques using the formulae of Siri (1961) or Brozek (1963). Although, the actual formulae and procedures are well known, it is good practice to include them. Where formulae are relatively straightforward, such as in studies of thermoregulation calculating mean skin temperature (Ramanathan, 1964), the formula can easily be stated in the method. Where a less common or less well-known procedure is undertaken, the formula should always be provided. For example, during studies examining the effectiveness of hand cooling on performance the amount of heat lost from the hands to water during the hand cooling procedure is calculated using the method of Livingstone et al. (1989). As this formula is less well known, it would then be provided and the components listed or defined.

3.3.1.vi   Presumed procedures

It is important to note that many statements regarding equipment preparation are often presumed or expected to have occurred. Many students include discursive or superfluous statements to try and demonstrate that they have a good appreciation of what has been done. Some common statements are: 'Douglas bags were evacuated before use', although this is clearly important before collecting samples it is standard procedure and expected to have occurred; 'Data was recorded in a results sheet', again, where data has been noted it is expected that it was written down or recorded somewhere; 'Equipment was checked before use to ensure it was working properly'. This would be inherent in the calibration procedures, some of which are most likely done before each laboratory class without the students being aware of them. If the laboratory class is, for example, based around calibration procedures or producing a dose response curve to determine solute content of given samples, such procedures are important to describe.

3.3.1.vii   Naming equipment

Within your methods section it is imperative that sufficient information is given so that the study could be repeated. It is common practice to name the piece of equipment used for each variable (or groups of variables) measured. As different analysers and equipment exist to measure your variables there is potential for different calibration methods etc. to be undertaken. The reader will then know specifically what equipment was used to collect and analyse the data and they can then form their own opinion as to its appropriateness, reliability and validity. More specifically, it is standard to provide the name of the equipment, the city and country of origin. For example, 'Exercise was performed on a cycle ergometer (Monark 814E, Varberg, Sweden)' or 'Heart rate was continuously monitored using a heart rate monitor (Polar Electro, Kempell, Finland)'.

3.3.2   Nomenclature and units

The majority of journals will often refer authors to an excepted list of standard units or 'SI units'. The 'SI' refers to the '*Système International*' or in its full form '*Le Système International d'Unités*' and is the modern metric system of measurement (Thompson and Taylor, 2008). As with most standard references these are available in pdf format from various websites (e.g. the International Bureau of Weights and Measures). Examples of the use of SI units are seconds (s) for time, metres (m) for length and kilograms (kg) for mass. There are also a number of non-SI units which are often used and are accepted for use with the International System of Units, e.g. minute (min), hour (h) and litre (l) (Thompson and Taylor, 2008).

Some variables do not have units or may be expressed as ratios or 'arbitrary units'. Ratios represent one variable in proportion to another. A good example is work-to-rest ratios, such as of 60 seconds of exercise followed by 30 seconds of rest. Here, the work-to-rest ratio is 60 s : 30 s or 2 (i.e. 60/30). Here, the units have to be the same and are effectively cancelled out in the calculation. The other main ratio variables within sport and exercise science are pH and respiratory exchange ratio (RER). Similarly, with respect to units, the Borg Scale for ratings of perceived exertion (Borg, 1973) does not have units. It is also worthy of note that the Borg scale provides a 'rating' and not a 'rate' and it reports 'exertion' not 'exhaustion'. In some studies, you may see data reported in Arbitrary Units or International Units (IU) which represents analysis based on relative changes.

3.3.2.i Formatting

With the use of word processing being widespread throughout universities and colleges for the production of laboratory reports and dissertations, there is no reason why more complex formatting applications available within word processing packages can't be used. Many word processers have equation options facilitating production of professional looking (and correct) equations and formulae. Admittedly, being required to produce complex chemical formulae or mathematical equations is relatively uncommon in sport and exercise science; however, there are a number of formatting options which will be of tremendous use. The key ones are subscripts and superscripts and the use of '$\dot{V}$' rather than 'V'.

3.3.2.ii Subscripts and superscripts

Subscripts relate to smaller characters at a lower level typesetting than the main characters, for example, $\dot{V}O_2$ or $\dot{V}O_{2max}$. These can simply be achieved by typing '$\dot{V}O2$' as normal in the document, highlighting the required text and applying the subscript option, usually in the font formatting option of the word processing software. The same can be done for superscripts; smaller characters at a higher level typesetting than the main characters. These are most common in addressing variable units such as 'beats·min^{-1}' or 'litres·min^{-1}'. Many students do use subscripts and superscripts but not always in the right way. For example, which is correct; O_2 or O^2? A common mistake is to type the number 2 as a superscript rather than a subscript – usually this can be remedied during proof reading. The different positions though do mean very different things in terms of the molecule's chemical properties, so it is important to get them right.

When letters have a dot above them, it infers that there is a time element to the unit of measurement, in other words, it is a rate. For example, '$\dot{V}$' is often used in conjunction with minute ventilation, oxygen consumption or carbon dioxide production giving $\dot{V}E$, $\dot{V}O_2$ and $\dot{V}CO_2$, respectively. These variables have units of litres per minute and therefore have both a volume and a time base in their measurement. Similarly, cardiac output is also measured in litres per minute, so is generally represented by $\dot{Q}$. The procedures for producing these symbols are straightforward and given in Appendix 3.

3.4   Validity, reliability and biological variation

3.4.1   *Reliability and validity*

As you will know from your research methods classes all the procedures that you use should be valid. By this we mean that they should measure what they are purported to measure. Procedures should also be reliable or repeatable. In other words, when you repeat the test or measure after an appropriate duration of time and under the same conditions you should expect to get the same results. If conditions under which your tests are undertaken are the same for both tests (sometimes referred to a 'test re-test'), this gives a measure of your own variability in undertaking the test and therefore how reliable the test is when you undertake it. In other words, what your level of error is. Consider the example of a group of familiarised participants undertaking a Wingate anaerobic test on two separate occasions with a week separating each test (producing peak power values of 829 ±54 Watts and 845 ± 48 Watts for test one and test two, respectively). If you calculated the difference between tests for each participant and the subsequent mean difference for the group (e.g. 16 ±26 Watts), you would then have calculated the bias or expected variation between tests. This procedure is actually part of the calculation for the Limits of Agreement in assessing the repeatability of measures (Bland and Altman, 1986, 1995). You can then use this value in consideration of the variation in your data and the meaningfulness of your data. In other words, differences between tests or treatments of greater than 16W may be biologically important. However, for lab reports establishing the error is unlikely to be a key focus of the class as you are learning to use equipment and processes (which may go wrong) which are just as important as the data collected. Likewise, for your final-year project data although you would be expected to have practised your required techniques you would not have the time for an in-depth assessment of measurement error. However, postgraduate students would most certainly be expected to report the reliability or typical error of their measurements. Clearly, the lower the error the more accurate the data and the greater the potential for observing significant differences.

As well as informing you about accuracy of your data collection and reporting, the reproducibility (reliability) of your techniques assessing the variability is important in discussing how meaningful any change in your variables actually is. There is a wide range of factors contributing to the error of your data collection. Usually, the more steps there are in the analysis procedures the greater the potential for error to exist. However, once you are well practised at a technique your measurement error should be considerably reduced and certainly more consistent. Although manufacturers will usually provide data for the reproducibility of their operating procedures you should always determine your own values. The repeatability of data is not only important for physiological or biochemical variables. Questionnaires need to be properly developed and psychometrically tested and developed upon or for the population you are testing (Kyrgidis and Triaridis, 2010). Using the appropriate scales for your participants is an extremely important component of the validity of the data collected (Brink and Louw, 2012).

3.4.2 Biological variation

From the factors described earlier, you can see that there are a number of components contributing to your measurement error or measurement variability. However, there is also biological variability. To put this into context, if you were to measure your resting heart rate every morning, would it always be exactly the same? For psychological variables, is your mood the same every day? Would your muscle activity and recruitment of fibres be exactly the same for a given movement? Would your technique for a given skill always be exactly the same? The answer here is no and the differences are predominantly due to biological variability. In determining the biological variation in $\dot{V}O_{2max}$ assessments Katch et al. (1982) reported that both biological variation and technological error amounted to ±5.6%. However, of this variation 90% was biological variation. Similarly, when assessing biological variation in residual lung volume measurement and the subsequent effect on body fat percentage values Marks and Katch (1986) calculated that biological variance accounted for 72% of within-subject variance.

Controlling for circadian rhythms, menstrual cycle and learning effects can all help to reduce the biological variation. However, other factors can also affect a participant's performance. For example, improvements in performance of a range of exercise tests have been observed when verbal encouragement has been provided (e.g. Wingate performance, Karaba-Jakovljević et al., 2007; elbow flexor strength; McNair et al., 1996) and when the encouragement is more frequent (maximal treadmill test, Andreacci et al., 2002). Therefore, when undertaking performance tests strong verbal encouragement is often provided and stated in the method. This process should also be standardised as far as possible. Wherever possible you should state how random errors and systematic errors were reduced (Kyrgidis and Triaridis, 2010).

3.5   Calibration

Having briefly considered validity and reliability and factors contributing to them, it is pertinent to consider equipment calibration. Calibration of your equipment is extremely important as it ensures that the readings from your equipment or analysers are accurate. For example, common procedures requiring calibration prior to analysis include blood variables such as blood lactate and blood glucose concentrations and gas analysers for the determination of oxygen and carbon dioxide concentrations. Calibration essentially involves the output from the analyser being compared to a known value or standard. If the difference between values is within acceptable limits, then the calibration is usually accepted, and the results obtained should be accurate. Many calibration procedures use a two-point calibration (i.e. two known values) as the electrical output from many analysers in response to different samples is linear. However, the more values you check the more confident you can be that your data is accurate. Analysing your standard solution as your first proper sample is a good way to check this. Using a range of known values or standards can provide you with what is termed a 'linearity check'. In addition, the standards used usually reflect the physiological range of values expected (e.g. for expired gas, 15% oxygen and 5% carbon dioxide, for blood lactate between 1 and 10 mmol.l^{-1}).

Calibration checks can provide you with information regarding the normal variation of your measurements. If you were to get a difference between mean blood lactate concentrations of 0.5 mmol·l^{-1} and your own error compared to a known sample is 0.2 mmol.$^{-1}$, then the difference is greater than your error and could be down to your experimental treatment. For undergraduate lab reports you will not personally have to calibrate equipment (with the exception of some exercise protocols such as the Wingate anaerobic test) as it will have been undertaken behind the scenes by technical staff prior to the class. However, postgraduate students will most certainly be responsible for calibration of their own equipment. When reporting calibration procedures, many authors state the reference standards used and that all procedures were calibrated in accordance with the manufacturer's guidelines.

3.6   Use of schematics

For many undergraduate and postgraduate dissertations as well as some journal articles the experimental procedures can be helpfully represented using some form of a schematic diagram. Such diagrams are helpful when there are a large number of variables or time points considered or where the design is more complicated. For laboratory classes, these are unlikely to be required or where your project has a relatively straightforward design (experiments don't have to be complicated to be informative and worthwhile!). Schematics are usually a must for any oral presentation of your work and very helpful in explaining procedures to your audience. Schematic diagrams are also useful

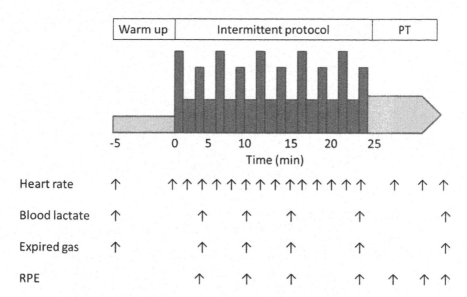

Figure 3.2 Typical schematic diagram for an intermittent exercise protocol. PT = performance trial

in helping you plan out your protocol and are extremely useful to have to hand during your first few experimental trials. The latter ensures that you don't miss any data collection points when testing. An example of a schematic for an intermittent exercise protocol is given in Figure 3.2.

Exercise 3.4 Developing a schematic of your experimental protocol

If your experimental protocol is quite involved the following exercise may help you finalise your measurement times or explain your method. To help you develop a schematic of your protocol, list the variables that you are going to measure and the corresponding measurement time points. An example for both heart rate and blood lactate concentration is provided.

Variable	Measurement time point
Heart rate	. . . Rest, post warm-up, every 5 minutes of exercise, at exhaustion. .
Blood lactate concentration	. . . Rest, 5, 15, 30 minutes of exercise, after performance trial . . . .
. . . .	. . . .
. . . .	. . . .

. . . .

. . . .

. . . .

. . . .

. . . .

. . . .

. . . .

3.7   Statistical analysis

The statistical analysis section should be the last section of your methods (Knight, 2010). You should ensure that the analysis is consistent with the first section of the methods relating to study design and your research question. Within this section it is important to state any data manipulation (e.g. combining data, calculation of delta or 'change' variables), the statistical tests used and both the statistical package and the specific procedures used within the package (Knight, 2010). There is usually an initial statement noting that data is expressed as means and standard deviations along with any checks of data normality and distribution. You should then list the statistical tests (often in the order of complexity) and any differences to standard techniques applied. You will likely have the same statistical test for a number of variables, so these can easily be grouped together. Try Exercise 3.5 and read the examples provided. If you are not confident with statistics you may find it helpful to read the next chapter covering the results section of reports and also consult your supervisor.

Exercise 3.5   Describing your statistical analysis

With respect to the points noted in Section 3.7 write down the key tests that you are likely to use or have used in the analysis of your data. It may be helpful to consider this in relation to your research question or specific hypotheses and each variable measured. You can then organise or group your statistical tests ready for your description in the methods section.

Variable measured   Statistical analysis

. . . .

. . . .

Example statistical descriptions for each of the lab reports used throughout this book could include the following.

Lab 1 Maximal oxygen uptake

Data are expressed as means and standard deviations. Maximal oxygen uptake and maximal heart rate were analysed using one way analysis of variance (ANOVA). Significance was accepted at the level of $P<0.05$. Where significance was obtained Tukey post hoc analysis was undertaken. All data were analysed using the statistics function in Microsoft Excel.

Lab 2 Ground reaction forces

All data are expressed as mean ±standard deviation. The walking and running speeds achieved in each trial and the corresponding peak ground reaction forces were analysed using one way analysis of variance (ANOVA) using Microsoft Excel. Significance was accepted at the level of $P<0.05$. Where significance was obtained Tukey post hoc analysis as was undertaken as outlined by Vincent (1999). Correlations between body mass and ground reaction force were analysed using Pearson's correlation coefficient.

Lab 3 Anxiety and performance

All data are expressed as mean ±SD. Basketball shooting performance and mean heart rate during each trial were analysed using two way analysis of variance (ANOVA) with repeated measures on both factors (anxiety × experience). Significance was accepted at the level of $P<0.05$. Where significance was obtained Tukey post-hoc analysis as was undertaken. All data were analysed using SPSS (version 21, Chicago).

3.8 'General methods' sections

Although all PhDs are different with respect to the scientific approach and the number of experimental studies undertaken, all will have a number of studies which are linked together to help answer the main research question. As such there are often many common procedures or protocols undertaken across each study. To prevent repetition in the thesis, it is quite acceptable to present a general methods chapter which considers all these procedures together in one section. However, if you find that only factors such as ethics and participant recruitment or preliminary testing procedures are common, you may find it best to describe these in each section or potentially refer to the first study where they are reported (check with your supervisory team for preference). A general methods section is also the ideal chapter in which to present your calibration procedures, validation and reliability data and general procedures such as participant familiarisation. Presenting these aspects also helps to demonstrate a good understanding and awareness of the research process, data collection and generally good science. When you are writing up your thesis you may find this is a useful section to consider.

3.9　Writing your methods and common errors

As noted in Section 3.8, the methods section is often compared to a recipe (Foote, 2008) providing sufficient detail to repeat the experiment (Ng and Peh, 2010a). In addition, the order of the methods should be written in a systematic way, usually in the order that the study was carried out (Ng and Peh, 2010a). For final-year undergraduate students, postgraduate students and the majority of researchers, the methods section is likely to have already been written to some extent prior to data collection as it will have been included in research proposals and ethics application (Azevedo et al., 2011). There may be minor changes to add once pilot testing has been completed (ethics permitting), but the key procedures are likely to be written. However, to aid the development and reporting of your method the exercises in this chapter have considered key sections or potential subheadings within the method, a range of preliminary testing considerations, planning and description using schematics and describing your statistical analyses. In addition to this, there are a number of factors for less experienced researchers to consider when writing undergraduate laboratory reports. A range of these are considered here.

3.9.1　Length of the methods section

One common question from students is: 'How long should my methods be?'. The simple answer is as long as it takes to describe all the procedures undertaken in relation to the marking criteria. Concern arises where students talk to each other regarding their project write-ups but fail to realise that the methods for some projects are more straightforward in their design and description than others so will have a shorter methods section. Always consult your supervisor for specific feedback.

3.9.2 *Past tense, third person*

Methods sections are written in what is referred to 'past tense, third person'. With respect to past tense, the way to appreciate this is when reading your completed lab report or project the study has already been done, and therefore in the past. For example, you should state 'On arrival at the laboratory height and body mass *were* recorded' or 'Personality *was* assessed using . . .' not 'On arrival to the laboratory height and body mass *will* be recorded' or 'Personality *will* be assessed by . . .'. The latter examples are future tense. Your research proposal will have been written in future tense as the study had not yet happened. However, a good proof reading should overcome any lapses in wording, if you have cut and paste information from your proposal to your method. As regards third person, this takes out the 'personal touch'. A common student mistake is to state that '*We* measured body mass' rather than stating that 'Body mass was measured'. Once you get used to reporting the procedures in this way it is quite easy to reproduce in subsequent reports.

3.9.3 *Only include methods information*

As with other sections of lab reports and projects a common error is to include information that does not aid the description of your procedures or the inclusion of your results (Foote, 2008). Essentially, what is learnt within the study is contained in the results not the methods. Furthermore, if you have a large amount of information to justify particular methods, it may be more appropriate to include a section in your introduction or literature review covering this.

3.9.4 *Terminology*

Appropriate terminology has been covered in the 'General reporting of procedures' section (Section 3.3). An important point to re-emphasise here is describing the equipment used such as referring to analysers or instruments as machines.

Exercise 3.6   Critique part of a methods section

Using a journal article from your literature searches read the methods section and determine whether the study is clearly explained and whether it could easily be replicated. Also, consult the critical appraisal section in Chapter 2 (Section 2.8) to critique to methods section. What can you take from this appraisal to help improve your own method?

Key factors to consider and improve

1   . . . .

2   . . . .

3   . . . .

4   . . . .

5   . . . .

6   . . . .

7   . . . .

8   . . . .

9   . . . .

10   . . . .

3.10   Chapter summary and reflection

This chapter covered a range of factors that you should consider reporting within your methods section and should also be aware of with respect to your research design. The typical procedures and forms required before a study can be undertaken were also noted. Although you may have already collected your data prior to reading this chapter, the factors described may be useful in explaining the responses you obtained in relation to variability of your data. For lab reports where testing sessions will have timetable and participant constraints, these factors are most likely less of an issue but are still important for understanding your data. This chapter also considered how to plan and write your method with respect to common errors in student reports. To assess your understanding of methods sections, consider the following summary questions.

- What is the purpose of a methods section?
- What aspects are routinely reported in methods sections?
- How do your methods reflect your research question or hypothesis?
- What are the common errors when writing methods sections?

3.11   Further activities

Browse the websites of a journal that you regularly read or are aware of. Direct yourself to the author guidelines and consider the advice given for writing methods sections.

Use the critical appraisal tools in the introduction chapter to evaluate or critique journal articles as you undertake your background reading. Also, use these points to critique your work.

Consult your lab schedule and ensure that you understand each procedure you are undertaking. It will also be helpful to determine the reliability, the expected values and daily variation of each protocol you use from previous literature.

4   Results

In this chapter you will be able to:

*   appreciate the purpose of the results section

    (Section 4.1)

*   present data graphically

    (Section 4.2)

*   present data in tables

    (Section 4.3)

*   choose appropriate statistical tests to analyse your data

    (Section 4.4)

*   write and critique a results section

    (Section 4.4)

*   identify common errors in results sections

    (Section 4.7)

4.1   Purpose of the results section

The key purpose of the results section is to present the data you have collected in a clear, concise and meaningful way. Your results section usually includes some combination of figures or tables, the outcomes of any statistical analysis and a written description of the key findings. There are a number of ways in which you could present your data once it has been analysed. Each approach has its own advantages and disadvantages, but however you present your results they should be organised and in a logical sequence (Foote, 2009a; ICMJE, 2019). This chapter is designed to provide guidance on understating your data, appropriate ways to present your data,

DOI: 10.4324/9781003112426-5

how to be consistent in your reporting and highlight common errors in data presentation. From the range of examples provided it is hoped that you will be able to recognise the research design that you have undertaken and undertake your own analysis.

4.2   Presenting data graphically

Different authors have different opinions about what is the best way to present data. However, some figures lend themselves to certain types of data more effectively than others. The main types of figures presented in laboratory reports include block graphs, line graphs and various types of scatter graphs. Other types of figures, such as pie charts, are less common in sport and exercise science. With a few key points in mind the following section should provide you with enough guidance to plot the most appropriate and effective figures and should help answer the common question of 'What graph do I use and when?'

4.2.1   *Key considerations for plotting data*

There are a number of key points that will be of help when graphing your data. You should also consider completing Exercise 4.1 to test your initial understanding of the different types of data presentation.

1   Figures generally plot mean data with some form of dispersion value such as the standard deviation (SD) or standard error of the mean (SEM). Individual data is seldom plotted except for correlation analysis (which uses paired data), some performance data, individual results for an athlete report or laboratory reports when it is not possible to collect more than a small number of participants' data.
2   Data that is presented graphically is not usually concurrently presented in tables. Doing this simply duplicates the information which is presented.
3   If you have a large number of variables and are not sure which to plot, data that shows statistically significant responses and relates to your specific research question, and that you are likely to discuss the most, is probably the best bet. As a rule of thumb, it is useful to present the most exciting or significant findings visually with other more routine data as tables. If you plot a basic figure for each of your variables on your spreadsheet, you can easily visualise what has happened to each variable. This will help you decide which are most appropriate to plot and may also give you an indication of which data may be significant.

Exercise 4.1   What type of figure should I plot?

Consider the following sets of data. What type of figure would be most appropriate to display the key findings? The answers are given in Appendix 4a.

Data set	Potential figure
Relationship between personality score and performance anxiety	. . . .
Centre of gravity at heel strike during running in elite and novice runners	. . . .
Peak power during a Wingate anaerobic test in a group of cyclists before and after 8 weeks of sprint training	. . . .
Maximal oxygen uptake in a group of runners during two different exercise protocols	. . . .
Motivation to train in international rowers, national standard rowers and club standard rowers	. . . .
Blood pH at rest and every 5 minutes during an interval training session in a group of runners	. . . .
Core temperature at rest and every 10 minutes during prolonged exercise on two occasions, one week apart, one trial where participants were allowed to drink and one where they were not	. . . .

4.2.2   Block graphs

Block graphs are useful when you have data which compares variables represented by one value or in one instance rather than responses over time, such as performance measures (e.g. maximal oxygen uptake, peak power output, etc.). For example, if you were interested in peak power output during a sprint test in a group of endurance trained athletes and games players a block graph would be useful (Figure 4.1. Data taken from Hamilton et al., 1991). Further examples could be the maximal oxygen uptake ($\dot{V}O_{2max}$) scores during treadmill running, cycling and arm cranking in triathletes (Figure 4.2. Data taken from O'Toole et al., 1987) or pre-competition and post-competition anxiety scores in male runners (Figure 4.3; data taken from Sanderson and Reilly, 1983). These figures clearly show the differences in mean responses. Presenting such data visually rather than as a sentence in the written description can have much more impact.

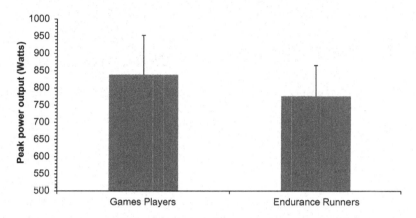

Figure 4.1 Peak power output for games players and endurance trained runners during treadmill running

Source: (data taken from Hamilton et al., 1991).

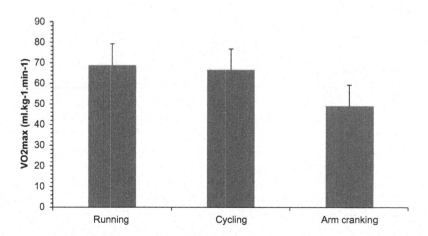

Figure 4.2 Maximal oxygen uptake ($\dot{V}O_{2max}$) for triathletes during treadmill running, cycle ergometry and arm crank ergometry

Source: (data taken from O'Toole et al., 1987).

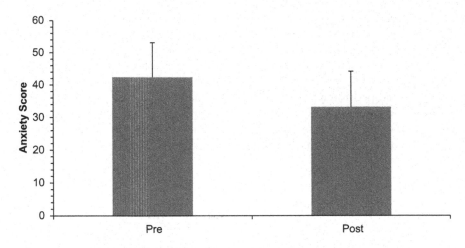

Figure 4.3 Pre- and post-competition anxiety scores (Speilberger trait questionnaire) in male runners

Source: (Data taken from Sanderson and Reilly, 1983).

4.2.3   Scatter plots

Scatter plots have a number of uses and tend to represent more dynamic data rather than descriptive data. The most common uses of scatter plots are for correlation analysis when there are paired data (see Section 4.4.2) and for displaying data series linked over time. The following sections will cover both types of figures in more detail. It will also be useful to consider the corresponding sections on statistical tests in conjunction with the use of figures.

4.2.3.i   Figures showing relationships

For correlation data (i.e. showing a relationship or association between variables) figures are quite straightforward. Consider the data provided in Table 4.1. This data shows energy intake measured by two methods. Method 1 involved calculating energy intake using nutritional tables and Method 2 involved using computer-based dietary analysis software. The relationship between each method is plotted as a scatter plot and shown in Figure 4.4. The figure shows that as energy intake calculated from nutritional tables increases so does that from the dietary analysis software. If both measurement techniques were valid, and all calculations were performed correctly, you would hope that this would be the case.

As well as any association statistics (r, r^2; Section 4.4.2), it is possible to add a trend line onto your figure and the equation of the trend line. The latter is useful for predicting one response from another. In brief, the r value

Table 4.1 Energy intake calculated both by hand from nutritional tables and from dietary analysis software

Participant	Sex	Method 1 (Kcal)	Method 2 (Kcal)
1	Female	2753	2802
2	Female	3589	2297
3	Female	3761	2528
4	Female	2368	1924
5	Female	1996	1713
6	Female	2641	2382
7	Female	2615	2262
8	Female	2849	2217
9	Female	1361	1815
10	Female	3541	3855
11	Female	1166	1231
12	Female	1885	2019
13	Female	1273	910
14	Female	1336	1185
15	Female	1101	1531
16	Female	2912	2212
17	Female	2673	2437
18	Female	2742	2064
19	Male	2311	2723
20	Male	3831	3107
21	Male	4657	4668
22	Male	4601	3902
23	Male	2515	1603
24	Male	1198	1126
25	Male	4760	3552
26	Male	3521	2142
27	Male	3487	4150
28	Male	1327	1408
29	Male	3874	3810
30	Male	2557	1979
31	Male	1988	2050
32	Male	3679	3146
33	Male	3120	2530
34	Male	2569	2298
35	Male	3609	2104
36	Male	2742	2213
37	Male	3516	1942

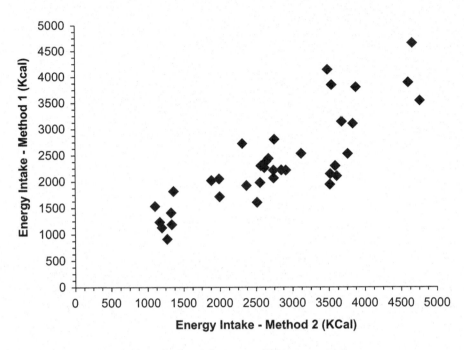

Figure 4.4 Energy intake calculated from two different methods

tells us the strength of the association between variables and the r² value represents the amount of variation in one variable explained by the other variable (Thomas and Nelson, 2001). The greater the r² value the better, as more variation is explained by one or other of the variables chosen. The r² value also helps to determine which type of trend line is best to fit to the data. Some data sets may be better suited to a curvilinear trend line rather than a linear one. If you are unsure which type of line to fit, whichever has the greater r² value can help you decide.

When using scatter plots you can also plot two different groups' data on one figure. For example, in our energy intake data we have data for both male and female participants and you may wish to distinguish between them. This can be done by setting out the data in your spreadsheet as shown in Table 4.2. In Microsoft Excel if you highlight the column headings on the top row (i.e. Method 1, Method 2 – Female, Method 2 – Male) and the corresponding data below you should produce the same figure but with male and female data indicated by different symbols (Figure 4.5). With this approach, you can also obtain a trend line for each group of participants. This is useful as both groups may share the same trend line – which is an important finding or produce different trend lines – which is also an important finding.

Table 4.2 Energy intake (Kcal) calculated both by hand from nutritional tables and from dietary analysis software for males and females

Participant	Gender	Method 1	Method 2 (Kcal)	Method 2 (Kcal)
			Female	Male
1	Female	2753	2802	
2	Female	3589	2297	
3	Female	3761	2528	
4	Female	2368	1924	
5	Female	1996	1713	
6	Female	2641	2382	
7	Female	2615	2262	
8	Female	2849	2217	
9	Female	1361	1815	
10	Female	3541	3855	
11	Female	1166	1231	
12	Female	1885	2019	
13	Female	1273	910	
14	Female	1336	1185	
15	Female	1101	1531	
16	Female	2912	2212	
17	Female	2673	2437	
18	Female	2742	2064	
19	Male	2311		2723
20	Male	3831		3107
21	Male	4657		4668
22	Male	4601		3902
23	Male	2515		1603
24	Male	1198		1126
25	Male	4760		3552
26	Male	3521		2142
27	Male	3487		4150
28	Male	1327		1408
29	Male	3874		3810
30	Male	2557		1979
31	Male	1988		2050
32	Male	3679		3146
33	Male	3120		2530
34	Male	2569		2298
35	Male	3609		2104
36	Male	2742		2213
37	Male	3516		1942

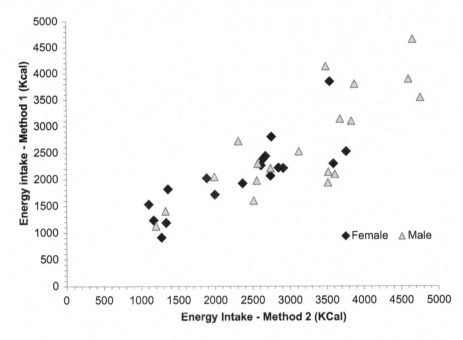

Figure 4.5 Energy intake calculated from two different methods for males and females

Using a scatter plot in conjunction with correlation data is a useful approach in comparing the relationship between variables and is particularly useful in determining the reliability or repeatability of measures (e.g. maximal oxygen uptake ($\dot{V}O_{2max}$) from an incremental exercise protocol) as well as for assessing the validity of measures (e.g. anxiety questionnaire scores versus heart rate or body fat percentage calculated from skinfold measure versus hydrostatic weighing). For example, if an established exercise protocol for $\dot{V}O_{2max}$ resulted in a large value you would hope that any new or alternative protocol developed would also produce a large value. This would demonstrate that those participants performing well on one test also performed well on subsequent tests. In addition, you could compare a subjective scale (such as anxiety rating) to a quantifiable physiological response (such as heart rate) to see if they are proportional to each other.

4.2.3.ii   Figures showing data over time

A large number of variables, especially in physiology and biomechanics, are measured at regular or varying intervals over time, for example, metabolic variables such blood lactate concentration or oxygen consumption during prolonged exercise or joint angles during a specified activity, such as during the gait cycle or during a javelin run up. Scatter plots can be used here, and it is common practice to join the data points together with straight lines. Straight lines are used as we haven't recorded data in between the chosen time points, so we don't specially know what has happened there (although it may appear intuitive). Such figures differ from scatter plots for correlation analysis as they join the data points together in series. Similar types of figures can also be plotted as line graphs. However, it is important to note that differences exist between scatter plots joined with straight lines and line graphs. The key point being that scatter plots enable data to be plotted with meaningful time intervals. With line graphs, the axis represents a set of labels rather than a continuous time scale. For example, consider Figure 4.6, where heart rate data from two trials of prolonged exercise with and without fluid replacement was recorded at 5, 15, 30, 45 and 60 minutes. Plotting as a scatter plot enables meaningful distances between time points to be illustrated. In Figure 4.6 you can see how the differences in time are presented between the two types of graphs. Although subtle, the scatter plot approach provides a better representation of the time scale.

Another useful point to note regarding plotting line graphs relates to the data labels in the column headings of your spreadsheet. When using Microsoft Excel, if columns are labelled as anything other than a number a standard time scale will not be plotted. By subsequently replacing your column label with a number will usually automatically change your figure. Where you have data recorded during recovery from exercise as well as during exercise or during separate exercise bouts or periods of a match, you will have to be careful how you label different parts of exercise protocols. For example, if you have 30 minutes of recovery data as well as 30 minutes of exercise, it is best to have recovery data labelled as 35, 40, 45 minutes, etc. rather than a second set of 5, 10, 15 minutes, etc. If you plot data with repeated timings you will soon see the figure is produced very differently (Figure 4.7). A continuous time scale is generally always best. Another example is for studies where potentially ergogenic aids are ingested, such as carbohydrate, caffeine or sodium bicarbonate to name but three. Here, the solutions may be ingested at various time intervals prior to exercise depending upon their physiological effects. For a 60-minute absorption period following ingestion, it is best to have pre-ingestion time as '-60', 15 minutes after ingestion as time '-45' etc. and 60 minutes following ingestion as time '0'. The warmup and exercise protocols can then be labelled as conventional time points. The y-axis can then be amended to cut the x-axis at '-60'.

Line graphs are useful when the important factor does not have to be time based (i.e. in minutes) or represents regular phases or intervals. For example, in coaching expressing the volume or intensity of training each month over a one-year cycle suits itself very nicely to written labels rather than an interval scale (Figure 4.8). Here, the focus is on the month label. A variation on figures being plotted over time is that of showing data in relation to exercise intensity. This reflects how data from many incremental exercise tests is presented, the classic example being lactate threshold or oxygen uptake (Figure 4.9).

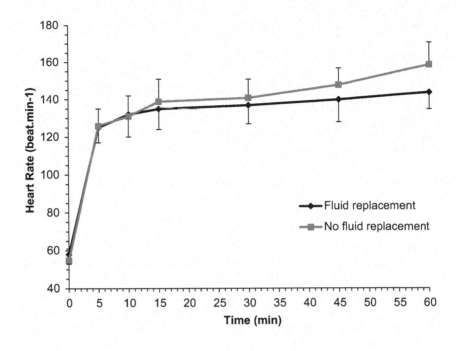

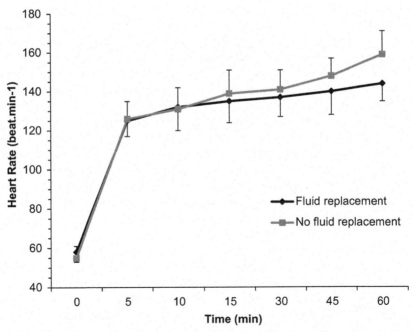

Figure 4.6 Heart rate during exercise for fluid replacement and non-fluid replacement trials. Plotted as a scatter plot (above) and as a line graph (below)

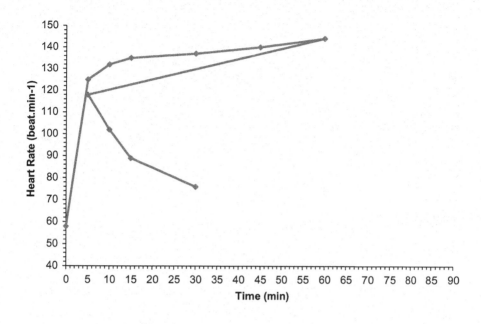

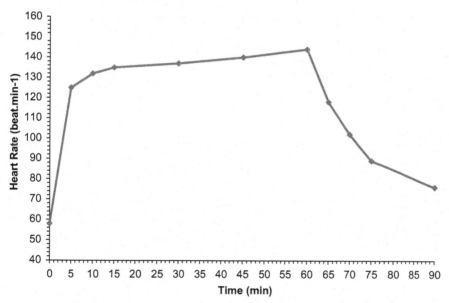

Figure 4.7 Heart rate during exercise and recovery. Plotted with a non-continuous (above) and a continuous (below) time scale

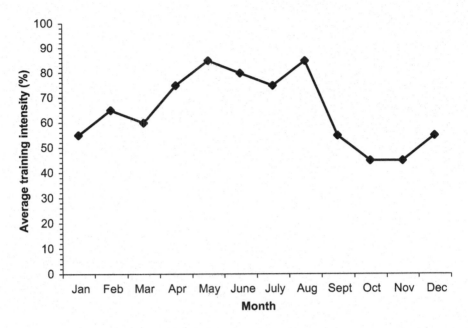

Figure 4.8 Exercise intensity over a twelve-month training cycle

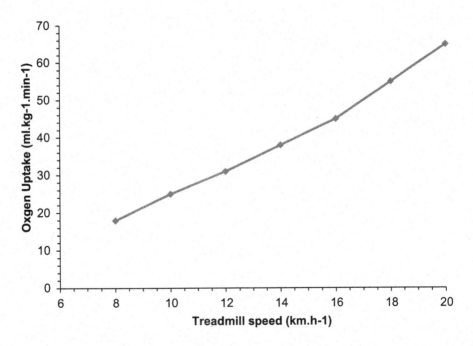

Figure 4.9 Oxygen consumption during incremental exercise

Exercise 4.2   Formatting your figures

How would you format your figures? Would you leave it as the figure automatically provided by your software or change it in any way? Consider the means and standard deviations for the following data sets (Tables 4.3a to 4.3c). Plot the data in your usual way and then consider the following points regarding formatting of figures.

Table 4.3a Time to exhaustion at 70% $\dot{V}O_{2max}$ (Data from Fallowfield et al., 1996)

		No Fluid	*Fluid*
Time to exhaustion	Mean	77.7	103.0
	±SD	7.7	12.4

Table 4.3b Ratings of perceived exertion (RPE) during prolonged exercise in cool and hot conditions (hypothetical data)

		Time (min)			
		5	15	30	60
Cool	RPE	12.0	14.0	15.0	15.0
	±SD	±0.5	±0.6	±0.8	±0.4
Heat	RPE	12.0	15.0	17.0	18.0
	±SD	±0.4	±0.7	±0.6	±0.5

Table 4.3c Exercise intensity per month over a one-year training cycle (hypothetical data)

	Intensity (%)
Jan.	40
Feb.	50
Mar.	55
Apr.	75
May	90
June	80
July	85
Aug.	80
Sept.	90
Oct.	60
Nov.	50
Dec.	50

4.2.4　*Formatting figures*

Although there is no right or wrong way to format a figure the key factor is to be clear and consistent. The following points will help you to produce consistent scientific figures. These suggestions will not change the figure, only different data can do this but will make it more appealing and help to get the point across visually.

4.2.4.i　*Titles*

The title should be meaningful and describe what is happening in the figure. Avoid using phrases such as 'A graph to show . . . '. The conventional approach is to use a format similar to 'Figure 4.1. Ratings of perceived exertion during exercise with and without music'. In addition, figure titles should be underneath the figure (and on top of tables). Some packages will automatically insert a title box for you to fill out. There is nothing stopping you from moving this text box to the bottom of your figure or simply deleting it. You can then write your own title below your figure once you have cut and pasted it into your word processing document. Try not to have duplicate titles for your figure, that is, the automatically formatted option embedded in the figure itself and one you have written in your main word processed document.

4.2.4.ii　*Axes*

Axes should have a clear title, usually the variable measured and appropriate units. Axes should always have a sensible scale and represent the range of data expected although you must consider the size of SEM or SD bars and make sure they can be seen. If you have values in the hundreds such as power output, it is probably best not to not start from zero. The scale should also increase in regular and conventional amounts. The number of decimal places should also be considered. In calculating the mean and standard deviation, most spreadsheet packages will provide a large number of values after the decimal place. It is up to you to decide what the appropriate number is. A common error is to present decimal heart rates or power outputs. Think, within sport and exercise can you have half or less of a heartbeat or a Watt? As a rule of thumb, you can use whatever number of decimal places the instrument or equipment measures to, although this may not always represent what is useful biologically. Consistency of decimal places is also important. Make sure that in your written description you show the same number of decimal places for the mean as you do for the SD or SEM and figure axes.

4.2.4.iii　*Figure size*

The size of the figure and all its components may initially be quite small. Arrange the figures so that it is clear without factors such as gridlines. For example, in Microsoft Excel you can enlarge the actual graph component within the figure so that the legend is incorporated within it rather than outside of it. This makes your figures much clearer for the reader.

4.2.4.iv   Legend

The legend should be clear and relate to the name of the trial undertaken or, in most instances, the condition tested rather than the variables measured. The latter is usually noted in the title. If you are printing out your work in black and white make sure that you have formatted the data markers so they can be easily distinguished from each other.

4.2.4.v   Indicating significance

If you consult journal articles you will see that an asterisk (*) is commonly used to indicate significance between two points on a figure. Other symbols such as $, † and ф are also commonly used for different comparisons. These can easily be added by using text boxes (see also Section 4.4. Using statistical tests). A note regarding what each symbol represents can then be added to the figure legend.

4.3   Constructing tables

Annesley (2010) provides a thorough overview of constructing tables in scientific articles. When producing tables, the main formatting guidelines are similar to those for figures in terms of titles but this time they go on top of the table (easy to remember as we put objects on the top of tables), units, decimal places, indicating significance, etc. However, if you consult author guidelines for journal articles most tables will have the following stipulations: no vertical lines, horizontal lines between the column headings and first variable and a horizontal line at the bottom of the table. How you design your table is up to you and will depend on the data collected. Different examples are shown here for guidance (Tables 4.4 and 4.5).

Table 4.4 Example table for participants' physiological characteristics

Characteristic	Mean ±SD
Age (years)	19.2 ±2.4
Height (m)	1.73 ±0.07
Body mass (kg)	81.3 ±5.6
Body fat (%)	15.3 ±7.5
Training sessions per week	2.5 ±1.3

Table 4.5 Example table for mean ±SD heart rate and pH data from high-intensity
interval training (HIT) and continuous exercise training (CET) sessions

Time (min)							
		0	*2*	*4*	*6*	*8*	*16*
Heart rate	HIT	57	107	171	116	173	108
(beats·min^{-1})		±8	±9	±7	±11	±12	±10
	CET	60	135	139	139	138	140
		±6	±11	±9	±12	±9	±13
pH	HIT	7.40		7.37		7.34	7.29
		±0.02		±0.03		±0.03	±0.02
	CET	7.41		7.37		7.39	7.40
		±0.02		±0.04		±0.02	±0.04

Exercise 4.3   Plotting figures and tables

Using the data presented for each of the typical sport and exercise lab
class examples (Appendices 1a to 1c) consider how you could present
the data.

4.4   Using statistical tests

Before starting this section, you will find it helpful to complete Exercise 4.4
to review your understanding of statistics and Exercise 4.5 to determine the
statistics to be used for your own project.

Exercise 4.4   Which statistical test to use?

For the experimental designs presented in Table 4.6 determine which
statistical test or test you could undertake to effectively analyse the
data. It will be useful to repeat this activity once you have read the next
section on reporting statistics. The answers are shown in Appendix 4b.

Table 4.6 Choosing a statistical test for Exercise 4.4

Data set	Potential test
Relationship between personality score and performance anxiety	. . . .
Differences between centre of gravity at heel strike during running in elite and novice runners	. . . .

Difference in peak power during a Wingate anaerobic test in a group of cyclists before and after 8 weeks of sprint training ....

Maximal oxygen uptake in a group of runners during two different exercise protocols ....

Motivation to train in international rowers, national standard rowers and club standard rowers ....

Blood pH at rest and every 5 minutes during an interval training session in a group of runners ....

Core temperature at rest and every 10 minutes during prolonged exercise on two occasions; one where the participants were allowed to drink and one where they were not ....

Exercise 4.5 Determine the analysis for your pending report

For your pending laboratory report or project consult the marking scheme or criteria, coursework guidelines or laboratory schedule provided by your tutors and determine what data you have in relation to the aims of the report. Are you likely to be determining a difference or relationship? Determine the type of statistical analysis you will need to undertake. You can complete this exercise again at the end of the chapter to check your learning.

Data set or variable	Test required
....	....
....	....
....	....
....	....
....	....
....	....
....	....
....	....

4.4.1 *Initial data checks – do you remember the assumptions?*

Although this book is not designed to be a statistics text it is important to review the assumptions of statistical tests prior to undertaking your analysis (consider your research methods and statistics course notes). Understanding your statistics is more than simply routinely undertaking statistical analysis for assessment, it is also about understanding your data. These initial checks will help you appreciate your data as well as what the subsequent statistical tests are actually doing.

You will likely have come across the terms parametric and non-parametric when referring to statistics. Parametric statistics are based on a number of assumptions, those being:

1 data is parametric (i.e. data lies on an interval scale)
2 data is normally distributed
3 data should have equal variances (i.e. conforms to homogeneity of variance) and
4 data should be randomly selected

Where these parametric assumptions are not met, or 'violated', alternative approaches can be used. These approaches are usually non-parametric statistics and will still assess differences between data sets but do not have the assumptions of parametric statistics. Indeed, non-parametric statistics are often referred to as 'distribution free' (Nahm, 2016). Most statistical packages will provide equivalent non-parametric test options. If parametric tests are used when assumptions are violated there is a greater chance of failing to detect a difference when one actually exists, that is, a Type II error (Hopkins et al., 2018). For an overview of the advantages and disadvantages of non-parametric tests, see Nahm (2016).

4.4.1.i *Normality*

Normality refers to the distribution of the data set. There are a number of ways to check this assumption, both statistically and visually (Ghasemi and Zahediasl, 2012). Let's take the example of a typical exercise physiology laboratory where peak power output achieved during 10×6 second sprints has been collected (Appendix 4c). To initially visually inspect the data, you need to construct a histogram; most software packages will provide this in their normality options. Essentially, the data is grouped into general categories, for the peak power data this could be every 50 Watts, and the number of performances in each category (the frequency) is plotted (Figure 4.10). For a normal distribution a bell-shaped curve is expected, meaning that the most common power output category is in the middle of the range of values (reflecting the group mean), and the greatest power outputs and the lowest power outputs, with fewer occurrences, are reflected in the two tails of the curve.

There are a number of tests that can be undertaken to determine the normality of the data set. Two commonly used tests of normality within sport

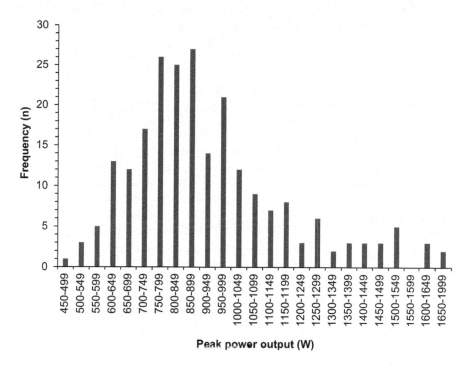

Figure 4.10 Data distribution for peak power during 10-second sprints (*n*=23, 230
   data points)

Source: NB: All data for each of the ten sprints has been pooled to enable a larger data set for illustration purposes only. In reality you would determine the distribution of each of the ten sprints.

and exercise science are the Kolmogorov–Smirnov and the Shapiro–Wilk
tests. Of these, the Shapiro–Wilk test has been considered the most powerful test for a range of distribution shapes (Yap and Sim, 2011). If the test
returns a significant result (i.e. P<0.05), it means that the data is different
from the expected normal distribution. To overcome any lack of normality,
non-parametric statistics rank the data and undertake analysis based on
the ranks rather than the actual data. It is important to note that when the
sample size is small, the distribution may not appear normal (Kim, 2013).

4.4.1.ii   Kurtosis and skewness

Two descriptive parameters provided in most descriptive statistics outputs
that help understand data distribution are kurtosis and skewness. Kurtosis
is often considered to represent how peaked or flat the data distribution is;
however, statistically, kurtosis relates to the 'tailedness' of the distribution
(McAlevely and Stent, 2018). Indeed, there has been quite a debate within the
statistics literature regarding the improper definition of kurtosis (Westfall,
2014). Where there are relatively short tails and a greater frequency of points
are close to the mean, the distribution can appear more pointed. Conversely,

where the tails are longer and there is a more even distribution of data across categories, these can appear flatter. It is also important to check the type of kurtosis value reported by your software. An absolute kurtosis value of 3 is considered normal, however, where 'excess kurtosis' is reported this relates to the deviation from the 'normal'. As such excess kurtosis is calculated as the absolute kurtosis minus three (McAlevely and Stent, 2018).

Skewness represents whether data is skewed to greater or lower values. For a normal distribution, skewness is expected to return values of zero. If the distribution is skewed to the right (i.e. the tail is longer on the right-hand side), then positive values are returned. If the distribution is skewed to the left (i.e. the tail is longer on the left-hand side), negative values are returned. It is important to note that the skew is where the tail lies, not the majority of the data. Comparing your data to norm values or previous research will help provide a clearer indication as to whether the values you have are as expected for the population tested.

If the lab report you are writing relates to a process or technique that you have not done before, you may well have skewed data. The likelihood of odd data or outliers in your first data collections is likely greater than for your final-year project where you will have had much more practice collecting your outcome variables. It is also possible that such preliminary data checks may uncover outliers from erroneous data input such as with decimal places (e.g. height as 18.1 m instead of 1.81 m). As well as the outcome variables, you can also check the distribution of your participant characteristics. Doing this may help to characterise your sample with respect to body mass, height, skinfolds, etc. Some participant groups though may be expected to be skewed or quite kurtotic for certain variables (e.g. such as height in basketball players), but this may help in validating your sample.

4.4.1.iii   Homogeneity of variance

The homogeneity of variance assumption refers to the variability within each group of participants tested. If you are using the same participants on multiple occasions (i.e. two occasions; paired data or three or more occasions; repeated measures), variability in outcome measures would likely be similar as it is the same people being tested. However, where different groups are being tested, variability may be greater in one group than another. For the lab class example assessing $\dot{V}O_{2max}$, if one group of participants ($n=10$) undertook all three modes of exercise on three different occasions, the variability should be similar across testing sessions (all other factors being equal; training status, fatigue, motivation, time of day, etc.). Alternatively, if a greater number of participants ($n=30$) were allocated to three different groups ($n=10$ per group) each undertaking one mode of exercise, the variability in performance could differ depending on how they were allocated to their group. Matching participants and inclusion criteria are considered in the methods chapter. There are a range of tests to assess homogeneity of variance assumptions for different statistical approaches, many of which are built into the various statistical analyses. Helpfully, there are often amendments that can be made in the test calculations to overcome any challenges to this assumption. These tests are considered later in the chapter for each of the statistical tests covered.

4.4.1.iv   A note on P values

When generating statistical outputs, the researcher is generally interested in whether differences between groups are significant, that is, the 'P value', is usually set at being less than or equal to 0.05. The use of this value represents a 1 in 20 occurrence of a random or chance result and is often heralded as the holy grail of the statistical outcomes. In recent years, many journals have taken to requesting specific P values to be reported rather than whether they are more generally less than or greater than 0.05. Consider a non-significant result reported as 'P>0.05', this could be achieved by values of P=0.051 or P=0.999. Conversely, a significant result could easily be P=0.049 or P=0.001. In the borderline examples (P=0.051 and P=0.049), the addition or loss of one participant's data (if withdrawing from the study) could mean the difference between significance or non-significance and very different conclusions. Indeed, Fisher (1933), often associated with the choice of P<0.05 convention, stated that this threshold represents a result worth taking a second look or 'taking a bet on' and that researchers should decide on their own cut-off points. The 0.05 threshold concept has recently been revisited (Nuzzo, 2014) suggesting a range of other approaches in conjunction with P values is good practice. Although some authors have more light-heartedly noted that 'surely God loves the 0.05 as much as the 0.06?' (Thomas and Nelson, 2001), there is an important notion of 'what is significant'. Considering differences between trials or treatments in conjunction with what is biologically meaningful, typical daily variation or error, effect size and statistical power all help to put significance or values that may 'approach significance' into context. Indeed, Nuzzo states that we should be asking how much of an effect there is rather than if there is an effect (Nuzzo, 2014).

Exercise 4.6   Determine the normality of data for the three typical laboratory classes (Appendices 1a, 1b, 1c). Complete the following table for the distribution components discussed so far.

	$\dot{V}O_{2max}$ lab	Anxiety lab	GRF lab
Normality			
Kurtosis			
Skewness			

Answers are in Appendix 4d.

Challenge yourself

Obtain normality information for each sprint in the 10 × 6 second sprint data provided. What statistical approach would you take if only half of the sprints were normally distributed?

4.4.2   *Relationships between variables: correlation*

Correlation determines the association or relationship between two variables, it does not determine cause and effect – this can only be considered in relation to your research design. Correlation can be univariate or bivariate. For example, univariate correlation analyses the relationship between data for one variable recorded on two occasions, such as motivation scores from two different assessment tools. Bivariate correlation analyses the relationship between two variables, such as perception of effort and heart rate during exercise. In this instance, variables don't necessarily have to have the same units, but each participant has to have two (paired) data points. For these tests, data should be linearly related which can be visually assessed from a simple scatter plot. The most common parametric correlation is Pearson's product–moment correlation coefficient. Where data is not normally distributed the non-parametric equivalent of Spearman's rank order correlation coefficient can be used. An extension of Spearman's test is Kendall's tau, which can be used when there are multiple tied ranks in a small data set (i.e. numerous occurrences of the same value in the data set, which would give the same tied rank) (Akoglu, 2018).

4.4.2.i   *Main output from correlation*

Whether parametric or non-parametric tests are used, the key result you will obtain from your correlation output is the 'r' value. Table 4.7 shows a typical output from a correlation analysis involving two hypothetical variables: pre-competition anxiety score from a 0–10 scale and introversion score on a scale of 0–100%. If you have more than one variable (e.g. ratings of perceived exertion, heart rate, blood lactate, oxygen consumption, pH) and there are a number of correlations that you are interested in you can often obtain the r values from a correlation matrix (Table 4.8). Here you can see how all the variables you are interested in are related to each other. However, within such a blanket approach there may be a number of relationships that make less sense (e.g. heart rate versus pH) or a number that will always provide good relationships as they are derived from similar source data (e.g. absolute ($l \cdot min^{-1}$) and relative ($ml \cdot kg^{-1} \cdot min^{-1}$) $\dot{V}O_{2max}$ values or body mass and body mass index). You will need to consider which relationships are of importance in answering your research question. If you want to compare all variables together, then you should seek help on multiple regression techniques (e.g. Winter et al., 2001; Scheider et al., 2010).

Table 4.7 Output table from a typical correlation test undertaken in Microsoft Excel

	Anxiety score	*% Introvert*
Anxiety score	1	
% Introvert	0.97338	1

Table 4.8 Correlation matrix for more than two variables from Microsoft Excel

	RPE	*Heart rate*	*Blood lactate*	*Oxygen consumption*	*pH*
RPE	1				
Heart rate	0.972044	1			
Blood lactate	0.958478	0.95144	1		
Oxygen consumption	0.947041	0.938334	0.893833	1	
pH	–0.79249	–0.7352	–0.77018	–0.61832	1

NB: Variables are still considered in pairs when the analysis of more than two variables is undertaken simultaneously.

4.4.2.ii *Describing results from correlations*

In reporting the results of correlations there are two factors to consider. First, you can describe whether the correlation is 'low', 'moderate' or 'high'. Vincent (1999) notes a general rule where correlation values between 0.5 and 0.7 are considered low, between 0.7 and 0.8 are considered moderate and over 0.9 are considered high. Second, you can state whether the correlation is significant. It is good practice to report both the correlation coefficient and significance, so the reader can interpret the importance of the results themselves irrespective of the descriptions. As noted earlier, it is becoming more common for authors to report the actual P value rather than simply 'P<0.05' or 'P>0.05' for all statistical tests.

To determine the significance of a correlation, you can obtain the P value directly from the given statistical output (such as correlation in SPSS or through linear regression in Excel) or look up the r values required to achieve significance from statistical tables. For the latter, you will require the degrees of freedom (usually n-2 as the data is paired) and the desired level of significance (i.e. P<0.05 or P<0.01). Most research methods and statistics textbooks provide such tables and are relatively easy to use. From these tables you will notice that as the number of data pairs increases (i.e. a greater number of participants) the correlation required for significance decreases. Conversely, if you desire a greater level of significance (e.g. P<0.01 rather than P<0.05) the r value required for significance is also greater.

A further way to assess the strength of a relationship is using the r^2 value, or coefficient of determination, as mentioned earlier in the section on scatter plots (Section 4.3). This is simply the r value multiplied by itself and indicates the amount of variation in one variable explained by the other variable (for further explanation, see any research methods or statistics textbook). As an example, a correlation of $r = 0.97$ provides an r^2 of 0.94, thus meaning that 94% of the variation is accounted for. Conversely, 6% of the variation is unaccounted for. Furthermore, a correlation of $r = 0.62$ provides an r^2 of 0.38. Here, there is a weaker relationship with much more of the variation between variables being unaccounted for. Such variation may be due to the conditions under which the data was collected or due to other factors being of greater explanatory importance.

4.4.2.iii   *Describing the results of correlation analysis*

From the correlation result in Table 4.8 you can see that the correlation is large. The relationship between variables also turns out to be significant. Complete Exercise 4.7 and describe the correlation results. Written examples are provided following the exercise.

Exercise 4.7   Describing correlation results

Try describing the results from the correlation outputs provided earlier.

Description: . . . .

. . . .

. . . .

. . . .

. . . .

. . . .

You could describe this result in either of the following ways:

1   'The correlation between anxiety and introversion was significant ($r = 0.973$, $P<0.05$)'.
2   'The correlation between anxiety and introversion ($r = 0.973$) was significant ($P<0.05$)'.
3   'The relationship between anxiety and introversion provided a correlation of $r = 0.973$ ($P<0.05$)'.

If you have multiple variables, such as in Table 4.8, you could word your description as:

> A summary of correlations between key variables is shown in Table 4.8. Strong positive correlations were observed for RPE against heart rate (r = 0.972), blood lactate (r = 0.958) and oxygen consumption (r = 0.947; P<0.05). A moderate negative correlation was observed for pH and blood lactate (r = 0.770; P<0.05).

If you have a large number of correlations, you can provide a table based on the r values from the correlation matrix. However, do make sure that only the meaningful values are presented.

Exercise 4.8

For the data provided for the typical sport and exercise lab classes provided consider what associations may be of interest and list them in the following table. Generate a correlation matrix for those associations you consider important. For this exercise you can use either parametric or non-parametric tests; however, in reality you would determine the appropriate test with your initial data checks.

Lab class	Potential associations	r	r^2	P
$\dot{V}O_{2max}$				
Anxiety				
GRF				

Answers are in Appendix 4e.

4.4.2.iv   Correlation or regression?

Correlation assesses the association between two variables. However, if you are interested in how a number of variables may be able to predict an outcome measure, such as performance, regression analysis may be more appropriate. Regression analysis can be used to determine which variables are the best predictors of your outcome variable. Take the example of factors that affect grip strength. You may consider forearm girth to represent the cross-sectional area of the active muscle and thus grip strength. However, a measure of forearm girth includes not only muscle mass but also skin, bone, fat, blood vessels, etc. Thus, by considering these other aspects you may get a closer association between grip strength and be able to predict strength from other measures. By using skinfold measures and bone widths you could, with some anthropometric assumptions, get a greater insight into the tissue proportions contributing to forearm girth as well as other known grip strength factors (for example research, see Manoharan et al., 2015; Jürimäe et al., 2009; Macdermid et al., 2002).

As regression is possibly a less common statistical technique undertaken for undergraduate sport and exercise science laboratory classes, it is beyond the scope of this text to overview regression techniques. However, it is worth noting three key assumptions for regression, which include: there should be at least five (and ideally twenty) participants for every independent variable considered, the dependent and independent variables should be linearly related (otherwise non-linear regression techniques should be considered) and the independent variables should not be related (Tabachnick and Fidell, 1996).

4.4.3   Differences between groups: t-tests

T-tests are parametric tests used to determine the difference between the means of two groups. These may be for the same participants undertaking the same tests on two occasions (e.g. electromyography activity during a maximal dead lift before and after a period of weight training), different participants performing the same tests (e.g. motivation to train in elite and non-elite athletes) or comparing a group's scores to an established criterion or standard (e.g. cholesterol measurements in a group of athletes compared to national averages). These examples represent the use of paired (dependent) t-tests, unpaired (independent) t-tests and differences between a sample and population mean, respectively. The first two tests are much more common than the last. The non-parametric equivalent for the paired t-test is the Wilcoxon matched pairs test, and the non-parametric equivalent of the independent t-test is the Mann-Whitney U test.

The output for your t-tests will differ depending upon the statistical package you are using. For example, Excel presents options for t-tests 'assuming equal variances' or 'assuming unequal variances' whereas SPSS presents specific options for paired or independent t-tests. The latter package provides an output to help determine which test you should choose. This is explained later in this section (4.4.3.ii).

4.4.3.i   Main output from t-tests

The key parameter you will obtain from your t-test output is the 't' value and its associated significance (P value). The majority of studies simply report whether the difference between variables was significant, that is, was the value less than or equal to a P value of 0.05? You do not have to report the whole results table (unless requested by your tutor). Look at any journal article that has used a t-test analysis and observe how the authors have presented their data. An example t-test output from Excel is shown in Table 4.9. These results are obtained from a hypothetical study examining motivation to train among elite and non-elite athletes. Here, a 'Motivation to train questionnaire' was completed by each athlete. The questionnaire produced values between 0 and 25 with greater values representing greater motivation.

Within the results table for t-tests you may have significance values for both one-tailed and two-tailed tests. If you know, from your literature review and hypothesis, the likely direction of the comparison, then you should concentrate on the one-tailed value, for example, maximal strength in elite weightlifters compared to non-elite. If you do not know the possible direction, such as pre-match anxiety levels in male and female hockey players, then concentrate on the two-tailed result. For our example, we could assume that elite athletes would be more motivated to train – although this may not always be the case!

4.4.3.ii Describing results from t-tests (Excel)

Table 4.9 shows a typical t-test output from Microsoft Excel for the example of motivation to train in elite and non-elite athletes (Data from Appendix 4f). The resultant t statistic is shown as t–5.95. If checking significance by using statistical tables, such as those provided in Vincent (1999), this value would have to be equal to or greater than the critical value within the tables for it to be significant (i.e. 1.73 for a one-tailed test and 2.10 for a two-tailed test at the $P<0.05$ level of significance). As our value is greater than the critical value our means are statistically significantly. However, the table shows the actual P values for both one-tailed (P = 6.18E-06) and two-tailed (P = 1.24E-05) tests, so you don't have to consult any further statistical tables.

Table 4.9 Example t-test output from Excel (using the two samples assuming equal variance option)

t-Test: Two-Sample Assuming Equal Variances

	Elite	Non elite
Mean	20.2	12.1
Variance	5.733333	12.76667
Observations	10	10
Pooled Variance	9.25	
Hypothesized Mean Difference	0	
Df	18	
t Stat	5.955238	
P(T<=t) one-tail	6.18E-06	
t Critical one-tail	1.734064	
P(T<=t) two-tail	1.24E-05	
t Critical two-tail	2.100922	

All you need to know for this output is that the difference between both one and two tailed tests is significant

In Table 4.9 the P values are expressed to the power of E-06 and E-05. This format is mathematical shorthand and indicates the number of zeros following the decimal point before you get to '124' for the one-tailed test or '618' for the two-tailed test; in other words, P = 0.00000618 and P = 0.0000124, respectively. The use of the 'E-' means that the output does not have to show all the zeros – if a response is highly significant, there can be quite a lot of these. Generally, if the result is reported as 'E-' it is likely to be significant. Other statistical software, such as SPSS, may just show P = 0.000. Here you can simply report as 'P<0.05'. Table 4.9 also shows the degrees of freedom (df) for the test. When describing t-test results you may see the actual t value provided along with the degrees of freedom (df) in brackets such as '$t_{(18)}$ = 5.95' for the example shown in Table 4.9.

From the t-test outputs (Table 4.9) you can see that both the one- and two-tailed comparisons are significant. Complete Exercise 4.8 and describe the t-test results. Written examples are provided following the exercise.

Exercise 4.9   Describing t-tests results

Try describing the results from the t-test output provided earlier.

Description: . . . .

. . . .

. . . .

. . . .

. . . .

. . . .

The t-test results in Table 4.9 could be reported as follows:

The motivation to train in elite athletes was greater than for non-elite athletes (P<0.05).

Adding some descriptive values would result in the following:

The motivation to train in elite athletes (20.2 ±2.4) was greater than that for non-elite athletes 12.1 (±3.6) (P<0.05).

Alternatively,

The motivation to train in elite athletes was 20.2 ±2.4 whereas for the non-elite athletes it was 12.1 ±3.6. The difference between groups was significant ($t_{(18)}$ = 5.95; P<0.05)

4.4.3.iii   Describing results from t-tests (SPSS)

Although Excel provides options for t-tests assuming equal or non-equal variances, the actual homogeneity of variance is not presented within the outputs (there is a separate data analysis option for this). In contrast, within SPSS, options for undertaking specific paired and independent t-tests are provided. For the latter, the output table provides an assessment of the homogeneity of variance through Levene's test. When your study design involves testing different (i.e. independent) groups of participants, each group may well elicit differences in the variation (i.e. variance) of the measured responses; a factor that may be reduced by well-matched participants and specific inclusion criteria. The variation between groups needs to be determined to ensure one of the criteria for the use of parametric statistics is upheld. In contrast, where the same group of participants is involved in the study design and experimental conditions, participant motivation etc. are equal across trials, it would be expected that similar variation occurs across the group each time they are tested. Thus, the variation within the group should be similar. If not, this would likely be an important discussion point. A typical output from SPSS for independent groups t-test using the same data as earlier is shown in Table 4.10.

Table 4.10 returns a P value of 0.154 for the Levene's test ('Sig' column in SPSS). As this is greater than our alpha level of 0.05, there is no difference between the variances of the elite and non-elite athletes. We can therefore proceed with the top line of the table, 'Equal variances assumed', to obtain the independent samples test P value (P = 0.000). If the Levene's test output had been significant (i.e. P<0.05), we could proceed by using the bottom line of the independent samples test.

Challenge yourself: homogeneity of variance tests

Levene's test is just one of many tests to establish homogeneity of variance across groups. For example, Conover et al. (1981) assessed 56 different homogeneity tests in skewed data distributions and in a later study a further twelve tests (Conover et al., 2018). Jayalath et al. (2016) undertook a two-step process where they first established the skewness of the data and then applied an appropriate homogeneity test. Li et al. (2015) assessed seven different tests, including two for their specific research area. Therefore, there is more the homogeneity testing than meets the eye! Although the studies stated here were not from the sport and exercise science area, you can read them to get more insight into homogeneity tests and how they are used.

Table 4.10 Example t-test output from SPSS (using independent groups option)

Independent samples test

	Levene's test for equality of variances		t-test for equality of means					95% Confidence interval of the difference	
	F	Sig.	t	df	Sig. (2-tailed)	Mean difference	Std. error difference	Lower	Upper
Motivation Equal variances assumed	2.216	0.154	5.955	18	0.000	8.10000	1.36015	5.24244	10.95756
Equal variances not assumed			5.955	15.727	0.000	8.10000	1.36015	5.21254	10.98746

4.4.3.iv Non-parametric t-tests

When the assumptions of parametric tests are not met, the use of non-parametric tests may be warranted. The equivalent of the t-test in non-parametric statistics are the Wilcoxon matched pairs and Mann-Whitney U tests for paired and independent groups, respectively. Non-parametric tests use ranks of the data instead of the absolute data per se, thus partly overcoming the violation of normality. Although Excel does not provide non-parametric tests other statistics packages do. The data set-up is generally the same as for parametric tests and although their outputs may be considered less complex than parametric test outputs, a P value is still provided and often an indication of how the ranks in each group or condition have changed. Consider the data sets provided (Appendix 1) and attempt Exercise 4.10.

Exercise 4.10

For the three typical sport and exercise science lab report data sets (Appendices 1a, 1b, 1c), determine what test you would use and whether a difference exists between:

1   $\dot{V}O_{2max}$ (or 'peak') in arm crank ergometry and cycle ergometry
2   Heart rate in high anxiety conditions in novice and expert players
3   Ground reaction force during walking and running

Answers are in Appendix 4g.

4.4.4 Combination of correlation and t-test analysis

For some data sets it is useful to undertake both correlation and *t*-test analyses (providing you have paired data). This is particularly so for examining how valid and/or reliable or repeatable responses are. We have already used the example of $\dot{V}O_{2max}$ values being produced from an established exercise protocol and a new exercise protocol (Section 4.2.2.i). This is essentially testing the validity of the new protocol. Here, providing the new protocol was valid, you would expect those participants who performed well on the first trial to also perform well on the second trial (giving a high correlation, Figure 4.11, r = 0.989; P<0.05) with no difference between the values (as determined from a t-test, Table 4.11). In this instance, the new protocol would appear to relate well to an existing protocol and provide similar values, thus being valid.

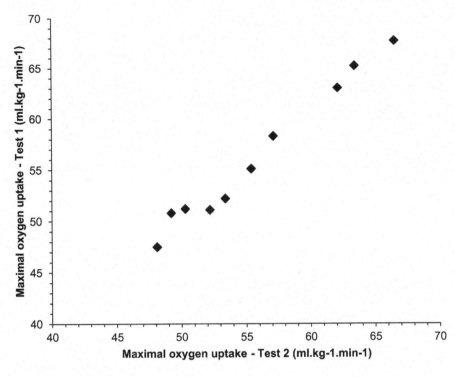

Figure 4.11 Maximal oxygen uptake during two exercise protocols

Table 4.11 t-test output from Microsoft Excel for maximal oxygen uptake during exercise on two separate occasions

t-Test: two-sample assuming equal variances

	Test 1	*Test 2*
Mean	55.77	56.24
Variance	40.62233	49.16044
Observations	10	10
Pooled variance	44.89139	
Hypothesised mean difference	0	
df	18	
t Stat	–0.15686	
P(T<=t) one-tail	0.438552	
t Critical one-tail	1.734064	
P(T<=t) two-tail	**0.877104**	
t Critical two-tail	2.100922	

Note: The two-tailed significance is considered here (highlighted row) as we are not sure which exercise protocols values would be correct.

In reporting the results from the output, you could state the following:

> There was no difference between trials for $\dot{V}O_{2max}$ (P<0.05) and a significant correlation was observed between trials (P<0.05).

Alternatively,

> There was no difference between trials for $\dot{V}O_{2max}$ ($t_{(18)}$=-0.15; P<0.05) with a significant correlation observed between trials (r=0.989; P<0.05).

Once a test has been validated, it should also be checked for reliability to ensure that it gives repeatable results. Remember, a test can only be valid if it is also reliable. Conversely, a test can be reliable but not valid, this means that the test consistently gives the same results, but they are not the correct ones. For a reliable protocol, you would hope that when tested twice using the same procedures that similar values would be achieved. Again, a correlation shows those performing well did so on both tests whereas the *t*-test can determine whether there are any differences – which hopefully there wouldn't be in this instance. It is good practice, especially for postgraduate students using the same procedures throughout a number of studies, to know the repeatability of each procedure that you use and thus, essentially what your level of error or variation is when doing so. Knowing this can help determine how meaningful your results are. If you are interested in the reliability or repeatability of test data using the same protocol you should consider techniques such as Limits of Agreement developed by Bland and Altman (1986, 1995). These are explained in the following section.

Exercise 4.11   Combining difference and relationship analysis

Consult a range of journal articles examining the reliability or validity of the procedures involved in your project. These studies will have potentially used both *t*-test and or correlation analyses. For each study complete the following table. Include enough detail within the 'Main aim' column so that you can see why the authors have used the given statistical test. For the 'Written description' column comment on how the authors have reported their data.

Statistical authors' test used	Main aim	Written description

t-test . . . .

. . . .

. . . .

Correlation . . . .

. . . .

. . . .

t-test and correlation

combined . . . .

. . . .

. . . .

. . . .

4.4.4.i   Bland–Altman analysis

Bland and Altman (1986) presented an alternative method for assessing the repeatability of measurements called 'limits of agreement', which has since become a common procedure within sport and exercise science. Their original example related to the respiratory measurement of peak flow, a measure you may well have encountered in your lab classes. The question posed was how well do peak flow measures from two different instruments agree. An equivalent example within sport and exercise science per se would be how well two $\dot{V}O_{2max}$ values compare from two different exercise protocols (see earlier) or for repeating the same protocol twice. Any similar example across disciplines could be used, providing the paired measures evaluated have the same units. Refer to Table 4.12 as we work through the following calculations.

To determine the agreement between two $\dot{V}O_{2max}$ measures two initial calculations are required; the mean of the two values for both trials for each participant (i.e. we are not sure which value is correct so the mean is taken) and the difference between measures from both protocols for each participant. When calculating the difference, you need to ensure that you always take test 2 from test 1 (as in the following example) or vice versa as the direction of the difference is key. From this we calculate the overall mean and standard deviation for the group mean of both tests (i.e. 67.2 ±6.7 ml·kg⁻¹·min⁻¹) and the mean and standard deviation of the differences between tests (i.e. 1.3 ml·kg⁻¹·min⁻¹) for the group. This latter value is termed the bias. Finally, we calculate plus and minus two standard deviations for the bias (i.e. +2.4 and –2.4 ml·kg⁻¹·min⁻¹). When considered in relation to

Table 4.12 Data and resultant values for calculation of Limits of Agreement example

	Test 1	Test 2	Mean	Difference
	57.1	58.3	57.7	1.2
	53.4	52.2	52.8	−1.2
	62.1	63.1	62.6	1.0
	55.4	55.1	55.3	−0.3
	63.4	65.3	64.4	1.9
	48.1	47.5	47.8	−0.6
	50.3	51.2	50.8	0.9
	49.2	50.8	50.0	1.6
	52.2	51.1	51.7	−1.1
	66.5	67.8	67.2	1.3
Mean	66.5	67.8	67.2	1.3
SD	6.4	7.0	6.7	1.2

the mean bias this represents the limits of agreement and should incorporate the majority of the population studied (i.e. ±2 standard deviations). So, for the bias +2SDs this results in 1.3 +2.4 = 3.7 ml·kg^{-1}·min^{-1} and for the bias −2SDs this results in 1.3−2.4 = −1.1 ml·kg^{-1}·min^{-1}. From this we can state that the bias is 1.3 ml·kg^{-1}·min^{-1} with limits of agreement of −1.1 and + 3.7 ml·kg^{-1}·min^{-1}. Although this test is available on many statistics packages it is quite straightforward to undertake from a standard spreadsheet and helps to understand the process. Please note, it is unlikely that we can truly measure to one decimal place for $\dot{V}O_2$ relative to body mass, however, we have done so simply to illustrate this example.

Now that we have the required values we can plot the Bland–Altman figure. The column of data for the mean of the two tests (x-axis) is plotted against the difference between tests (y-axis) as a scatter plot (Figure 4.12). You then simply draw on a line representing the bias and the two limits of agreement. Ensure that you have clicked on the figure to edit it as normal before you add your lines (in Excel), otherwise, when you copy and paste to other documents the lines won't go with it. When interpreting the plot, we can see that all except one data point is within the limits of agreement, and this is only slightly outside, so we can be confident that the majority of data is within ±2SDs of the bias. In addition, there may be a bias for the second protocol to elicit greater $\dot{V}O_{2max}$ values than the other as seven points are below the bias line. However, three are very close to the bias (within 1 ml·kg^{-1}·min^{-1}), as are the two points above the bias line, and three are ~2 ml·kg^{-1}·min^{-1} from the bias. Such small values are most likely within the error of the measurement and not too meaningful. By undertaking this analysis on the same protocol with the same equipment on two separate occasions in familiarised participants will determine your measurement error.

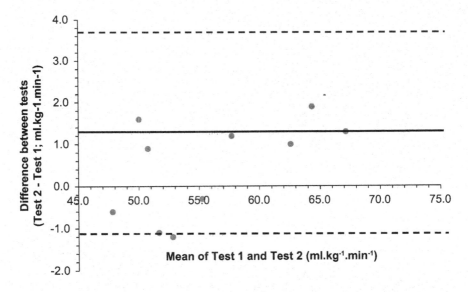

Figure 4.12 Bland–Altman plot for $\dot{V}O_{2max}$ achieved in two different exercise proto-cols. Solid line represents the bias (1.3 ml·kg⁻¹·min⁻¹) and dotted lines above and below represent the limits of agreement (3.7 and –1.1 ml·kg⁻¹·min⁻¹, respectively).

Doing this will allow you to address your error specifically and directly in your interpretation of any results. A benefit of the Bland–Altman analysis is that it is open to your interpretation without relying on a specific P value to determine if data is different or not; significance tests though are often undertaken alongside this approach.

Challenge yourself: repeatability

Read the original article by Bland and Altman (1986). What are the reasons why limits of agreement may be preferred to using t-tests and correlation coefficients in reliability analysis?

Read Price and Campbell (1997). What does this tell us about the validity and repeatability of arm crank exercise protocols?

4.4.5   *Differences between groups: analysis of variance (one-way analysis of variance)*

Most students are confident with the use and reporting of correlations and t-tests. It is after this point when the analysis gets more complex that students may feel a little bemused, such as with analysis of variance. As you will have read in most research methods textbooks, analysis of variance (ANOVA) is an extension of the t-test but this time the key value is the F ratio and its associated significance. Let's first review when to use ANOVA.

The first aspect of ANOVA that students are often confused about is when to use this test. A useful guide is to consider the number of comparisons that you have. Let's consider the example of long jump distance (dependent variable) in different groups of athletes. If there were just two groups of athletes (e.g. elite versus non-elite), there would be two sets of data and just one comparison, therefore, you would use an independent t-test. If you had a scenario where there was the possibility of using more than one t-test (e.g. long jump distance in three groups of athletes (e.g. under 19, under 21 and senior athletes) resulting in three possible comparisons (i.e. under 19 versus under 21; under 19 versus seniors, under 21 versus seniors) then ANOVA is required. In this instance, it is often referred to as 'one-way ANOVA'. The number of 'ways' relates to the number of factors involved in the analysis. For one-way ANOVA there is only *one* key factor affecting your variable. In our example for the analysis of the under 19, under 21 and senior athlete long jump data the 'way' would be the age group, of which there are three different levels. If we took this analysis further and were interested in the same age groups but had long jump distances for both male and female athletes this would give us a second 'way' (i.e. sex). Here we would subsequently use two-way ANOVA (Section 4.4.6).

There are a number of different approaches for ANOVA and the options differ with the research design, software that is used and the preference of the user. A good description of ANOVA procedures using SPSS is given by Ntoumanis (2001). For Microsoft Excel users there is only one option for one-way analysis of variance. However, both software packages will provide you with an ANOVA analysis and you should decide in conjunction with the advice of your tutors what the most appropriate test is for your data. In general, as with t-tests you need to consider the groups that you have. In the long jump example, we have three different groups or an independent group design. This also represents a cross-sectional study. If we tested the same people three times, such as pre-season, mid-season and at the end of the season, this is a repeated-measures design, essentially the ANOVA equivalent of the paired t-test. The following section will overview statistical outputs from Excel and then for typical independent and repeated-measures designs from SPSS.

4.4.5.i   *Output from one-way ANOVA (Excel)*

When considering a typical ANOVA analysis output, we will continue with the example of the long jumpers used earlier. The data set for analysis is shown in Table 4.13 with the resulting output for Excel shown in Table 4.14 and SPSS, using one-way analysis through the general linear model, univariate

Table 4.13 Long jump data set for one-way analysis of variance for under 19 years (U19), under 21 years (U21) and senior athlete age groups

Long jump distance (m)

U19	U21	Senior
7.28	7.21	7.98
7.37	7.31	7.82
7.25	7.48	7.75
7.55	7.29	7.56
7.08	7.65	7.46
7.51	7.55	7.58
7.33	7.65	7.77
7.05	7.59	7.90

Table 4.14 One-way ANOVA statistical output for Excel

Anova: Single Factor

SUMMARY

Groups	Count	Sum	Average	Variance
U19	8	58.42	7.3025	0.032307
U21	8	59.73	7.46625	0.03017
Senior	8	61.82	7.7275	0.03225

ANOVA

Source of Variation	SS	df	MS	F	P-value	F crit
Between Groups	0.735175	2	0.367588	11.64151	0.000396	3.4668
Within Groups	0.663088	21	0.031576			
Total	1.398263	23				

P value is less than 0.05

analysis, shown in Table 4.15. The main value of interest is the F ratio and the accompanying P value. Both results tables show a significant F ratio ($P < 0.05$). This tells us that there is a difference somewhere between the sets of data. However, as there are three possible comparisons (i.e. U19 versus U21; U21 versus senior; U19 versus senior) we don't yet know where the specific difference or differences are. This is where post hoc testing is important (Section 4.4.5.iii). Selecting one of the post hoc options in SPSS will enable you to find where the differences are (Table 4.16). Excel, however, does not have a post hoc option so you would have to do this manually (see Vincent, 1999).

4.4.5.ii   Output from one-way ANOVA (SPSS)

When using SPSS for the long jump example there is a specific option for the independent groups design. This option is 'One-way ANOVA' available

Table 4.15 One-way ANOVA output (using 'One-way ANOVA/compare means option) for SPSS

ANOVA

Long_jump_distance

	Sum of Squares	df	Mean Square	F	Sig.
Between Groups	1.156	2	.578	19.503	.000
Within Groups	.622	21	.030		
Total	1.778	23			

P value for group is less than 0.05

through the 'Compare Means' option. Table 4.15 shows the output. As with Excel you can see that there is a significant difference somewhere in the data. If you selected the post hoc analysis option to determine where the potential differences exist this will be displayed in the output for you (Section 4.4.5.iii).

4.4.5.iii   Post hoc testing

Post hoc testing enables you to determine where differences exist in data sets containing multiple comparisons (e.g. one-way and two-way ANOVA). There are two approaches to this. One approach is where the analysis software calculates the significance between various comparisons and displays the actual P value. The second approach is where you calculate the difference required between two means for it to be significant. How to undertake post hoc testing manually is explained by Vincent (1999). Here, examples for using the Tukey and Scheffé post hoc procedures are provided. If calculating by hand you are essentially determining the difference required between two means for the difference to be significant. For the long jump example, let us consider that we require a difference between group means of 0.22 m or greater for the difference to be significant. The mean long jump distances for the under 19, under 21 and senior athletes are 7.30 ±0.18, 7.47 ±0.17 and 7.73 ±0.18 m. Therefore, calculating the differences between means for each group, we can see that the difference between under 19 and under 21 groups (7.30 m – 7.47 m = 0.17m) is not significant. However, the difference between the under 19 and senior athletes is significant (7.30 m – 7.73 m = 0.43 m) and so too is the difference between the under 21 and senior athletes (7.47 m – 7.73 m = 0.26 m). You can annotate such significance on any figure that you may produce.

For the SPSS output (Table 4.16) you can see that both Tukey and Scheffé post hoc results have been generated – in reality you would likely have chosen a test appropriate for your research design. Here you can see the three groups (coded 1, 2 and 3) compared against each other. From the 'sig' column you can then determine where any significance exists.

Table 4.16 Post hoc output from SPSS for long jump distance in the three groups (age groups coded as 1 for U19, 2 for U21 and 3 for senior athletes)

Pairwise comparisons

Measure: Distance

(I) Point_ of_season	(J) Point_ of_season	Mean difference (I-J)	Std. error	Sig.b	95% Confidence interval for differenceb	
					Lower bound	Upper bound
1	2	−.004	.033	.912	−.081	.074
	3	−.164*	.021	.000	−.213	−.115
2	1	.004	.033	.912	−.074	.081
	3	−.160*	.022	.000	−.213	−.107
3	1	.164*	.021	.000	.115	.213
	2	.160*	.022	.000	.107	.213

Based on estimated marginal means.
*. The mean difference is significant at the .05 level.
b. Adjustment for multiple comparisons: Least Significant Difference (equivalent to no adjustments).

4.4.5.iv   Describing results from one-way ANOVA

For the results of ANOVA tests, it is a good habit to report the overall result and then any post hoc testing if appropriate. As with t-tests you may see the F ratio itself reported with the accompanying degrees of freedom for the between groups and within (error) groups comparisons. For the examples in Tables 4.14 and 4.15 these would be 2 and 21, respectively and reported as $F_{(2,21)}$=11.642. Complete Exercise 4.8 and describe the one-way ANOVA results. Written examples are provided following the exercise.

Exercise 4.12   Describing one-way ANOVA results

Try describing the results from the one-way ANOVA outputs provided earlier.

Description: . . . .

. . . .

. . . .

. . . .

. . . .

. . . .

. . . .

From the statistical outputs obtained, you could report the results in the following ways:

1   There was a significant difference between groups for long jump distance ($P<0.05$) with the senior athletes achieving greater distances (7.73 ± 0.18 m) than both the under 19 athletes (7.30 ± 0.18 m; $P<0.05$) and the U21 athletes (7.47 ± 0.17m).

2   There was a significant difference between groups for long jump distance ($F_{(2,21)}=11.642$; $P<0.05$) with the senior athletes achieving greater distances (7.73 ± 0.18 m) than both the under 19 athletes (7.30 ± 0.18 m; $P<0.05$) and the U21 athletes (7.47 ± 0.17 m).

3   There was a significant difference in long jump performance between groups ($P<0.05$). Post hoc analysis revealed differences between the under 19 and senior athletes and the U21 and senior athletes but no differences between the U21 athletes and U19 athletes.

4   Long jump distances for the U19, U21 and senior athletes were 7.30 ± 0.18, 7.47 ± 0.17 and 7.73 ± 0.18 m., respectively ($P<0.05$). Distances for the U19 and senior athletes and the U21 and senior groups were significantly different ($P<0.05$) whereas those for the U19 and U21 athletes were not ($P>0.05$).

5   Long jump distances for the U19, U21 and senior athletes were 7.30 ± 0.18, 7.47 ± 0.17 and 7.73 ± 0.18 m, respectively ($F_{(2,21)}=11.642$; $P<0.05$). Distances for the U19 and senior athletes and the U21 and senior groups were significantly different ($P<0.05$) whereas those for the U19 and U21 athletes were not ($P>0.05$).

You will have seen the term 'respectively' was used within the written description. This is commonly used in journal articles and scientific analyses and enables a list of values to be given in relation to the trials they belong to without too much repetition in the text. Also note that use of '$P>0.05$' when significant is *not* found.

4.4.5.v   *Output from repeated-measures ANOVA*

The previous examples used different groups but tested on the same outcome measure. Also noted earlier was that we could have one group of participants tested at different times of the season (or different jumps within one testing session over time). Here, we use the term 'repeated measures' as we are repeating the measurement in the same group.

A specific repeated-measures option for ANOVA analysis is provided by SPSS through the 'general linear model' option. Let's continue with the long jump example but testing one group of athletes pre, mid and post season (Table 4.17). The SPSS output is shown in Table 4.18. Within the 'Sig' column for repeated-measures designs there are a number of options to choose from for significance. The first option in the table is 'sphericity assumed'. Sphericity

Table 4.17 Long jump data set for repeated-measures analysis of variance for a group of long jumpers pre-, mid- and post-season

	Point of season	
Pre	*Mid*	*Post*
7.18	7.25	7.32
7.27	7.32	7.48
7.15	7.21	7.31
7.35	7.34	7.52
6.98	7.05	7.21
7.41	7.21	7.49
7.23	7.18	7.32
6.95	6.99	7.18

Table 4.18 One-way ANOVA with repeated-measures output (using repeated-measures/general linear model) for SPSS

Tests of within-subjects effects

Measure: Distance

Source		Type III sum of squares	df	Mean square	F	Sig.
Point_of_ season	Sphericity assumed	.140	2	.070	26.267	.000
	Greenhouse–Geisser	.140	1.454	.096	26.267	.000
	Huynh–Feidt	.140	1.737	.081	26.267	.000
	Lower-bound	.140	1.000	.140	26.267	.001
Error (Point_of_ season)	Sphericity assumed	0.37	14	.003		
	Greenhouse–Geisser	0.37	10.177	.004		
	Huynh–Feidt	0.37	12.156	.003		
	Lower-bound	0.37	7.000	.005		

relates to an assumption of the repeated-measures ANOVA test and requires that the variance–covariance matrices in each measure are equal, in other words, the variances between measures are equal and thus they are from the same population (Mauchly, 1940; Ntoumanis, 2001). This is similar to testing the equality of variance for t-tests. If you assume sphericity you can simply read off the P value from the first line of the table. Alternatively, if you determine the amount of sphericity that exists by referring to the Mauchly's test result (i.e. the epsilon value in the SPSS output) and the result is significant this means that the assumption is violated. An epsilon value of 1.0 represents complete sphericity. As the values get smaller the degree of assumption violation increases. However, if violations occur you can choose an amended P value from the lines headed Greenhouse–Geisser or Huynd–Feldt. In general, if epsilon is less than 0.75, you can select the Greenhouse–Geisser value and if greater than 0.75 select the Huynd–Feldt value (Ntoumanis, 2001).

For the SPSS output (Table 4.18) the 'Tests of within-subjects effects' returns significance values of P<0.05 for all possibilities whether sphericity is assumed or violated. However, as with the previous example we don't know where the significant comparisons exist. The post hoc analysis ('pairwise comparisons' i.e. comparing pairs of data) is shown in Table 4.19. Here, the results inform us that there are differences between time point 3 and both time points 1 and 2 in the season. In other words, long jump performance improved at the end of the season when compared to pre- and mid-season. The overall result can be described in a similar way to those in Section 4.4.5.iv for the independent groups ANOVA.

Table 4.19 Post hoc output from SPSS for repeated-measures ANOVA analysis of long jump distance in the three groups (pre-, mid- and post-season)

Pairwise Comparisons

Measure: Distance

(I) Point_of_Season	(J) Point_of_Season	Mean Difference (I-J)	Std. Error	Sig.[b]	95% CI Lower Bound	95% CI Upper Bound
1	2	-.004	.033	.912	-.081	.074
	3	-.164*	.021	.000	-.213	.115
2	1	-.004	.033	.912	-.074	.081
	3	-.160*	.022	.000	-.213	.107
3	1	.164*	.021	.000	.115	.213
	2	.160*	.022	.000	.107	.213

Based on estimated marginal means

*. The mean difference is significant at the .05 level.
b. Adjustment for multiple comparisons: Least Significant Difference (equivalent to no adjustments).

Challenge yourself: post hoc tests

When you were setting up the analysis of the ANOVA data you will have seen a number of different post hoc test options. Read articles such as Kim (2015) to understand how post hoc tests work and see a range of post hoc tests that are available. Consider these different tests and what comparisons they are suited to.

Exercise 4.13

For the three typical sport and exercise lab reports data (Appendices 1a, 1b, 1c) determine what test you would use to determine whether differences existed between:

1   $\dot{V}O_{2max}$ in arm crank ergometry, cycle ergometry and treadmill running
2   Heart rate in high anxiety conditions in novice, intermediate and expert players
3   Ground reaction forces during walking, jogging and running

Answers are in Appendix 4h.

4.4.6   *Differences between groups: factorial ANOVA*

Factorial analysis of variance is a common statistical test in sport and exercise science. Here, there are a number of factors that are being studied. As noted earlier in the chapter for the long jump study design, if you have different age groups (U19, U21, senior) and both male and female athlete data then you have two factors (i.e. age and sex) and the analysis can be referred to as two-factor or two-way ANOVA. In practice, researchers rarely use designs greater than three-way ANOVA, but these can be undertaken and interpreted; the output tables are just larger. There are most likely three main research designs that you will come across that can be analysed with two-factor ANOVA:

1   Repeated measures on both factors
2   Independent groups on both factors and
3   Repeated measures on one factor and independent on the other ('mixed model')

The following sections will provide an overview of typical outputs for these designs.

4.4.6.i Repeated measures on both factors

A 'repeated measures on both factors' design is probably one of the most common in sport and exercise science. Here, the same participants are used in all trials, usually some form of control trial and a treatment trial (i.e. a placebo compared to carbohydrate ingestion, cool compared to warm environmental conditions). Consider a study where you are interested in blood lactate responses during a continuous exercise training session (CON) and an interval training session (INT). We will assume that both sessions are matched for total work done and energy expenditure (e.g. as in Christmass et al., 1999) with blood lactate concentration measured at rest and 4, 8 and 16 minutes of exercise. Here, the dependent variable is the blood lactate concentration as it *depends* upon the protocol undertaken and the time at which the measurement is made. However, we are interested in not only how blood lactate concentration changes over time (one way/factor) and how the blood lactate differs between training types (a second way/factor) but also how the two interact. In other words, how does the blood lactate response change in relation to the type of training session *and* time. This third comparison is called the interaction. A typical data set organised in Excel is shown in Table 4.20.

Table 4.20 Typical data set for blood lactate concentration for a two-way ANOVA design

	Time (min)			
	0	4	8	16
CON	1.8	5.4	4.1	3.2
	0.8	4.9	4.1	3.8
	1.5	5.1	4.7	3.1
	1.6	3.8	3.1	2.5
	1.1	4.1	3.9	2.9
	0.9	5.3	5.1	4.7
	1.2	4.9	3.9	3.2
INT	1.6	5.6	6.8	7.4
	0.9	4.9	5.6	6.9
	1.4	6.1	7.1	7.9
	1.3	4.5	5.9	7.3
	0.8	4.9	5.7	6.9
	1.3	6.1	7.2	8.1
	0.9	5.6	6.8	8.3

Remember that it is the same participants in both exercise protocols with an appropriate recovery between trials (e.g. one week) and a counterbalanced test order (same number of participants undertaking the CON trial first has undertook the INT trial first).

4.4.6.ii Main output from factorial ANOVA (repeated measures on both factors)

As with one-way analysis of variance both Excel and SPSS have functions to compute various types of two-way ANOVA. The statistical output from the analysis of the blood lactate concentration data using Excel's 'Two-way ANOVA with replication' and from SPSS's 'General Linear Model/repeated measures' are shown in Tables 4.21 and 4.22, respectively. If we take the Excel output first you can see a large amount of information in the results table. The first few sections provide the number of data points and the sum, mean and variance for each variable. These are all the stages required to calculate the final F ratio (to appreciate the calculation process, refer to any research methods or statistics textbook).

To begin with you need to focus only on the final section of the output which provides the F ratio and the accompanying significance values. Here you will see a line of results for each of 'Sample', 'Columns' and 'Interaction'. Before we discuss these results, it is important to know the aspects of the data they represent. First, consider how you have set up your data in Excel (Table 4.20). The 'Sample' refers to the two types of training (i.e. CON versus INT). The 'Columns' relate to the time component of the data (i.e. each time point in a separate column on the spreadsheet). The 'Interaction' relates to how these two factors interact with each other. These concepts are shown in Tables 4.23a–4.23c. As a simplified view, the 'Sample' analysis is concerned only with the responses of the continuous versus interval training data as a whole and is effectively comparing two means (and the associated variance), one representing all the data for CON group and one for INT group. Therefore, this is a general group comparison and is not concerned with the time aspects. The 'Column' analysis is concerned only with the responses over time, it is not concerned with the differences between training type. Here, the analysis effectively compares a mean value (and associated variance) for all the resting data, all the 4, 8, and 16 minutes data across both samples. As these comparisons relate to general rather than specific responses they are referred to as main effects. The interaction is concerned with how the group and time factors interact specifically with each other. This is shown in the Figure 4.21c where the factors overlap. Here, time 0 minute for CON could be compared against time 0 minute for INT or time 4 minutes for CON or time 8 minutes for CON or time 16 minutes for CON, etc. In other words, the specific comparisons you would be interested in if you were to do multiple t-tests – which of course you wouldn't do!

Table 4.21 Typical statistical output for two-way ANOVA (Excel; two-way ANOVA with replication)

Anova: Two-Factor With Replication

SUMMARY		0	4	8	16	Total
	CON					
Count		7	7	7	7	28
Sum		8.9	33.5	28.9	23.4	94.7
Average		1.271429	4.785714	4.128571	3.342857	3.382143
Variance		0.139048	0.368095	0.405714	0.509524	2.126706
	INT					
Count		7	7	7	7	28
Sum		8.2	37.7	45.1	52.8	143.8
Average		1.171429	5.385714	6.442857	7.542857	5.135714
Variance		0.092381	0.394762	0.469524	0.319524	6.319418
	Total					
Count		14	14	14	14	
Sum		17.1	71.2	74	76.2	
Average		1.221429	5.085714	5.285714	5.442857	
Variance		0.109505	0.449011	1.845934	5.131868	

ANOVA

Source of Variation	SS	df	MS	F	P-value	F crit
Sample	43.05018	1	43.05018	127.6236	4.03E-15	4.042652
Columns	173.1234	3	57.7078	171.0766	1.26E-25	2.798061
Interaction	38.73054	3	12.91018	38.27263	8.83E-13	2.798061
Within	16.19143	48	0.337321			
					P values less than 0.05	
Total	271.0955	55				

Note: P values are indicated for main effects and interaction.

In general, we are most interested in the interaction term. If the interaction P value is significant we know that there is a difference somewhere in the data. You can then undertake post hoc tests to determine where the specific differences are, as you would for a one-way ANOVA. If the interaction term is not significant, then you can examine the main effects for each factor involved in the ANOVA. These results are not as specific but can provide useful general information. The results table for the SPSS analysis (Table 4.22) shows essentially the same information as in the Excel output, however, there are two

Table 4.22 Typical statistical output for two-way ANOVA (SPSS; general linear model)

Tests of Within-Subjects Effects

Measure: Blood_Lactate

Source		Type III Sum of Squares	df	Mean Square	F	Sig.	Partial Eta Squared	Noncent. Parameter	Observed Power[a]
Protocol	Sphericity Assumed	43.050	1	43.050	205.642	.000	.972	205.642	1.000
	Greenhouse-Geisser	43.050	1.000	43.050	205.642	.000	.972	205.642	1.000
	Huynh-Feldt	43.050	1.000	43.050	205.642	.000	.972	205.642	1.000
	Lower-bound	43.050	1.000	43.050	205.642	.000	.972	205.642	1.000
Error(Protocol)	Sphericity Assumed	1.256	6	.209					
	Greenhouse-Geisser	1.256	6.000	.209					
	Huynh-Feldt	1.256	6.000	.209					
	Lower-bound	1.256	6.000	.209					
Time	Sphericity Assumed	173.123	3	57.708	234.725	.000	.975	704.174	1.000
	Greenhouse-Geisser	173.123	1.674	103.439	234.725	.000	.975	392.852	1.000
	Huynh-Feldt	173.123	2.246	77.090	234.725	.000	.975	527.125	1.000
	Lower-bound	173.123	1.000	173.123	234.725	.000	.975	234.725	1.000
Error(Time)	Sphericity Assumed	4.425	18	.246					
	Greenhouse-Geisser	4.425	10.042	.441					
	Huynh-Feldt	4.425	13.474	.328					
	Lower-bound	4.425	6.000	.738					
Protocol * Time	Sphericity Assumed	38.731	3	12.910	121.780	.000	.953	365.311	1.000
	Greenhouse-Geisser	38.731	1.468	26.390	121.780	.000	.953	178.729	1.000
	Huynh-Feldt	38.731	1.825	21.218	121.780	.000	.953	222.298	1.000
	Lower-bound	38.731	1.000	38.137	121.780	.000	.953	121.780	1.000
Error(Protocol*Time)	Sphericity Assumed	1.908	18	.106					
	Greenhouse-Geisser	1.908	8.806	.217					
	Huynh-Feldt	1.908	10.952	.174					
	Lower-bound	1.908	6.000	.318					

[a]. Computed using alpha = .05

Note: P values are indicated for main effects and interaction.

Table 4.23a Schematic representing 'Sample' concept

	Time (min)			
	0	4	8	16
CON	1.8	5.4	4.1	3.2
	0.8	4.9	4.1	3.8
	1.5	5.1	4.7	3.1
	1.6	3.8	3.1	2.5
	1.1	4.1	3.9	2.9
	0.9	5.3	5.1	4.7
	1.2	4.9	3.9	3.2
INT	1.6	5.6	6.8	7.4
	0.9	4.9	5.6	6.9
	1.4	6.1	7.1	7.9
	1.3	4.5	5.9	7.3
	0.8	4.9	5.7	6.9
	1.3	6.1	7.2	8.1
	0.9	5.6	6.8	8.3

Data in each sample represents all data with respect to each group (i.e. CON and INT). This represents the 'main effect' for sample and is not concerned with any other factor

Table 4.23b Schematic representing 'Columns' concept

	Time (min)			
	0	4	8	16
CON	1.8	5.4	4.1	3.2
	0.8	4.9	4.1	3.8
	1.5	5.1	4.7	3.1
	1.6	3.8	3.1	2.5
	1.1	4.1	3.9	2.9
	0.9	5.3	5.1	4.7
	1.2	4.9	3.9	3.2
INT	1.6	5.6	6.8	7.4
	0.9	4.9	5.6	6.9
	1.4	6.1	7.1	7.9
	1.3	4.5	5.9	7.3
	0.8	4.9	5.7	6.9
	1.3	6.1	7.2	8.1
	0.9	5.6	6.8	8.3

Data in columns represents all data with respect to time. This represents the 'main effect' for time and is not concerned with any other factor

Table 4.23c Schematic representing 'Interaction' concept

	Time (min)			
	0	4	8	16
CON	1.8	5.4	4.1	3.2
	0.8	4.9	4.1	3.8
	1.5	5.1	4.7	3.1
	1.6	3.8	3.1	2.5
	1.1	4.1	3.9	2.9
	0.9	5.3	5.1	4.7
	1.2	4.9	3.9	3.2
INT	1.6	5.6	6.8	7.4
	0.9	4.9	5.6	6.9
	1.4	6.1	7.1	7.9
	1.3	4.5	5.9	7.3
	0.8	4.9	5.7	6.9
	1.3	6.1	7.2	8.1
	0.9	5.6	6.8	8.3

Where the group and time shapes overlap represent the possible interactions of these factors and each set of data which can be compared against each other noticeable differences. First, the main effects are labelled according to how you have labelled the SPSS data sheet columns – in this instance – 'protocol' and 'time'. The interaction term is labelled 'protocol*time'. Second, the output is much larger as it contains the various options associated with sphericity for both main effects and the interaction, as outlined earlier. SPSS though does not automatically provide post hoc results for interactions so you will have to determine where the differences lie as you would have to for the analysis in Excel.

4.4.6.iii   *Meaningful post hoc comparisons*

When you have a significant interaction term you can compare any two means with each other. However, there is the possibility that you may have a large number of potential comparisons. So, which post hoc comparisons are useful to report? In some instances, there may only be one or two that you find so it is quite easy to report them. In other instances, especially if you calculate the post hoc values by hand, you will need to decide which comparisons are useful.

Imagine if you had core temperature measures every 5 minutes over a 60-minute duration of exercise and recovery for two or three different trials there would be a large number of potential comparisons. So, which means should you compare? Consider the figure for blood lactate against time relating to the previous example for two different training sessions (Figure 4.13).

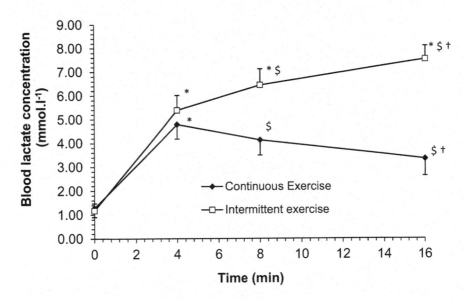

Figure 4.13 Blood lactate concentration during continuous (CON) and interval (INT) training

Note: * different from resting values (P<0.05), $ different from CON at same time-point (P<0.05), † different from 8 minutes (P<0.05).

The number of useful comparisons will usually relate to your research question. Although we may primarily be interested in whether there is a difference in blood lactate concentration between the training types at each time point, it is also important to see where differences in responses begin to appear within each trial and if there are differences at the end of exercise. In the blood lactate example, the figure shows the most likely differences would be not only at the end of exercise but also where blood lactate increases during one trial but decreases in the other. Here it may be useful to be able to state whether these changes were significant. Some useful comparisons to consider for most experimental designs are suggested here.

1   **Comparing resting values.** This comparison tells you if the resting data is the same. Hopefully, this will be the case, so each participant is in the same physiological or psychological state, unless your study design suggests otherwise. Either way, it is useful to compare.
2   **Differences at given time points.** This is important to determine whether differences exist *between* trials.
3   **Changes over time in specific trials.** This is important to determine whether differences exist *within* trials. This could involve comparing values within one trial to resting values or between different time points in that trial. This comparison may reveal different trends and adaptations between trials.
4   **Differences at the end of exercise.** For many research designs this is the important comparison and will tell you if differences exist at the end of the experiment as a result of a given treatment.

4.4.6.iv   Describing results for factorial ANOVA interaction

Similar to one-way ANOVA the first aspect you would normally report is the overall significance. In the case of two-way ANOVA that is the interaction along with any specific comparisons from the post hoc analysis. For example, the results in Tables 4.21 and 4.22 show a significant interaction between blood lactate concentration with respect to time and with training type. From post-hoc analysis we would have also determined that significant differences exist between blood lactate concentrations at the following points:

1   Between 4, 8 and 16 minutes compared to rest for the both trials
2   Between CON and INT trials at 8 and 16 minutes
3   Between 8 and 16 minutes within both training types

As with t-tests and one-way ANOVA, you can express the results of two-way ANOVA using the F ratio and degrees of freedom as well as the P value. As you have three different results for two-way ANOVA (two main effects and the interaction), there are three different combinations of degrees of freedom to report. The format of reporting requires two degrees of freedom values. First, the value for the specific result you are reporting and second, the degrees of freedom for the error (or within) term. This second term is the same for each result. For the two-way ANOVA outputs provided in Tables 4.21 and 4.22 these would be: $F_{(1,48)}$, $F_{(3,48)}$ and $F_{(3,48)}$ for the main effect for group, main effect for time and the interaction, respectively. Complete Exercise 4.14 and describe the two-way factorial ANOVA results. A written example is provided following the exercise.

Exercise 4.14   Describing two-way ANOVA results

Try describing the results from the two-way ANOVA outputs provided earlier.

Description: . . . .

. . . .

. . . .

. . . .

. . . .

. . . .

. . . .

You could report this data in the following way:

> Blood lactate concentration at rest and during exercise for the two training types is shown in Figure 4.13. A significant interaction was observed (P<0.05). There were no differences for resting values between trials (1.3 ± 0.4 and 1.2 ± 0.3 mmol·l⁻¹ for CON and INT, respectively; P>0.05) with blood lactate concentration increasing from rest at 4 minutes in both trials (4.8 ± 0.6 and 5.4 ± 0.6 mmol·l⁻¹, respectively; P>0.05). During interval training blood lactate continued to increase from this point until the end of exercise (7.5 ± 0.6 mmol·l⁻¹; P<0.05) whereas values decreased during the continuous trial (3.3 ± 0.7 mmol·l⁻¹; P<0.05). Blood lactate at the end of exercise was greater following INT than for CON (P<0.05).

4.4.6.v   Describing results for factorial ANOVA main effects

Let us consider a scenario where the results in Tables 4.21 and 4.22 did *not* give a significant interaction. In this instance we can fall back to the main effects to examine general responses. In sport and exercise science there is very often a significant main effect for the 'time' factor due to most variables being elevated with exercise (e.g. heart rate, oxygen consumption) or in some instance decrease with exercise (e.g. blood pH and blood bicarbonate concentration), so this won't really tell us a great deal. The key factor to examine here is probably the main effect for the treatment (e.g. training type or 'group'). However, as there were only two training types that we were interested in we already know that there is a difference between them, so a post hoc analysis here won't provide any further information. Indeed, in SPSS you would come across an error message in the results output stating that 'no post hoc analysis was undertaken for group as there were fewer than three groups'. This does not mean you have done anything wrong, just that the next level of analysis won't be completed as you effectively already have the answer. If we had three types of training (continuous exercise, interval training, interval training at a different intensity), we then could undertake a post hoc analysis of the training types in order to find which training type provided the greatest blood lactate values – in general. However, if there was no significant interaction observed we couldn't be any more specific than that. In the aforementioned case you could describe the data in the following way:

> No interaction was observed for blood lactate concentration between time and training type (P>0.05). However, a significant main effect was observed between trials (P<0.05) with the interval training eliciting greater blood lactate concentration than for the continuous exercise training.

4.4.6.vi   Independent groups on both factors

In this design, the data for both factors are obtained from different groups. A typical example could involve the number of injuries obtained across a number of sports ('sport' factor; basketball, hockey, softball, athletics) and between male and female athletes ('sex' factor). As such, there are no repeated measures. However, the main effects and interaction concept, post hoc analysis and written descriptions are the same as for repeated measures. Table 4.24 provides data for the sports injury study suggested with the SPSS output tables presented in Tables 4.25 and 4.26. (For an equivalent analysis Excel requires equal numbers in each comparison.) The main output table (Table 4.25) shows that the interaction between sport and sex is not significant (P=0.401). So, considering the main effects, there is a main effect for sport (P<0.05) but not sex (P=0.955). The pairwise comparisons for the main effect of sport (Table 4.26) indicates that sport 2 (hockey) elicits more injuries that the other sports. Therefore, we could report the results as:

> There was no interaction between sport and sex for the number of injuries obtained (P=0.401), however, a main effect was observed for sport (P<0.05). Post hoc analysis of the main effect for sport demonstrated hockey elicited more injuries than any other sport (P<0.05). There was no difference in injuries between the sexes (P=0.955).

Table 4.24 Number of injuries acquired across sports for male and female athletes

	Basketball	Hockey	Softball	Athletics
Male	1	5	2	3
	2	6	3	0
	1	8	2	2
	4	4	3	3
	0	5	4	1
	1	3	1	4
	2	2	0	
	4		0	
			1	
Female	0	7	4	1
	2	8	3	2
	0	5	2	0
	1	6	1	2
	2	5	0	1
	3	3	3	2
		5		1
				2

Note: a value of zero represents a return of no injuries, not an empty cell.

The description could also provide key values. As a point of critique, you would need to consider the definition of an injury, time period considered, competitive standard and inclusion criteria, etc.

4.4.6.vii   *Repeated measures on one factor and independent on the other*

The third example for two-way ANOVA is where there is a repeated measure on one factor but not the other, often termed as mixed model. A common repeated measure in sport and exercise science is that of time, where data is recorded every 5 minutes etc. during an exercise protocol or simply pre and post exercise or pre and post a period of training. Where the interest is how two different groups' responses differ, the 'group' represents the independent factor. Examples of this factor could be males and females, able-bodied athletes and wheelchair athletes, old and young athletes, different competitive standards, etc. Here, there may well be more than two levels of the same factor, such as participants who are 18–29 years, 30–49 years and 50–69

Table 4.25 Statistical output for injury data (SPSS)

Dependent Variable: Injuries

Source	Type III Sum of Squares	df	Mean Square	F	Sig.	Partial Eta Squared	Noncent. Parameter	Observed Power[b]
Corrected Model	127.271[a]	7	18.182	8.696	.000	.554	60.872	1.000
Intercept	383.813	1	383.813	183.574	.000	.789	183.574	1.000
Sex	.007	1	.007	.003	.955	.000	.003	.050
Sport	119.188	3	39.729	19.002	.000	.538	57.006	1.000
Sex * Sport	6.269	3	2.090	.999	.401	.058	2.998	.255
Error	102.448	49	2.091					
Total	614.000	57						
Corrected Total	229.719	56						

a. R Squared = .554 (Adjusted R Squared = .490)

b. Computed using alpha = .05

Note: P values for two main effects (sex, sport) are indicated.

Table 4.26 Pairwise comparison for the sport main effect

Multiple Comparisons

Dependent Variable: Injuries

Scheffe

(I) Sport	(J) Sport	Mean Difference (I-J)	Std. Error	Sig.	95% Confidence Interval	
					Lower Bound	Upper Bound
1	2	-3.5000*	.54652	.000	-5.0823	-1.9177
	3	-.2905	.53733	.961	-1.8461	1.2652
	4	-.0714	.54652	.999	-1.6537	1.5108
2	1	3.5000*	.54652	.000	1.9177	5.0823
	3	3.2095*	.53733	.000	1.6539	4.7652
	4	3.4286*	.54652	.000	1.8463	5.0108
3	1	.2905	.53733	.961	-1.2652	1.8461
	2	-3.2095*	.53733	.000	-4.7652	-1.6539
	4	.2190	.53733	.983	-1.3366	1.7747
4	1	.0714	.54652	.999	-1.5108	1.6537
	2	-3.4286*	.54652	.000	-5.0108	-1.8463
	3	-.2190	.53733	.983	-1.7747	1.3366

Based on observed means.

The error term is Mean Square(Error) = 2.091.

*. The mean difference is significant at the .05 level.

Note: Sports labelled as 1 (basketball), 2 (hockey), 3 (softball) and 4 (athletics).

years of age. Let's take the example of mood score in two sports teams before a competitive match, at half time and at the end; the data is shown in Table 4.27. The repeated measure is the time of measurement (pre, half-time, end) whereas the independent groups would be the two teams. When considering the outputs, the repeated measure is termed the 'within factor' and the independent group comparison is termed the 'between factor'. These are terms that you may well have seen in the previous SPSS output tables.

Table 4.28 shows the output table for factorial ANOVA relating to the repeated measure factor, that is, time. The table heading states 'Tests of Within Subjects Effects' which relates to the main effect for time per se and the interaction – which involves the time factor. The significance values for the various sphericity options are presented. For this example, each case for the time main effect and the time × team interaction provides a significant result (i.e. $P < 0.05$). Table 4.29 shows the results for the effect of the independent variable ('Tests of Between Subjects Effects'). Here, there is also a significant result for each of the sphericity options. The results can be

Table 4.27 Mood scores for two teams before competition, at half time and at the end of the match

		Pre game	*Half time*	*Post game*
Team 1	1	89	56	100
	2	79	78	99
	3	92	85	97
	4	85	79	89
	5	86	61	93
	6	84	79	94
	7	76	62	88
	8	73	59	81
	9	68	59	79
	10	71	63	100
		Pre game	*Half time*	*Post game*
Team 2	1	87	76	60
	2	75	81	58
	3	85	95	57
	4	87	86	48
	5	80	84	53
	6	86	86	59
	7	81	79	48
	8	78	85	51
	9	75	87	53
	10	75	89	45

Table 4.28 Output from SPSS for analysis involving repeated-measures factors

Tests of *within-subjects effects*

Measure: *Measure_1*

Source		Type III sum of squares	df	Mean square	F	Sig.	Partial eta squared	Noncent. parameter	Observed power[a]
Time_point	Sphericity assumed	640.300	2	320.150	8.902	.001	.331	17.804	.960
	Greenhouse–Geisser	640.300	1.740	367.950	8.902	.001	.331	15.491	.939
	Huynh–Feldt	640.300	2.000	320.150	8.902	.001	.331	17.804	.960
	Lower-bound	640.300	1.000	640.300	8.902	.008	.331	8.902	.805
Time_point * Team	Sphericity assumed	8153.033	2	4076.517	113.353	.000	.863	226.706	1.000
	Greenhouse–Geisser	8153.033	1.740	4685.167	113.353	.000	.863	197.255	1.000
	Huynh–Feldt	8153.033	2.000	4076.517	113.353	.000	.863	226.706	1.000
	Lower-bound	8153.033	1.000	8153.033	113.353	.000	.863	113.353	1.000
Error (Time_point)	Sphericity assumed	1294.667	36	35.963					
	Greenhouse–Geisser	1294.667	31.323	41.332					
	Huynh–Feldt	1294.667	36.000	35.963					
	Lower-bound	1294.667	18.000	71.926					

a. Computed using alpha = .05

Table 4.29 Output from SPSS for independent factors of mixed model ANOVA

Tests of between-subjects effects

Measure: Measure_1

Transformed variable: Average

Source	Type III sum of squares	df	Mean square	F	Sig.	Partial eta squared	Noncent. parameter	Observed power[a]
Intercept	351594.150	1	351594.150	3964.271	.000	.995	3964.271	1.000
Team	770.417	1	770.417	8.687	.009	.326	8.687	.796
Error	1596.433	18	88.691					

a. Computed using alpha = .05

reported as for the previous examples for factorial ANOVA considering the interaction and main effects as is pertinent.

Now that you have practised writing results descriptions for each of the statistical tests covered, read the results section of previous journal articles using ANOVA techniques and complete Exercise 4.15. You can then go on to critique a range of written descriptions (Exercise 4.16) and then write the results section for your own data (Exercise 4.17).

Exercise 4.15   One-way and two-way ANOVA results

Consult a range of journal articles to find those which have used one- and two-way ANOVA analysis. For each study complete Table 4.30. Include enough detail within the 'Main aim' column so that you can see why the authors have used the given statistical test. For the 'Written description' column, comment on how the authors have reported their data.

Table 4.30 One-way and two-way ANOVA results from previous research studies

Statistical test used	Authors	Main aim	Written description
One-way ANOVA	. . . .	. . . .	. . . .
			. . . .
			. . . .
			. . . .
Two-way ANOVA	. . . .	. . . .	. . . .
			. . . .
			. . . .
			. . . .

Exercise 4.16   Critiquing a written description

For the following data (Table 4.31), the accompanying figure (Figure 4.14), statistical output (Table 4.32) and written descriptions provided, comment on how these could be improved. There are two different written descriptions to critique. The data is for a hypothetical study examining the effects of music tempo on ratings of perceived exertion during continuous exercise at 60% $\dot{V}O_{2max}$ for 30 minutes. Example comments for the following descriptions are given at the end of the exercise.

Table 4.31 Data set for Exercise 4.16

	Time (min)			
	5	*10*	*15*	*30*
Slow tempo	12	13	14	14
	11	12	13	14
	13	13	14	15
	14	13	14	15
	12	11	12	13
	11	13	13	12
	13	13	14	14
Fast tempo	14	15	15	15
	12	13	14	15
	14	15	16	16
	14	15	16	16
	13	13	14	14
	13	14	14	14
	14	15	15	15

Written description 1

As you can see from the graph there is an increase in RPE. One trial is higher than the other. There are differences between trials.

Comments: . . . .

. . . .

. . . .

. . . .

. . . .

. . . .

Written description 2

The results are shown in the graph. RPE is similar at 5 minutes of exercise giving values of 12.3 and 13.4. At 10 minutes values go up to 12.6 and 14.3. Values then increase at 15 minutes to 13.4 and 14.9. At the end of exercise values go up to 13.9 and 15.0.

Comments: . . . .

. . . .

. . . .

. . . .

. . . .

. . . .

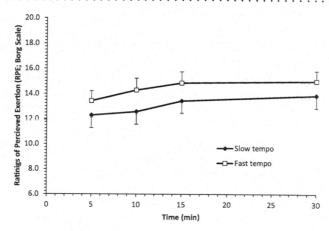

Figure 4.14 Rating of perceived exertion during continuous exercise in the presence of fast or slow tempo music

Table 4.32 Statistical output for Exercise 4.16

ANOVA

Source of variation	SS	df	MS	F	P-value	F crit
Sample	25.78571	1	25.78571	31.16547	1.08E-06	4.042652
Columns	21.14286	3	7.047619	8.517986	0.000122	2.798061
Interaction	0.785714	3	0.261905	0.316547	0.813332	2.798061
Within	39.71429	48	0.827381			
Total	87.42857	55				

Comments for written description 1 include:

1   Specific figure is not stated.
2   Specific trial where greater values are found is not stated.
3   No description of values obtained.
4   Where were the differences found between trials?

Comments for written description 2 include:

1   Specific figure is not stated.
2   Every mean is provided in the description making it more of a catalogue of values than a true description of key results.
3   No standard deviations are provided.
4   No statistical results are provided.

You could report this data in the following way:

> Ratings of perceived exertion (RPE) for both the fast and slow music trials are shown in Figure 4.14. There was no interaction observed between music tempo and time ($F_{(3,48)}=0.32$; $P>0.05$). However, significant main effects were observed for music tempo ($F_{(1,48)}=31.17$; $P<0.05$) and time ($F_{(3,48)}=8.52$; $P<0.05$). RPE for the fast tempo trial was consistently greater than for the slow tempo trial ($P<0.05$). RPE increased from values at 5 minutes of exercise (12.3 ± 1.1 and 13.4 ± 0.8 for the slow and fast tempos, respectively) to 13.4 ± 0.8 and 14.9 ± 0.9 at 15 minutes. Values then remained at similar levels until the end of exercise (13.9 ± 1.1 and 15.0 ± 0.8, respectively).

Exercise 4.17   Producing your own written description

Using the pointers in Exercise 4.16 produce a written description for your own factorial ANOVA data. For extra practice you could consider writing a results section for each of the typical lab class examples used throughout this book.

Written description for your own data: . . . .

. . . .

. . . .

. . . .

. . . .

. . . .

. . . .

. . . .

Exercise 4.18

For the three typical sport and exercise lab report areas, what test you would use to determine whether a difference exists between:

1 $\dot{V}O_{2max}$ in arm crank ergometry, cycle ergometry and treadmill running in males and females
2 Heart rate in novice, intermediate and expert players in high and low anxiety conditions
3 Ground reaction force during walking, jogging and running when wearing shoes and barefoot (in the same participants)

Answers are in Appendix 4i.

4.5 Don't be afraid of error messages!

Most statistics packages or spreadsheets with statistics options normally provide error messages if something is not quite right with the data set-up or analysis procedures. Although these are designed to help you they may seem daunting at first glance and mean little to you. However, if you think about what they are saying you can usually workout what the problem is. For example, Excel will tell you that 'Output will overwrite existing data' if the output region for the statistics analysis will cover something else already on your spreadsheet. In this instance simply direct your output to a different cell or area on your spreadsheet or to a new spreadsheet. Also, as noted earlier, for two-way analysis of variance in SPSS you may get the message 'No post hoc results for group as fewer than three groups'. This just means that there are only two groups to compare for main effects, the results for which you would already have from your two-way ANOVA output. If you had three or more groups to compare this would not appear.

4.6 Common errors in results sections

There are a number of common errors that many students display when writing their results sections. The following are the most common to be avoided. Doing so will help to improve not only the flow of your results section but also your marks for this section.

4.6.1 Discussing results

Within your result section you should present and describe only the results. It is very common for students to try and explain or discuss their results within the results section. Try to avoid this as you have a discussion section specifically for this purpose.

4.6.2 Reporting variables not described in the methods

You need to ensure that all the results you present have been adequately described in the methods. Conversely, you need to also ensure that all the variables described in the methods are reported in the results. Otherwise, what was the point of measuring them? Even if variables do not result in any significant differences, a single sentence may be all that is required to inform the reader of the main finding.

4.6.3 Duplicating data in tables and figures

Avoid duplicating your data by presenting results in both figure and table formats. The description of your data should be sufficient to provide the key responses and any specific values of interest.

4.6.4 Poor description of results

Poor written descriptions do not help demonstrate the key findings of the study. Always make sure that you have reported the key statistical results and any values which aid this description. In addition, the actual statistical outputs from each test (i.e. the output tables) are seldom required in written reports. You may need these tables within your project lab file as evidence of data analysis or even as appendices (check your coursework guidance), but they are not usually contained within the results section per se. A common error is when your data may look as if it would yield a strong correlation, but you have not actually undertaken a correlation analysis. Here, many students state that 'there is a positive correlation' but, if you have not done the analysis it is better to state as 'a linear relationship', for example.

4.6.5 Unclear reporting of statistics

If you are not confident with the statistical analysis, it is likely that you will also not be confident in reporting the key findings of each test. Try to keep the message simple. Focus on stating whether the results for each test were significant in conjunction with reporting whether the P values were greater than or less than 0.05. Also make sure that you have the greater than ($>$) and less than ($<$) symbols written correctly. Confusing these symbols could have important implications on your results and demonstrating your understanding of statistics. It is becoming more common for authors to report the actual P value rather than simply 'P<0.05' or 'P>0.05'.

4.6.6 Repeating the statistical tests used

You do not have to repeat the statistical tests undertaken as this will have been described in the methods section.

4.6.7 Inconsistent reporting of values and units

As noted in the methods it is important to use the correct units for all variables and an appropriate number of decimal places. It is also important not to forget to state the standard deviation values with each mean value reported.

4.6.8 Lack of reference to figures and tables

If you have figures and tables in your report, it is important to state which figure your description relates to (see the example written descriptions earlier in this chapter). If figures and tables are not labelled clearly, the flow of the results from the readers', or assessors', perspective will be affected.

4.7 Chapter summary and reflection

This chapter considered different ways of analysing and presenting your results. Different types of figures may be more effective than others in displaying the key findings of your study. The main statistical tests for different types of research design were also considered. This chapter also considered how to write your results section through a series of exercises relating to each statistical test. To assess your understanding of results sections, consider the following summary questions.

- What is the purpose of a results section?
- What are the main ways of expressing your key findings?
- How do your results reflect your research question or hypothesis?
- What are the common errors when writing results sections?

4.8 Further activities

Browse the websites of journals that you regularly read or are aware of. Direct yourself to the author guidelines and consider the advice given for writing results sections.

Use the critical appraisal tools in the introduction chapter to evaluate your own results section.

Consult your lab schedule and ensure that you understand the expected results for each variable you have measured.

5   Discussion

In this chapter you will be able to:

- appreciate the role of the discussion

  (Section 5.1)

- consider the components of a discussion

  (Section 5.2)

- plan your discussion

  (Section 5.3)

- practise writing part of your discussion

  (Section 5.4)

- consider what your results mean

  (Sections 5.5 & 5.6)

- appreciate the role of the conclusion

  (Section 5.7)

- identify limitations and future work

  (Section 5.8)

- reflect upon your research question and hypotheses

  (Section 5.9)

- identify common problems when writing discussions

  (Section 5.6)

5.1   Purpose of the discussion

Once the research study has been designed and the data collected and analysed, it is time to explain what it all means. For many readers of scientific

DOI: 10.4324/9781003112426-6

articles, the discussion is often the key section to be read and, along with the methods, is a key section for critique (Section 2.8). The discussion should emphasise the new and important aspects of the study without repeating information and details from other sections (ICMJE, 2019). The discussion should also compare and contrast the results to previous research studies (Foote, 2009b; ICMJE, 2019) to put the results into context and assert their value (Skelton, 1994). Importantly, the discussion should explain how the results help to answer and support the research question posed (Foote, 2009b). Finally, the discussion is also the opportunity to present your study limitations and suggestions for future work (ICMJE, 2019).

The guidance provided for writing your lab report discussion can take many forms. For example, in your first year of study you may have a series of questions to answer relating to your data thus providing the focus required. Alternatively, you may simply be asked to 'discuss your results'. The latter is certainly likely for final-year dissertations and postgraduate theses. Having written lab reports in the formative years of your studies you may be expected to already know how to approach your discussion. This chapter provides an overview of what may be expected to appear in your discussion and some guidance as to how to plan and write your discussion. As with previous chapters, it will be useful to consult the information on critical appraisal of journal articles (Section 2.8) to appreciate those areas often lacking in discussion sections.

5.2 Components of your discussion

The discussion, along with the results section, has been considered to be the most difficult section of scientific reports to write (Foote, 2009b). Indeed, the discussion is often a section which clearly discriminates between students of different abilities or grades, probably more so than other sections of the report. However, when written well the discussion provides an excellent opportunity to achieve good marks. Therefore, it is important to grasp the key factors required. So, how do you go about writing your discussion and what actually needs to be contained within it? It may seem obvious to state that this is the section where you discuss your results but what does this actually mean? The following paragraph should help to start you off prior to the 'planning your discussion' section.

To put discussions into context both Wells (2006) and Alexandrov (2004) have considered three- and four-part or 'paragraph' approaches, respectively (Figure 5.1). Although these authors were concerned with providing guidance for writing journal articles, the concept is essentially the same for both dissertations and lab reports. Wells (2006) suggests a three-part approach akin to the 'three paragraph' approach used for writing introductions. Here, the first part considers the general background to the study, the second contains a brief description of the main results and the third looks at how the new results add to the field of research. Alexandrov (2004) suggests a

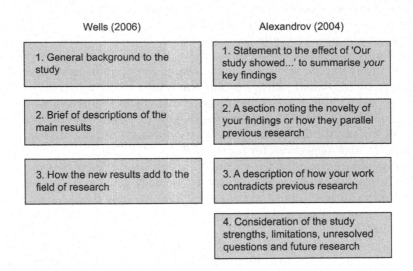

Wells (2006)

Alexandrov (2004)

1. General background to the study

1. Statement to the effect of 'Our study showed...' to summarise *your* key findings

2. Brief of descriptions of the main results

2. A section noting the novelty of your findings or how they parallel previous research

3. How the new results add to the field of research

3. A description of how your work contradicts previous research

4. Consideration of the study strengths, limitations, unresolved questions and future research

Figure 5.1 Three- and four-component models for discussions

four-part model that starts with the statement 'Our study showed . . . '. The second section notes the novelty of the findings or how they parallel previous research. In the third part there is a description of how your work contradicts previous research and the final paragraph considers the study's strengths and limitations, any unresolved questions and looks towards future research. For those authors struggling to begin writing discussions for journal articles, Branson (2004) considers a more specific eight-part (or paragraph) approach (Table 5.1).

All of the aforementioned aspects suggested by the authors are important to include in your discussion. However, as a more straightforward approach for undergraduate students, you need to essentially consider all the variables measured within your report and what they mean. Try not to miss any out. As you progress through your studies your level of understanding will increase and so will the expectations of critique and explanation. Therefore, it will also be useful to consider the critical appraisal tools in Chapter 2 and the comments relating to discussion sections. The following section will consider ways to plan your discussion and get your writing started.

Many students are concerned that they are repeating information from their literature review or introduction within their discussions. This is understandable as many of the key journal articles used may well be the same. Wells (2006) summarises the differences between introductions and discussions as follows; introductions consider what was known before the experiment was done and discussions compare the new results found in the study and integrates them with previous literature (Wells, 2006). Furthermore, the information within your lab report introduction often sets the scene for the

Table 5.1 Generic construct for writing the discussion (Branson, 2004)

Paragraph	Objective
1	Describe the major findings Answer the research question Don't make conclusions
2	Interpret your findings Explain what you think the main findings mean Don't over interpret
3–5	Compare your results with the current literature on the same or similar topics Use references to support your interpretation of your findings and the current literature Make sure to explain the literature that conflicts with your data and explain why the reports conflict
6	List the limitations of your study Describe the generalisability of your result to other situations Discuss any problems you encountered in the methods
7	List unanswered questions Propose further research that should be undertaken
8	Conclusion Answer the research question and explain your interpretation of the findings Don't make conclusions unsupported by the results

tests to be undertaken whereas your dissertation introduction should develop the rationale for your research question (see chapter 2). A common question from students is 'can I use the same references in the discussion as in the introduction?'. The answer is of course, yes you can. As your discussion is attempting to explain your lab results and answer your research question you will, of course, have to refer to studies cited in your introduction or literature review. The main difference is how you use the sources within your discussion. Consider Exercise 5.1 to determine how source may be used differently in introductions and discussions.

Exercise 5.1   Distinguishing between introductions and discussions

First, read the discussion of a journal article and compare it to the introduction. How does the use of information differ between them?

Key focus of the introduction: ....

....

....

....

....

Key focus of the discussion:..

....

....

....

....

Where the authors have used the same references in both sections, consider how the reference has been used. What key information is included in both sections? How is the information used different?

Reference:..

How used in introduction:...

....

....

....

How used in the discussion:...

....

....

....

....

5.3   Planning your discussion

There are a number of ways to plan your discussion and you will no doubt find one that works best for you. As such there is no right or wrong way to do this provided all the relevant information is considered. You may go straight into writing without much planning and see what evolves. However, as for exams, this approach could result in writing off topic or forgetting something that is crucial to your work. For all reports and scientific studies, it is essential that you relate back to your aims and hypotheses to see if you have managed to answer your research question. As with other sections of your report always have your research question in mind. The following may help you to start considering what the important factors are in your data.

1   With your results section or your spreadsheet of data open in front of you consider the responses for each variable you have measured. It may be helpful to produce a (basic) figure or some plot of your mean

data to visualise what has happened. You can do this prior to your statistical analysis too. You can then view your responses and consider what they show. It may also be helpful to add a sentence of initial thoughts as to what has happened under each figure on your spread-sheet. By doing this you will at least consider the underlying responses for each variable you have measured. Remember, everything you measured was measured for a reason.

2   Consider each group of variables that you have measured, that is, cardiorespiratory, metabolic, perceptual, EMG, kinematic, personality, mood, performance (e.g. power, speed, agility), etc. What are the logical links between them? Do the responses complement each other? Would you expect them to? You can then plan specific themes throughout your discussion.

3   What is the logical order or progression of the data? Do you have performance measures and some corresponding variables relating to underlying mechanisms? Do some variables lend themselves to explaining others? For example, how were different levels of anxiety provoked in your study and what were the resultant heart rate responses reflecting this? For the peak oxygen uptake data, peripheral fatigue during upper body exercise (evidenced by ratings of perceived exertion for the arms) may help explain lower peak exercise values.

4   Consider the subheadings you have in the method and results sections. This is a good model to follow for your discussion. You don't neces-sarily have to keep the subheadings in the text in your final version, but it may help your planning.

5   Refer to your research question. Have you managed to answer it? Can you reject or accept your hypotheses?

Exercise 5.2   Structure of a discussion

Read the discussion section of a journal article related to your lab report or project. Choose one or two words to describe what each paragraph discusses.

Paragraph 1: ....
Paragraph 2: ....
Paragraph 3: ....
Paragraph 4: ....
Paragraph 5: ....
Paragraph 6: ....
Paragraph 7: ....
Paragraph 8: ....

Examine your list of areas covered within the journal articles discussion and examine the flow of information. Is there a logical progression? How did the discussion evolve? In what order did the authors discuss their findings?

Compare your descriptors to what is contained within the results section. Were all the results considered? How were the variables grouped within the discussion?

Now we have considered the components of a discussion and how you plan it in the next stages to actually write it.

5.4   Writing your discussion

As you may have noticed from your background reading of journal articles, across sport and exercise disciplines, authors' writing styles differ considerably. If there was a magic formula to produce an ideal discussion writing, it would be formulaic, not allow you to add your own personal slant in explaining your data and as a result most likely be uninspiring. However, although developing your own writing style is of great importance, there are a number of factors you should consider when writing your discussion. These are by no means the only way to present your discussion points but do attempt to provide a focus for contextualising your results.

After reading Section 5.3 relating to planning your discussion, you should at least have an idea of what your data is showing you in terms of its absolute values that is, what increased, what decreased and by how much. If you stop at this point and do not explain the responses, your discussion will be descriptive and not explanatory. This is not the foundation for a good report and likely to achieve lower marks. You need to make sure you take your discussion to the next level. Consider the purpose of the main body of the discussion noted in Section 5.1. The discussion should:

1   Emphasise the new and important aspects
2   Compare and contrast the results to previous research and put them into context
3   Explain how the results help to answer the research question

The following sections will consider each point and how you may demonstrate them.

5.4.1   Emphasise the new and important aspects

You need to make it clear what your new findings are. This is closely related to your research question and the uniqueness of your study. If you have not examined anything 'new', then your results are likely to be more confirmatory than novel. This is more of an important consideration for postgraduate students and other researchers who desire to publish their work rather than for undergraduate students. If you have not found anything 'new' (whether statistically significant or otherwise), this is not a major problem. Please note that results which are not statistically significant are just as important as those which are significant – especially if you were expecting a considerable difference. However, it is also important not to overestimate the importance or implications of your key findings if significance is not evident.

5.4.2 Comparing and contrasting to previous research – putting the results into context

This second aspect is extremely important. By comparing your results to other studies helps you to contextualise your data. However, not everyone knows what 'contextualise' means. If you consult a thesaurus for variant words and phrases for 'context' you will find such entries as 'connection', 'frame of reference' and 'relation' (Collins Shorter Thesaurus, 1994). Therefore, contextualising your results means that you relate your findings to previous research studies and determine how your results fit in with the current body of knowledge. For example, are your peak power values from the Wingate anaerobic test similar to other studies examining similar populations? Are your personality profiles as expected for trained athletes? Are your ground reaction forces within the normal range? Are your $\dot{V}O_{2max}$ values lower than for elite athletes but greater than those of untrained participants? Here you should include a selection of the most pertinent references (Alexandrov, 2004) but not an exhaustive list of the literature. In a review of research articles, Clarke and Chalmers (1998) and Clarke et al. (2002) noted that although previous studies were cited within the discussion sections it was often unclear as to whether these studies represented similar study designs or why they had been included. Therefore, in general, consider referencing those studies which have used a similar population, protocol or methods to your own. If studies are used that are not similar (which may often be the only literature available), note this and explain what the differences between those studies and your own may be.

Comparison of your results to previous studies can also be used to demonstrate that your data is of good quality. For example, are your resting values or performances similar to what is expected? For undergraduate dissertations this is a good illustration of the accuracy of your data collection techniques, for postgraduate students a high level of accuracy would certainly be expected or presumed. Consider the example of measuring blood lactate concentration in midfielders and defenders during a simulated soccer match. You may not have found significant differences between your groups but were the overall values within the expected range? Discussing this aspect demonstrates your knowledge of the general responses to a simulated soccer match which is important at many levels of study. A discussion of such responses also helps to validate your data. Likewise, you may not have observed any performance differences in basketball shooting ability in high and low anxiety conditions but was the performance of the players as good as expected for their level of experience or the test used? This may lead you on to reasons why accuracy may differ between studies, thus initiating study limitations and stimulating future research ideas. For example, if we had found no difference in shooting performance between the expert and novice basketball players in our psychology lab (Appendix 1b), you could consider the following.

> No difference was observed between the expert and novice players in shooting performance. The performance of both groups was poorer than for those reported by Jones et al. (2000) for elite basketball players. The lack of performance differences between novice and expert players is therefore most likely due to the groups being based upon basketball playing experience rather than skill level.
>
> (NB: The reference used is fictitious.)

Although comparing your data to previous studies is important you must be careful not to be purely descriptive in your approach but to explain any similarities or differences in comparison to your own.

5.4.3   Explain how results help to answer the research question

When you are planning your discussion, it is important to note that what is important or of interest to one author may not be of importance or interest to another. Therefore, the focus of a discussion for a given set of results could differ between authors. However, no matter how opinions or approaches may differ between authors your discussion must address your research question. Theoretically, this aspect should be straightforward as you have the results of your statistical analysis to inform you whether your results differed between conditions or groups. For example, consider the hypothesis that a group of basketball players who compete regularly would exhibit less anxiety in a high-pressure shoot-out situation than a novice group of basketball players. If your anxiety data is statistically lower in the trained group, you can accept your hypothesis. If there is no difference (or experienced players are more anxious), then you can reject it. Although one result may be more expected than another you can provide a decision on your hypothesis based on the statistical analysis. However, if there are confounding variables that may have affected the data, you need to explain them.

5.5   What do your results actually mean?

If you understand how to relate your results to previous literature and how to put your results into context, then you are well on the way to understanding what your results actually mean. As well as discussing the main statistical findings it is useful to reflect upon the factors which contributed to your research design and those considered to reduce the potential variability in your data. Furthermore, these factors may also help explain why your results are different from other studies as a result of protocol, population or procedural differences. These factors may therefore help to explain your results, thus putting them in context. The following paragraphs will consider general student concerns relating to discussions, biological and statistical significance and essentially the meaningfulness of your data.

5.5.1 General discussion concerns

Frequently voiced concerns by undergraduate students include 'I haven't found any significance so I have nothing to write about' and 'what happens if my results aren't very good?' Part of this can be answered by Section 5.4.2 with the examples of blood lactate responses to a simulated soccer match and the accuracy of shooting performance in different anxiety conditions. In light of no differences being observed between specific comparisons, the general responses to a protocol or treatment can be considered (NB: these should be considered anyway in terms of underlying processes). For example,

> No differences were observed between the blood lactate concentrations between midfielders and defenders. However the values observed for both groups were similar to other simulated soccer protocols (Smith et al., 2003; Jones et al., 2006) demonstrating the imbalance between lactate production and removal during repeated high intensity efforts (Smith and Jones, 2004).
>
> (NB: The references used are fictitious and a greater level of detail explaining the underlying physiological responses would likely be expected)

You should certainly discuss the underlying processes that explain your results for the majority of the variables measured. Discussing responses in this way also helps to put your result into context. Remember, the difference between your study design and previous studies may have been the crux of your research question. Consider the comforting statement from Foote (2009b) that if the results are not as expected it is not a sign of failure.

As regards the student concern that their data is 'not very good' just remember what your project signifies. It is not designed to win Nobel Prizes or to produce the basis of a classic research article (although some dissertations may contain publishable data). The aim very often includes demonstrating an ability to undertake an independent piece of research. The data is usually only one part of the assessment. Although you will likely feel more confident about your discussion if you have clear and good quality results you still need to discuss them effectively.

With respect to data quality at an undergraduate level you may have some results with large standard deviations or erratic or irregular responses. Here it is best to consider what may be producing these responses. Are the large standard deviations due to outliers? Is there an erroneous value in the spreadsheet that has gone unchecked? Are your resting data responses quite variable but the exercise responses less so? A number of these factors can probably be answered by perusing your data set and explaining the potential reasons in your discussion.

5.5.2   *Statistical significance versus biological significance*

If you find that you have no statistically significant data, all is not lost. As well as putting your data into context with previous research, you can also put data into context with respect to the biological significance. Biological significance refers to factors such as whether your (nonstatistically significant) differences are greater than you may expect with respect to daily variation or measurement error (Section 3.4). For example, consider a performance trial where there were no statistically significant differences in the mean values, but the values appear to be different. You could have a scenario here where all participants improved, but by small amounts, or where no one actually performed worse. You can consider your data on an individual level identifying those participants who performed better than others and those who did not and assess whether these participants exhibited any specific characteristics. Although this approach may be useful for performance data it is by no means a licence to ignore your statistical outputs. If the statistical tests find no difference then there is no difference to report. Many students report in their results section or discussion that that 'there were no differences between trials' and then state that one value was greater than another.

Incorporating biological significance may provide greater scope for discussion particularly when you have previously determined the reliability or the magnitude of daily variation for your specific populations and variables of interest. Skelton and Edwards (2000) note that in quantitative research a central aim of the discussion is to reinterpret the significance as relevance and requires subjective interpretations of the data. The authors further note that future hypotheses are generated from the 'maybe' or 'perhaps' of speculative statements. However, you must be sure not to over speculate above what your data shows.

Interpreting biological significance is of importance for performance data. Where you are writing athlete feedback reports or case studies it is vital that you know what is a meaningful change or adaptation. As case studies generally have a sample size of one (n=1) and you are unable to undertake statistical analysis this is particularly important. Some authors have considered the 'smallest worthwhile change' (Hopkins et al., 1999) in relation to this and is worthy of consideration with respect to whether performance may be improved or not.

5.5.3 *Effect size and statistical power*

Not all undergraduate students will initially be aware of the concepts of effect size and statistical power. These concepts though are reasonably straightforward and can help in assessing the meaningfulness of your data. It may seem strange to consider statistical procedures within the discussion rather than in the results, but it is the interpretations of these values which is important, and that occurs within the discussion. As well as the statistical significance and meaningfulness of your data you should also consider the practical significance (Vincent, 1999). Therefore, there are a number of measures that can be calculated to help provide additional information to the P value.

Vincent (1999) notes that if the number of participants in an analysis is large, the standard deviations are small and a repeated measure design is used, then it is possible to find statistical differences between means that are actually quite similar. In this situation although you may have a statistical difference, how meaningful is it? An estimation of the magnitude of the responses you have reported can be obtained by calculating the effect size (Schäfer and Schwarz, 2019), or more simply put, the size of the effect you have found. A large effect size usually results in greater statistical power with the latter usually expressed as a percentage of one (i.e. a power value of 0.89 is 89%). With greater statistical power you can be confident in your statistical outputs and whether you are able to accept or reject your hypotheses.

There are a number of different types of effect size calculation which fall into two classifications; those for differences and those for relationships (Schober et al., 2018). Common effect size approaches in sport and exercise science are considered here. For t-tests, Cohen's d can be used whereas for analysis of variance, omega squared or Cohen's f are often reported (Kotrlik et al., 2011). Cohen's d represents the ratio of the difference between means to the standard deviation of the control group or the pooled standard deviation if there is no control group (Vincent, 1999). Cohen's f and omega squared estimate the total variance which may be explained by the influence of the dependent variable (Thomas and Nelson, 2001), more specifically, for the sample (Cohen's f) and population (Omega squared) (Kotrlik et al., 2011). For t-tests effects size values of 0.2 are generally considered to be small, 0.5 moderate and greater than or equal to 0.8 large (Cohen, 1988). For analysis of variance (Cohen's f) equivalent vales of 0.10, 0.25, 0.40 can be applied (Cohen, 1988) and for omega squared values 0.01, 0.06 and 0.138–0.15 (Kirk, 1996; Keppel, 1991) (see Kortrlik et al. for a summary of effects size tests and their interpretation). Effect sizes can therefore be used in addition to P values to express the size of the effect achieved.

Speed and Andersen (2000) provide effect size calculations for a range of commonly used statistical tests. The authors also noted that the reporting of effects size and statistical power was rare within sport and exercise science research and adequate interpretation of them was even rarer. However, considering these values may help guard against Type I and Type II errors and assist in determining the meaningfulness of your data. In addition, Nevill (2000) notes that it is possible to reduce TI and TII errors by ensuring any assumptions of statistical tests are met. Likewise, performing tests for homogeneity of variance and normality of data should always be undertaken prior to your main data analysis (see Chapter 4).

Challenge yourself

Read the overview of effect sizes by Kotrlik et al. (2011) for greater insight into the area and then consider the 'admonitions' by authors such as Correll et al. (2020) and Thompson (1999).

5.6   Other discussion considerations and common errors

There are a range of common errors which, as for the other sections of your report, can be easily avoided. This section will cover the most common errors including: repeating information from other sections of the report, not discussing your data, not presenting key ideas within paragraphs, over speculation and not providing specific information in comparison to previous studies.

5.6.1   Repeating information from other sections of the report

An important consideration for discussions is not to repeat information or details from other sections of your report (ICMJE, 2019; Gaafar, 2005, Alexandrov, 2004). Common errors in writing discussions include: repeating sections of the literature review or introduction, the methods used or statistical analysis and statistical tests and restating the results without discussing them. There may be some of these aspects which have affected your results or the outcomes of your study and therefore require discussion, but do exactly this, discuss them and discuss them in context of your research question.

5.6.2   Discussing YOUR data

A common problem for students writing either lab reports or dissertations is not actually discussing their own data. You may have cited previous literature and reported your findings correctly, but if you haven't discussed your results it doesn't take your discussion to the next level. In this instance, the reader will know how your results compared to previous studies but not what is new, novel or important. Similar to not discussing your own data another common error is explaining other people's results rather than your own. This is quite an easy trap to fall into thinking that you have explained why results may differ but with the focus on other people's results rather than your own. You can read other people's results in their articles, so make sure that you explain yours.

5.6.3   *Presentation of key ideas within each paragraph*

Each paragraph should really consider only one aspect of interest. If you try and introduce too many arguments or discussion points into one paragraph it can at best result in overly long paragraphs and at worst confuse the reader. Refer to the chapter on introductions (Chapter 2) where it was suggested that you should be able to read each paragraph and provide one or two words to describe what is being discussed. Try that approach for your discussion. You may well have a number of variables that help to explain a response but try not to overwhelm the reader. If you have a range of theories that are pertinent to what you have measured, you may want to use separate paragraphs for each one.

5.6.4   *Paragraph structure*

Similar to the aforementioned, consider the structure of each paragraph that you write. You need to state what you found, how it compares to previous work and what it actually means. Although this does not have to be in any specific order, as your approach may differ depending on each aspect discussed, each sentence should flow easily from one to another without making the reader ask themselves what the link may be. Consider the model given in Table 5.2. The below example follows this model and demonstrates how the same information may be written in different ways:

> The knee angle at take-off was found to be greater in the experienced long jumpers when compared to the novice jumpers. This consistent with the work of Smith et al. (2010) and demonstrated the differences in jumping technique between groups of athletes that differed in training status.

OR

> Smith et al. (2010) observed that more experienced long jumpers exhibited greater knee joint angles at take-off when compared to less experiences athletes. The results of the current study support this finding and emphasize the differences in jumping technique between groups.
>
> (NB: The reference used is fictitious)

Both of these examples present the same information but in different ways. However, both examples are purely descriptive and do not really provide

Table 5.2 Considerations for components of discussion paragraphs

Component	Possible wording
What was the finding?	Variable X was greater in condition 1 when compared to condition 2.
How did it compare to previous work?	This is similar to a study by A. This is in contrast to a study by B.
What does it mean?	The [similar] response demonstrates C and D. The [contrasting] response is possibly due to E and F.

much more of an insight into the underlying reason for differences in performance. Taking into account the advice from Section 5.4.2, we can add more information to make the paragraph discuss the results in relation to other variables.

> The knee angle at take-off was found to be greater in the experienced long jumpers when compared to the novice jumpers. This is consistent with the work of Smith et al. (2010) and demonstrated the differences in jumping technique between groups of athletes that differed in training status. Furthermore, the present study also demonstrated a faster running velocity at take off in the experienced group and a strong positive correlation between knee angle and jump distance. It is possible that the faster running speeds at take off could have contributed to differences in knee angle and consequently greater jump distance.

5.6.5   *Comparing your results to previous studies*

When comparing your data to previous studies, don't forget that you can use results from control trials, where no treatment has been administered, for general comparison. This is so even though the studies may have investigated different treatments to your own. For example, consider a study where you have examined the effects of caffeine ingestion on performance of repeated sprints. You may want to compare your performance data to what is expected for that protocol. However, what do you do if no studies have examined the responses to caffeine ingestion using this protocol (i.e. the reason why you are interested in studying this area) and you are unable to directly compare your data? The simple answer is that you can at least refer to the study's control trial using the same protocol as you have for an initial comparison of results. You can then consider the magnitude of any improvements (or decrements) in performance based on previous performance trial data reported in the literature, but for different protocols.

5.6.6 Be specific in your wording

When discussing previous work, it is important to make sure you include all the pertinent information regarding the studies that you are citing. The reader is then able to specifically compare the responses reported to those for your results. For example, it may be useful to clearly state the protocol or exercise intensity used, the specific time of measurement or the questionnaire used. Conversely, don't be too brief and produce writing that is only understood by experts in the field (Bem, 1995). It is also important to note the direction of any differences noted in previous research. Stating that previous studies observed a difference is not helpful to the reader. Was it an increase or a decrease?

5.6.7 Subheadings

Although some authors suggest that subsections in journal article discussion may break up the flow for the reader (Foote, 2009b), these may well have a place in dissertations. Using the same heading as in the results will help to focus your discussion and ensure that you have covered all the variables measured.

5.6.8 Speculation

Although we noted earlier that you are able to speculate what may have happened in your data it is important not to over speculate or discuss aspects that are too far reaching from your data (Skelton, 1994). Try and keep to the facts that you have presented in your results. Skelton (1994) undertook an analysis of original research articles in the *British Journal of General Practice* noting that markers of uncertainty, that is, using words like 'may', seems' or 'possibly' were common along with speculation. Moreover, many articles ended with a recommendation that was too imprecise to be operational.

Exercise 5.3   Components of your discussion

Once you have written your discussion, try the same exercise as previously suggested for the introduction. Read your discussion and write one word alongside each paragraph to describe the key point being discussed and assess the flow of your ideas.

Paragraph 1: ....

Paragraph 2: ....

Paragraph 3: ....

Paragraph 4: ....

Paragraph 5: ....

Paragraph 6: ....

Paragraph 7: ....

Paragraph 8: ....

Paragraph 9: ....

Paragraph 10: ....

Comment on the flow of your discussion.

....

....

....

....

....

5.7   Conclusions

Your discussion should end with an appropriate conclusion. This often takes the form of 'The results of this study suggest . . .'. However, try and avoid repeating the results without any application or interpretation; otherwise, you will have written a summary of findings rather than a conclusion. It is also helpful to link the conclusions with the goals of the study but avoid unqualified statements and conclusions not completely supported by the data (ICMJE 2019).

You may want to consider whether you can relate your data to more than your specific population, whether you can relate to your findings to field testing as well as lab tests or actual performance. The key factor is to present your take-home message from your study. This should also tie up with the concluding sentence of your abstract.

Exercise 5.4   Planning your conclusions

Now that you have written your discussion, what are the main findings you have considered and the application of your work? Note these and develop your conclusions around them. An example is given here.

Main finding	Application
....	....
....	....

....
....
....
....

Conclusions:

....
....
....
....
....
....
....

An important finding would be that the experienced basketball players demonstrated a smaller decrease in performance under high anxiety conditions. The application could be to consider how this is achieved in actual basketball games with a concluding sentence relating to the fact that experienced players may exhibit better coping strategies during competitive situations. Further work could then examine this.

5.8   Limitations and future work

5.8.1   *Limitations*

Your discussion provides the opportunity to also present any limitations that you have identified within your study. As with critical appraisal identifying limitations is not just about finding negative aspects of your work and what might have not gone to plan. Some limitations are readily accepted, and you probably could not have done much to prevent them. Don't forget that even the most sophisticated research designs are not perfect.

So, what could be a limitation to your study? Here, it is important to consider factors such as your research design and how well it enabled you to answer your research question. There may be factors which, in light of your results and factors that you could not have known before testing or analysing your results, would suggest modifications to your protocols or procedures may be appropriate. This is very common in research. If we had all the answers we wouldn't need to do the research in the first place, so modifications to protocols, research design or measurements are quite likely suggestions. As a consequence of this your limitations are closely linked to your suggestions for future work. This is particularly important for PhD students where the thesis contains a number of linked studies which often follow on from each other with respect to research questions and study design.

Typical limitations for undergraduate work may include the population tested and how applicable the results are. Your participant population may not have been as well trained as initially thought or you may not get a clear split between groups in terms of their physiological characteristics as you hoped for. There may also be a genuine reason for low participant numbers, that is, the population was not available at that point in the competitive season for example. However, you would have ideally considered this in your initial research design and when considering practicalities of data collection. The exercise protocols used may have been too intense or not intense enough, potentially needing adjustment after pilot testing or your first few trials.

Finally for limitations, a note of caution. There are two common limitations often stated by students. The first is having a small number of participants. This may be a limitation to the quality of the data but should really have been addressed in the initial stages of the project through participant recruitment or during data collection if participants dropped out of the study. Working with humans does mean that you have to accommodate such problems, something which all researchers have to contend with. The number of participants is usually the researcher's responsibility and not generally the key limitation of the study. However, if you express your small number of participants in terms of low statistical power and how it may have affected your results this is a much more considered approach to your possible limitation. Second, students may state equipment malfunction or being able to use 'better equipment' as limitations. Your laboratory equipment is likely to be much more up-to-date and effective than you may consider, and you should always have a back-up plan for your data collection in case of malfunction or heavy usage by other students. Don't use the limitations to air your personal gripes or views on resources, such comments will likely just vex your supervisor! There are much more important limitations to consider.

5.8.2 *Future work*

Standard viva questions for research degree candidates often include 'if you had to do the study again what would you change' or 'what would your next study be?'. As all research is driven by what has gone before, your suggestions for future work should be based on what you have found (or not found) and the limitations you have identified. Consider why you undertook your specific study in the first place, most likely as a result of a gap in the literature or a limitation to previous studies. As with your research question, there must be a rationale for future studies you recommend. If they do not relate to your findings or design, then you need to be clear as to why they are important. As with reporting limitations simply stating future work should use a greater number of participants or more measurements are not well-considered suggestions. Try Exercise 5.5 to try and link your limitations and future work.

Exercise 5.5   Linking your limitations and future work

Use Table 5.3 below to list the factors you think may be considered as limitations to your study and any future research that may overcome them. Consider what you can or can't explain with your data. Two examples are provided within Table 5.3 to help you.

Table 5.3 Limitations and future work

Potential limitation	Potential future work
Exercise protocol not intense enough.........	Modification of the existing protocol or development of a new protocol................
Participants aerobic fitness too low.........	Recruit specifically trained athletes or screen participants prior to inclusion in the study..
....	....
....	....
....	....
....	....
....	....
....	....
....	....

5.9   Chapter summary and reflections

In this chapter we have considered how to discuss your results. The organisation of ideas within a discussion, how to put your results into context and what to do if there are no statistically significant differences in your data were also noted. Once your results are discussed, you will have unearthed potential limitations to your study which should be related to future work. The discussion should always focus on the research question asked and whether you have been able to answer it. To assess your understanding of discussions, consider the following summary questions:

- What is a discussion?
- How does a discussion differ from an introduction?

- How can you put your results into context?
- How can you discuss your results if there is no significance?
- What should be included in your limitations and future work?
- What are the common errors discussion?

5.10   Further activities

Browse the websites of a journal that you regularly read or are aware of. Direct yourself to the author guidelines and consider the advice given for writing discussions.

Use the critical appraisal tools to evaluate or critique journal article discussions as you undertake your background reading. You should also try critiquing your own discussion.

6 Planning, referencing and general writing tips

In this chapter you will:

- be aware of Gantt charts and their potential components

  (Section 6.1)

- be aware of the purpose of referencing

  (Section 6.2)

- be aware of different types of referencing

  (Section 6.2)

- be aware of the basics of plagiarism

  (Section 6.3)

- appreciate some general writing tips

  (Section 6.4)

- identify common writing and referencing errors

  (Section 6.5)

- learn how to format a thesis

  (Section 6.6)

6.1 Gantt charts and project planning

The Gantt chart – as developed by Henry Gantt (e.g. Gantt, 1903) – is synonymous with project management. When submitting your final-year project proposal, or indeed any research grant application, you will usually be asked to provide some form of project plan, often referred to as a Gantt chart. Such charts are essentially an indication of the duration of the project, the various components that need to be undertaken to achieve it and both when and how these will be done. It is important to note that, with the exception of start and end dates, for most components of the project the dates you enter into

DOI: 10.4324/9781003112426-7

the chart are not set in stone. Indeed, when presenting your Gantt chart some contingency should be considered. Depending on how you work, sticking rigidly to a plan may cause additional stress – especially if it does not go as hoped. Therefore, having a backup plan is essential and can be built into the chart. An example chart incorporating some of the considerations noted in the following sections is shown in Figure 6.1.

6.1.1   Project component timings

In the first instance, it is useful to simply consider the start and end points of the project. Your project will likely begin with submission of your project proposal or the start of the term, for example, and end with submission of the final dissertation. Next, you will need to consider any finite deadlines that your course may have – such as a given block of time for data collection, deadlines for ethics applications, when your participants are available or when you may be allowed access to them; particularly if working with external teams or groups. If there are no set times for data collection during your final year this offers more flexibility, but you will certainly need to determine these deadlines for yourself rather than leave this to the last minute when there may be a rush for equipment and lab time. There are also other key aspects you must consider, such as ethics. You cannot collect data until you have the appropriate ethics approval from your institution and any other required research partners. You will no doubt have taught sessions regarding your institutions' ethics application procedures and should ensure that you are on top of these. Also consider the time it takes for the reviewers to consider your ethics application. Similar to the return of your coursework grades, there is probably a set time period for ethics reviewers to respond. Please do be aware that there could be multiple iterations of the review process to ensure everything is clear and in accordance with your course and institution requirements. Don't underestimate the time it may take to get all the documents together. One of the benefits of getting your ethics application submitted early is that this is essentially your methods section and thus a chapter of your dissertation drafted.

6.1.2   Reflections and supervisor meetings

Once your project has ethical approval you are free to start data collection and get your participants booked in for testing sessions. Consider all the aspects noted in the methods section of this book, such as pilot work, preliminary testing and familiarisation (NB: if you change any part of your methods you will likely need additional ethics approval for this, so check with your supervisor or ethics team). You may also have to provide a lab diary as part of your final submission. It is good practice to keep a reflective diary of your data collection experiences. There will likely be many more entries in the first few weeks as you become more confident with your testing

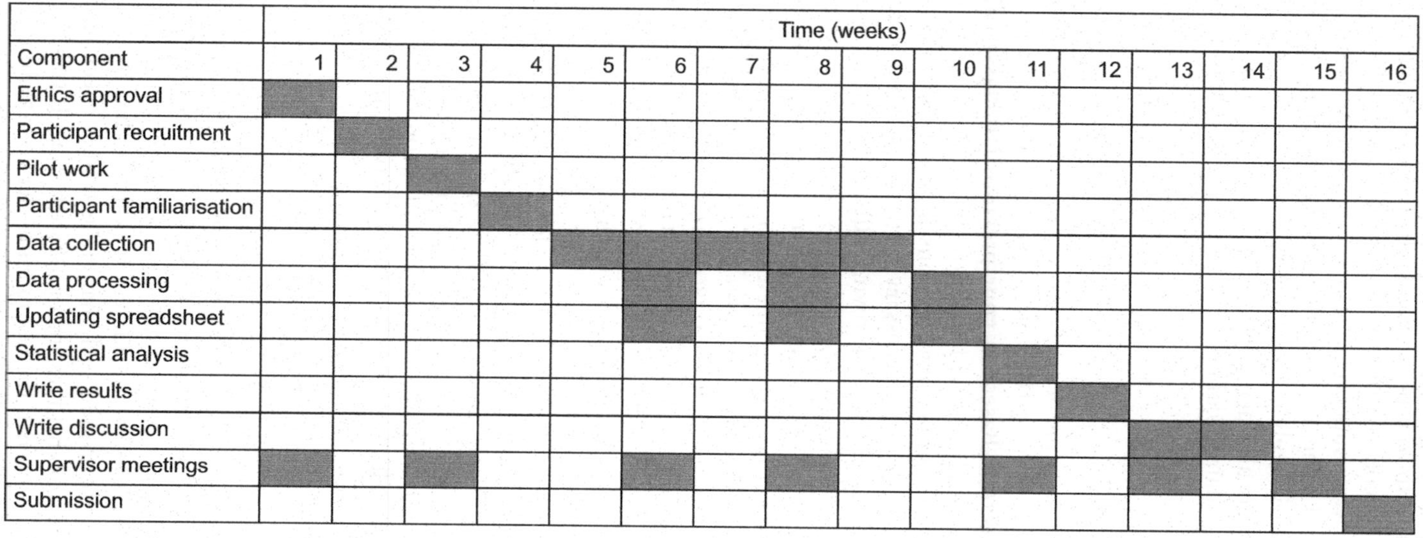

Component	1	2	3	4	5	6	7	8	9	10	11	12	13	14	15	16
Ethics approval	X															
Participant recruitment		X														
Pilot work			X													
Participant familiarisation				X												
Data collection					X			X	X							
Data processing						X	X	X								
Updating spreadsheet					X	X	X			X						
Statistical analysis											X					
Write results												X				
Write discussion													X	X		
Supervisor meetings	X					X		X			X		X		X	
Submission																X

Figure 6.1 Hypothetical Gantt chart considering typical final-year project components

Source: NB: Components are not exclusive, and timings will differ depending on your specific project and guidance provided by your project module leader or supervisor. Timeline begins from ethics approval and does not include vacation periods.

protocol, interacting with your participants, etc. than the latter sessions when your method will be second nature to you. You will no doubt find it helpful to give feedback to your supervisor how these initial sessions have gone, checking the expected values and potentially some much-needed moral support. Your supervisor is likely just as interested in your data as you are and meetings like these may also help to correct or prevent any errors you can't change once all your data is collected. Add regular supervisor meetings to your Gantt chart.

6.1.3   Lab time

One aspect of the project proposal Gantt charts which often receives considerable feedback is that of the amount of time required in the lab to complete data collection. Based on your previous lab classes throughout your course, you should have an idea of how long your various testing sessions will last. You also though need to consider the time it takes to set up your workstation, time for the necessary forms to be completed, the time to analyse your data (likely on your own, unlike many lab classes) and the time to clear away after each session or set up for the next participant. It is common to underestimate these and better to have spare time in between testing sessions rather than a long line of participants waiting at the lab door. As you become more proficient you can always amend your schedule. There is no 'one size fits all' here as some projects require longer periods of data collection (e.g. sprint protocols compared to prolonged exercise) and processing (e.g. EMG, biomechanical/motion analysis, interview analysis, etc.) when compared to others. This time should therefore be considered realistically.

Although it may seem obvious to consider any natural breaks in testing such as Christmas or exam periods, the last thing you want is to have completed three out of four sessions and then there to be a prolonged gap in testing which may affect your data. Depending upon the type of testing you have, you may find it helpful to complete one group of participants first rather than get them all booked in at once or have some form of rolling programme of bookings.

6.1.4   Equipment bookings

You should consider all the equipment you need for your study. Technical staff may request a full equipment list so it can be logged on the system for each booking. Any equipment that may be in constant demand and booked out regularly should also be considered. It is likely that the technical and teaching staff will liaise around such matters as well as checking the prompt return of equipment from field testing or offsite testing. If you have a participant cancel a session – even at the last minute – let your technical staff know as soon as possible, so someone else can use the equipment.

6.1.5   Be on top of your data

As you are collecting your data, it is good practice to add your results to your spreadsheet as they come in. You are then not faced with large amounts of data input in one go. Continually updating your spreadsheets means you can also see how your results are shaping up as they happen and which may help in understanding your data.

6.1.6   Postgraduate appraisals

In a centenary appreciation of the Gantt chart, Wilson (2003) noted how the original project management process considered 'two sets of balances of what each workman should do'. These essentially reflect the work that should have been done and the work that was actually done, highlighting any remedial actions required. Indeed, many postgraduate students, particularly PhD students, will have some form of annual appraisal. A Gantt chart is central to assessing progress as you can map where you currently are in your project with where you had intended to be. As noted earlier, some components may have delays whereas others may be started early, with the overall result being a project delivered on time.

6.2   Referencing

Throughout your studies you will be taught how to reference the various sources of information that you use in writing your assignments. You will also no doubt have been informed about plagiarism and how referencing all your sources should avoid this problem. Indeed, both referencing and plagiarism are often directly related. Amongst the range of textbooks available to students regarding academic writing many specialise in referencing or at least have chapters dedicated to these areas (for example, Deane, 2010; Neville, 2007). In addition, if you were to undertake a literature search for 'Plagiarism' you would find many scholarly articles across all research disciplines, such is its importance to academic and other forms of writing. Three potential problems have been associated with referencing, those being; the selection of references, the placement of reference citations and the accuracy of references (Foote, 2007). The selection of references was briefly considered in the introduction and discussion chapters. This chapter will provide the basics for referencing and why it is important.

6.2.1   Why reference?

Although the lab report or project you are writing is your own work you will have certainly used various sources to help you develop your research question and explain your findings. Subsequently, you will have used other people's work to get to your final conclusions. The information you have used is the evidence on which you have based your reasoning and discussion. One of the key rules of academic writing is to recognise this evidence and attribute it accordingly to those who provided it in the first instance (Creme and Lea, 2006). Therefore, the main aim of referencing is to show the reader where you have borrowed material from (Deane, 2010). However, there is a lot more to referencing than simply avoiding plagiarism (Neville, 2007). Foote (2007) notes that proper referencing brings authority, credibility and precision to scientific manuscripts. Furthermore, Neville (2007) notes nine points as to why you should reference including; tracing the origin of ideas, building a web of ideas, finding your own voice, demonstrating the validity of arguments, spreading knowledge, showing an appreciation of previous work, indicating the influences within your work, avoiding plagiarism as well as referencing being an essential part of marking criteria. This is why it is important to reference all your sources. There are a number of different referencing systems, and you should always follow the guidelines set by your university.

6.2.2 Different types of referencing

The golden rule of reference is to provide enough information for the reader to be able to quickly find the source you have cited (Neville, 2007). The two main referencing systems for doing this within academic writing are the Harvard and Vancouver systems. Both need to have an in-text citation every time the source is used with a corresponding list of references at the end of the work (Deane, 2010). The most common system in sport and exercise science is probably that of the Harvard system. The American Psychological Association (APA) has a useful online tutorial and explanation of referencing, formatting and writing scientific manuscripts for publication (www.apastyle.org). Many journals cite these guidelines as the favoured referencing system. The Harvard system involves 'author–date' referencing. Here the names of the authors for each source and the date of publication (or date of access in the case of web sites) are reported within the text. The full details of each source are then provided at the end of the report, usually in alphabetical order. For the Vancouver system, each source is referred to by a number in the text, corresponding to the numbered reference list at the end of the report. In this instance, the list is usually in the order in which sources were cited. However, there are variants of the both systems in term of specifics which can cause confusion amongst students (Deane, 2010). As noted earlier, you should always follow the guidelines set down by your university.

If you refer back to the introduction chapter (Chapter 2) you will have completed Exercise 2.3 ('Extracting and using information'). This exercise involved combining the information you considered important from four abstracts into a sentence or paragraph. When the information was integrated you will have seen that the 'author–date' system was used in different ways. The examples used in Exercise 2.3 involved primary referencing where you have read the original source yourself. If you have not read the original source yourself and quote it from someone else's work then you are using secondary referencing. There is nothing wrong with secondary referencing itself except you are trusting the interpretation of the original data by the authors to be correct, which on the whole it is likely to be. However, if you constantly use secondary referencing your tutors will know that you have not undertaken a particularly detailed literature search yourself and are relying on other people's opinions. There are different ways to cite secondary references in the text and in the reference list and you should consult your specific guidelines. However, always try to read the original document.

6.2.3 *Different ways to reference*

If you understand the key aspects of referencing and how to integrate them into your report you should be on the way to successful referencing and writing. You will find that within the author guidelines for every journal there will be examples of how to cite the authors and date effectively. The following examples will provide the most likely referencing methods you will require. Three common examples involving in-text citation of primary referencing of authors and dates are given here:

Price and Campbell (1997) observed that a cadence of 70 rev·min^{-1} elicited greater peak oxygen uptake than 60 rev·min^{-1} during incremental arm crank ergometry.

It was observed that a cadence of 70 rev·min^{-1} elicited greater peak oxygen uptake than 60 rev·min^{-1} during incremental arm crank ergometry (Price and Campbell, 1997).

Studies examining incremental arm crank ergometry protocols have examined crank rate (Price and Campbell, 1997) and ramp rate (Smith et al., 2004).

For secondary references you would normally state 'cited in' within the in-text citation. For example:

Price and Campbell (1997; cited in Smith and Price, 2007) observed that a cadence of 70 rev·min^{-1} elicited greater peak oxygen uptake than 60 rev·min^{-1} during incremental arm crank ergometry.

The reference for Smith and Price would be the one contained in the reference list.

If you want to use multiple studies for a given fact, it is perfectly acceptable (two or three will usually suffice). You will need to check your university guidelines as to whether they should appear in alphabetical or chronological order. In addition, there are different rules relating to how many authors are cited. In general, one author involves citing the sole author and date. If there are two authors, you would state both authors and the date. If there were three or more you generally cite the first author followed by 'et al.' (meaning 'and others'). However, there are differences between journals and guidelines as to whether you cite all authors in the first instance and then (where there are three or more authors) the first author and et al. with every subsequent use.

When citing textbooks, you also cite the author and date as for journal articles. When citing textbooks, or specifically chapters in textbooks where the chapter authors are different from the main author or editor of the book, you generally follow the same guidelines as for journal articles. However, in this instance the format of the reference list becomes more involved. The specific chapter is usually referred to first followed by the details of the main book it is contained within. An example is given here. Again, consult your own guidelines for referencing specifics.

Smith PM, Price MJ (2007). Upper-body exercise. In EM Winter, AM Jones, RCR Davidson, PD Bromley, TH Mercer (Eds.), *Sport and Exercise Physiology Testing Guidelines* (138–44). Abingdon: Routledge.

Exercise 6.1   Getting to grips with referencing

Consult your referencing guidelines or those of a recommended journal. For each type of referencing format, using your references, write an example of the in-text citation and how it would appear in the reference list.

Reference/sentence 1

. . . .

. . . .

. . . .

. . . .

. . . .

. . . .

Format of reference 1 in reference list

. . . .

. . . .

. . . .

. . . .

. . . .

. . . .

Reference/sentence 2

. . . .
. . . .
. . . .
. . . .
. . . .
. . . .
. . . .

Format of reference 2 in reference list

. . . .
. . . .
. . . .
. . . .
. . . .
. . . .

Reference/sentence 3

. . . .
. . . .
. . . .
. . . .
. . . .
. . . .

Format of reference 3 in reference list

. . . .
. . . .
. . . .
. . . .
. . . .
. . . .

6.3 Plagiarism

As noted earlier, you have to reference all of your sources so that any ideas or statements which are not your own can be attributed to the original authors. If you do not do this you are considered to be passing off other people's ideas as your own, an act which constitutes plagiarism. Incidences of plagiarism have increased in number considerably in recent years not only due to the internet enabling large amounts of work to be cut and pasted from a whole host of sites but also because of the ready availability of computer packages that can detect plagiarism. Plagiarism is not just a problem for the electronic age and can certainly occur when electronic data bases and sources are not used (see McNamee et al., 2007). Plagiarism also includes collusion between students, falsification of data and a range of exam cheating offences (Neville, 2007). These days all universities and colleges will have some form of plagiarism policy or statement and you should read yours carefully. Many universities also have informative referencing and plagiarism tutorials. The aim of this section is to provide you with some guidance to avoid plagiarism based on my experiences of first-year to final-year assignments being processed through plagiarism panels. Three key examples which are easily avoidable are given here.

6.3.1 'Chunking'

Many allegations of plagiarism, certainly at first-year level, may be down to poor referencing or what is termed 'poor scholarship'. However, as you progress through your studies this is no excuse as you are expected to know the specific and appropriate methods for referencing. 'Chunking' refers to large amounts of text being taken from a single source and not written in your own words (i.e. not paraphrased). There may be a cursory reference at the end of the section, but this is not enough. You need to write any information you require in your own words. Similarly, if you place a reference after each sentence it will be clear that you have simply cut and pasted a large chunk from one text. If you are able to use your university's plagiarism software prior to submitting your work, such an error should be highlighted in the output. Refer to Exercise 2.3 'Extracting and using information' in Chapter 2 regarding obtaining key information from your sources.

6.3.2 Patch-working

Patch-working refers to where a section of text has been cut and pasted and a number of words from the original text have been replaced by alternative words with the same meaning. Such an error should be evident from any software output. The fact that the section has not been rewritten should be very clear.

6.3.3 Poor note taking

Many students who have had allegations of plagiarism against them are genuine mistakes and maybe considered as poor scholarship. A common mistake relates to note-taking skills. This is especially true for students who write notes from a given source when researching their project and then days or weeks or even a few hours later use the information in their own written work. The problem arises when the notes taken by the students were not written in their own words as effectively as they may have been (i.e. they are not paraphrased). Consequently, when integrated into the text of their report it is detected by the plagiarism software as identical or exceptionally close to the original. When writing notes from books or journal articles, make sure you know what has been written verbatim and what was definitely written in your own words.

6.4 General writing tips

This section is by no means set out to teach students how to write grammatically correct English or even how to write scientifically. There are many excellent texts which already exist relating to those topics. This section is primarily designed to make you aware of what you are writing and how to describe the results of laboratory-based experiments. It is hoped that after reading the examples you will be able to reflect upon your writing so you can improve your writing. We are always learning how to write and, although it gets a lot easier with experience, there are always aspects to improve upon. You should also consider the intended audience as the language you use will differ. Are you writing a report to an athlete, a report to a funding body or a scientific journal article? This section will focus upon the conventional scientific report format. However, all types of report require clear concise writing.

There are a considerable number of articles and editorials in scientific journals addressing aspects of journal article production (Greenhalgh, 1997) and key aspects of science such as ethics (Winter and Maughan, 2009; Maughan et al., 2007), peer review (Baltzopoulos, 2004) and scientific writing (Winter, 2005; Bartlett, 2001). With respect to editors' comments on the clarity of manuscripts submitted for publication many authors have their own particular nemeses. However, most editors note that many articles rejected following peer review are often just badly written (Greenhalgh, 1997) and may lack the clarity and precision expected (Baltzopoulos, 2004). Furthermore, the many aspects of journal reviewing considered by reviewers and editors should not be confined to writing journal articles alone but also to scientific writing in general (Baltzopoulos, 2004). Most journals recommend that manuscripts should be proofread carefully, so why not laboratory reports and theses? Your reports and theses will indeed be read by other people, especially by your assessors. In the case of MSc and PhD theses, these will be read by the examiners and possibly by other postgraduate students and as such reflects you as the author. It is therefore important to make the thesis the best read possible. The aim of this section is to summarise a range of comments from editorials in sport and exercise science journals to emphasise recurrent errors in scientific writing, many of which can be easily avoided. These should be considered in conjunction with classic scientific writing texts such as Day (1998) and Turk and Kirkman (1989), which are often recommended for undergraduate and postgraduate students.

6.4.1   Abbreviations

You will find that many journal articles will abbreviate certain terms to aid the flow of reading. This is particularly evident for labels referring to experimental and control trials. The latter is normally abbreviated to CON and the former to some kind of acronym or shorthand. However, after this only standard abbreviations should be used and importantly, written in full prior to their use. This is a common error for undergraduate students. For example, many students may write that '$\dot{V}O_{2max}$ was measured'. If you have not defined this term, the reader may not know what $\dot{V}O_{2max}$ refers to, even though you may consider it standard terminology amongst your peers or all professionals working in your area. Not everyone reading journal articles in your area will be a student of your discipline. The example is better written as 'Maximal oxygen uptake ($\dot{V}O_{2max}$) was measured', not '$\dot{V}O_{2max}$ (maximal oxygen uptake) was measured'.

Bartlett (2001) notes that abbreviations are essential for mathematical equations but not always within the text of scientific manuscripts. Bartlett further states that abbreviations may be a 'word saving device' but can ultimately decrease the readability of the work. Consider the following sentence for a hypothetical study of pre-performance anxiety.

> Pre-performance anxiety (PPA) was measured in elite tennis players (ETP) and club level players (CLP) during a high anxiety (HA) condition and a control condition (CON). Heart rate (HR) was also measured to determine the severity of somatic anxiety (SOM).

If all terms had been abbreviated and used throughout the manuscript the sentence may read as follows:

> PPA was measure in ETP and CLP during a HA trial and CON. HR was also measured to determine the severity of SOM.

Although the word count is considerably reduced the reader has to remember a large number of definitions, which are not standard or regularly used. This is one reason why non-standard abbreviations are avoided. If you are using abbreviations, avoid starting sentences with the abbreviated form and avoid back-to-back abbreviations.

6.4.2   Readability

An important attribute of any piece of written work is its readability (Bartlett, 2001). Indeed, the readability of any manuscript has been considered as critical for communication and understanding (Winter, 2005). Within word processing documents you are able to assess the readability of your work. For example, Microsoft Word allows you to assess the readability of your work using the Flesch reading ease test and the Flesch–Kincaid grade level test. Both tests assess the readability of your work based on the length of sentences and the number of syllables per sentence. The former test provides a score out of 100 whereas the latter provides a grading based on the American school system of grades. The example provided by the Word help menu states that if you have a grade score of 8.0 a student in the eighth grade should be able to read it successfully. Try activating the analysis as directed by the help menu to determine your own readability scores. It may be quite enlightening.

6.4.3   Grammar and paragraph structure

In a large number of reports, and not just first-year students, there is often a lack of proper sentence construction and paragraph structure. Each sentence should ideally provide one main fact or idea. Sentences should be concise, not overly long and punctuated appropriately. If you have a sentence that is more than two or three lines long, it is probably too long. Sentences are then linked together to form paragraphs. I am often amazed at the number of reports where sentences are presented separately, appearing on a new line rather than in paragraph form. Paragraphs should link sentences together to provide one key and coherent idea for the reader. Throughout this book it has been suggested that you read each paragraph of your work and use one word to see what the content reflects. Also, try reading the first and last lines of each paragraph to see whether the main idea is clearly introduced and concluded.

6.4.4   Writing style and word use

Every author will develop their own writing style with time and experience, and it is not the purpose of texts such as this one to enforce a standardised writing style upon students. There are however a number of factors emphasised by journal editors which should be considered by those writing regularly. When you consider the following comments and put them into practice, your understanding of phrasing and wording will be much improved and the clarity of your writing style most likely enhanced.

Bartlett (2001) considered the excessive use of the 'passive voice' in writing and how it may hinder readability. Three specific examples were provided; using more words than is necessary; using meaningless or filler words, and the correct use of words. When considering the use of more words than necessary students are often concerned with word counts, so any word saving approach should be well received. The examples provided included stating 'the majority of' when compared to stating more simply 'most' and stating 'due to the fact that' instead to stating 'because'. Examples such as these may help to reduce the sometimes 'flowery' nature of some writing in an attempt to impress the tutor or make the writing appear more important. Using extra words can overcomplicate what you are saying, essentially you just need to get to the point.

Examples for the use of meaningless and filler words included stating 'game situation' versus 'game' or stating 'measures of anxiety levels' versus 'measure of anxiety'. In relation to this latter example and the correct use of words, Bartlett (2001) notes that the correct use of the word 'level' is in 'level playing field', 'sea level' and 'liquid level'. Therefore, when describing the performance ability of participants 'national level' should be replaced by 'national standard'. Similarly, 'force levels' should be referred to as the 'magnitude of force'. An example from my experience relates to 'lactate levels' where 'blood lactate concentration' should be correctly used instead. In a similar way to the comments noted earlier is the use of 'higher'. If a participant's heart rate is increased it should be described using 'greater' rather than 'higher', as higher pertains to height. This can also be applied to blood lactate concentration and other sport and exercise-related variables that may change with exercise.

Four further examples of common writing errors termed as 'brow furrowing writing' are provided by Winter (2005). The first example given was vernacular, such as stating 'This study looked at' rather than studies 'investigating' or 'examining'. The second example was tautological, such as stating 'There are many different types'. Winter notes that if there are many types then they must be different so the word different is not required. Third, the example of superfluousness which relates to Bartletts' earlier comment of extra words being used such as 'in order'. If these words are omitted it makes no difference to the sentence so they can be removed. Finally, the use of the phrase 'Participants were familiarised with procedures' was considered. Winter suggests it is better to phrase participants being familiarised as being 'habituated', 'accustomed' or 'well-practised'.

6.4.5 *Punctuation*

Most word processing software packages have both spelling and grammar checkers that can monitor your punctuation and sentence structure, usually providing indications of errors as you write. Even if you do not understand the grammatical terminology used to explain the errors, grammar checkers generally provide alternative ways of constructing your sentences which may help develop your writing. However, you should always try and develop your own writing style. A simple and common mistake is the misuse and overuse of commas. Commas can be used in a number of ways, such as for lists and to add extra information or context within a sentence. For example, consider the following sentence.

> The exercise protocol, which was undertaken by ten male participants, involved incremental exercise to exhaustion.

If the text between the commas is removed the general message of the sentence should not be affected. In other words,

> The exercise protocol involved incremental exercise to exhaustion.

Commas are often overused and can hinder the readability of your sentences. If you are using a large number of commas and your sentences are long consider splitting the sentence up into separate, more concise ones.

6.5   Common errors

There is a range of writing errors commonly noted by tutors when assessing work. Many can be avoided by careful proofreading. The following are some examples to watch out for.

6.5.1   Incorrect word use

Although we have considered using the correct words in describing how variables may differ between treatments (e.g. 'higher' versus 'greater'), there is a much simpler error and one that is not detected by spell checkers. In this instance, the word is spelt correctly but is just the wrong word. Common examples are shown in Table 6.1. My particular favourites over the years have been the 'lactate shuffle' and 'hydrogen iron'.

Table 6.1 Common wording errors

Affect/effect
There/their/they're
Ion/iron
Sources/sauces
To/too/two
Previous/pervious
Baseline/bassline
One repetition max/one reputation max
Food diaries/food dairies

6.5.2 In-text citation errors

We have briefly considered the citation of previous studies within your work using the author– date system. A key error is stating the author's initials, journal title or any other information in the text that should only be contained within the reference list. This shows your assessor that you have not grasped the format of referencing within the text. Only the name and date are required in the text.

6.5.3 Omission of cited references

If you cite a source of information it must be contained within the reference list (exceptions to this rule are 'personal communications' or articles 'in press', although these forms of referencing are unlikely to affect you during your undergraduate studies). A common error is to cite a study and not provide the details within the reference list or, conversely, listing a reference that has not been cited in the text. All the sources in the reference list must be used in the text and vice versa. A list of all the sources you have used in preparation for the report (i.e. background reading etc. and those sources not necessarily used for writing the report) is termed a 'bibliography'. However, we do not use bibliographies for academic writing.

6.5.4 Not reading original sources

Wherever possible, it is recommended that you obtain and read the original journal article or source of information. It is unlikely that many students will obtain original articles with publication dates prior to 1970, as this is the date where some search engines may not have abstracts available or online access. However, reading much older articles is very useful for becoming aware of how research has developed over time. If you cite much older articles your tutors will most likely, and often correctly, presume that you have not read the original article, even though you may have correctly listed the source in your reference list. A similar problem occurs if you do use an older research article or review article and take a lot of secondary references from it without acknowledging them properly. Here, you will have a lot of older references in your work and the field of research may have moved on considerably in the last thirty or forty years. This demonstrates to your assessors that you have not fully reviewed the literature and are over reliant on a potentially outdated source. Some students, however, may very much enjoy scouring original articles from the early twentieth century – and I do recommend it!

6.5.5 Use of quotes

To avoid disjointed writing and the potential for plagiarism to occur you should avoid using quotes. As you will have seen from your background reading it is very unusual for direct quotes to be used within sport and exercise science. The best method is to paraphrase the information you are interested and identify the key results in your own words.

6.5.6 Singular versus plural

A basic grammatical error concerns the use of singular or plural forms of words and descriptions. These are often highlighted on your word processing document as you write and should be taken note of. These errors are generally quite straight to correct when this occurs. For example, the plural of 'was' is 'were'; so stating 'Ground reaction forces and running time *was* measured' should be 'Ground reaction forces and running time *were* measured'. The second version is correct as there are two factors being considered, not one, so it is plural.

6.6 Formatting a thesis

When you are putting your lab report together, you will normally only need the headings of abstract, introduction, methods, results and discussion. However, for a thesis you will likely have chapter and section numbers to organise. There will no doubt be specific university guidelines for the format and structure of your undergraduate and postgraduate theses, but if not, the following may help when organising your headings. The organisation itself is relatively straightforward. The difficultly may arise in ensuring that the content of your section relates to the specific subheadings used. In general, the following example is typical (Figure 6.2) and there are not usually more

1.0 Main chapter title (e.g Introduction / literature review etc)

    1.1 Subheading level 1 (e.g. Anxiety and performance)

        1.1.1 Subheading level 2 (e.g. Anxiety and team sports)

            1.1.1.i subheading level 3 (e.g. Netball)

            1.1.1.iiSubheading level 3 (e.g. Hockey)

        1.1.2 Subheading level 2 (e.g. Anxiety and individual sports)

            1.1.2.i Subheading level 3 (e.g. Tennis)

            1.1.2.i Subheading level 3 (e.g. Athletics)

    1.2 Measurement of anxiety

        1.2.1 Physiological measures

        1.2.2 Questionnaire methods

        Etc.

Figure 6.2 Organisation of chapter subheadings

division of subsections after the third level (the use of i, ii, iii, iv etc). Remember, you do not have to separate each section with a different heading if it is not required. As a further example, this book has been organised using typical chapter and section numbering throughout.

6.7   Appendices

Within your project you may want to present some detailed information which may distract from the key point of the section and affect the flow of writing. Here you may find presenting information in appendices is more appropriate. Appendices are usually used for more methodological aspects such as presenting perceptual scales or full versions of questionnaires that have been used. The reader can then refer to the appendix if they are unfamiliar with the item or if they require further more specific information. Long descriptions of biochemical methods or calibration procedures can also be presented here in the absence of a general methods section.

6.8   A final note

Always proofread your work before you submit it as this will overcome a number of errors. Take time to do this rather than rushing it as you may miss more subtle, but important, errors. You may be able to see your tutors regarding coursework on a number of occasions prior to submission of your work. If you take advantage of this chance make sure you turn up prepared with ideas and ideally a draft of your work. Also, do this early as there will likely be a long queue of fellow students outside your tutor's door the week before the submission date.

Once you have received the mark for your work always read the feedback that is provided by your tutors. These days most coursework feedback from your tutors is likely given in a word-processed form, however, this may not always be possible. So, if you cannot read their handwriting, go and see them for clarification or further feedback. Also read any generic feedback documents that are provided. This will help you reflect upon your work and should help you improve for the next assignment. Finally, make sure you have a backup of your work in case of loss of files or damage to your data storage device.

6.9   Chapter summary and reflections

In this chapter we have considered why referencing is important and how to reference your information sources. We have also considered plagiarism and a range of techniques to avoid it. The second section of this chapter covered some general writing tips noted by journal editors and how these may affect the flow of your writing. Finally, we considered the organisation of your thesis with respect to numbering chapters and headings. To assess your understanding of this chapter, answer the following questions:

* What is a Gantt chart?
* Why is referencing important?
* What types of referencing systems are there?
* What is plagiarism?
* What are the common referencing and writing errors?

6.10   Further activities

Browse the websites of a journal that you regularly read or aware of. Direct yourself to the author guidelines and consider the advice given for referencing. Also refer to the journal articles that you read to see how the types of referencing and use of citations may differ.

Activate the readability function within the spell checker and grammar checkers of your word processing software and assess the first and final drafts of your work.

Appendices

Appendices

Appendix 1a

Example data and experimental details for typical sport and exercise science labs and projects

Lab report 1. Maximal oxygen uptake

Study: $\dot{V}O_{2max}$ assessed in a group of fit healthy sport science students for treadmill running, cycling and arm ergometry

Participants: N = 10 healthy, recreationally active but none specifically trained university students

Age (years)	19.3 (2.6)
Height (m)	1.79 (0.08)
Body mass (kg)	71.2 (7.1)

Protocols

Table A.1 Exercise protocols undertaken to determine maximal oxygen uptake ($\dot{V}O_{2max}$) for treadmill running, cycle ergometry and arm cranking

	Treadmill	Cycle ergometry	Arm cranking
Initial intensity	8 km·h⁻¹	70 W	50 W
Cadence	–	70 rev·min⁻¹	70 rev·min⁻¹
Exercise stage duration	3 min	3 min	2 min
Exercise intensity increment	2 km·h⁻¹	35 W	20 W

Oxygen consumption determined from Douglas bag technique in the final minute of exercise.

Heart rate continually monitored using a heart rate monitor.

Exercise testing performed at the same time of day. At least 5 days between tests.

Data

Data provided for maximal/peak oxygen uptake ($\dot{V}O_{2max}/\dot{V}O_{2peak}$; ml·k^{-1}g·min^{-1}) and maximal/peak heart rate (HR$_{max}$/HR$_{peak}$; beats·min^{-1})

	Treadmill	$\dot{V}O_{2max}/\dot{V}O_{2peak}$		HR$_{max}$/HR$_{peak}$		
		Cycling	Arm crank	Treadmill	Cycling	Arm crank
1	61.0	55.4	43.8	191	187	181
2	59.6	53.7	41.9	187	181	175
3	45.3	40.7	31.6	193	185	181
4	51.5	49.1	29.5	196	190	183
5	56.8	53.1	45.6	201	195	187
6	63.1	57.7	36.1	198	191	171
7	66.3	60.5	49.7	189	179	169
8	58.9	53.6	37.4	195	181	178
9	59.6	52.4	36.1	187	183	180
10	62.9	57.2	35.3	199	191	189
Mean	58.5	53.3	38.7	194	186	179
SD	6.1	5.5	6.4	5	5	6

Results

Maximal/peak oxygen consumption

Analysed by one-way ANOVA
Significant difference (P<0.05) between exercise modes
Treadmill and cycle ergometry $\dot{V}O_{2max}$ were greater than for arm cranking
Treadmill was greater than cycle ergometry

Maximal/peak heart rate

Analysed by one-way ANOVA
Significant difference (P<0.05) between exercise modes
Treadmill and cycle ergometry $\dot{V}O_{2max}$ were greater than for arm cranking
Treadmill was greater than cycle ergometry

Appendix 1b

Study: The effects of low and high anxiety levels on basketball shooting performance in a group of novice and experienced university basketball players.

Participants: $N=10$ in each group, novice players had been competing for less than two years, expert players had been competing for more than five years.

	Novice	Expert
Age (years)	18.9 (1.9)	19.1 (2.3)
Height(m)	1.87 (0.15)	1.81 (0.13)
Body mass (kg)	81.2 (6.1)	83.6 (5.4)
Experience (years)	1.7 (0.6)	8.3 (0.8)

Protocols

Participants took 15 basketball shots under both low and high anxiety conditions. The low anxiety condition was undertaken on a basketball court with only the experimenter present. The high anxiety condition was undertaken on the same basketball court with the full basketball squad present ($n=30$ players) producing a noisy atmosphere similar to competition. The number of baskets scored was the performance measure.

Heart rate was measured using a heart rate monitor to give an indication of the level of anxiety.

Data

Data provided for average heart during each trial (HR; beats·min^{-1}) and baskets scored (n/15 shots).

		Heart rate		Baskets scored	
		Low anxiety	*High anxiety*	*Low anxiety*	*High anxiety*
Novice	1	123	141	10	5
	2	128	135	11	7
	3	111	128	12	8
	4	118	131	13	7
	5	120	137	9	7
	6	118	143	11	8
	7	109	134	12	7
	8	127	142	7	6
	9	116	131	8	3
	10	109	126	9	7
Mean		118	135	10	7
SD		7	6	2	2
Expert	1	118	125	14	13
	2	116	131	13	13
	3	115	120	12	10
	4	120	129	11	11
	5	115	120	13	12
	6	107	119	12	10
	7	101	123	13	12
	8	119	124	13	11
	9	108	117	11	11
	10	101	121	10	9
Mean		112	123	12	11
SD		7	4	1	1

Results

Mean heart rate

Analysed by two-way ANOVA
Significant main effects ($P<0.05$) for conditions (anxiety level) and experiences novice versus expert).

Baskets scored

Analysed by two-way ANOVA.
Significant interaction ($P<0.05$) between conditions.

Post hoc analysis indicated that performance was poorer for the novice players in the high anxiety condition ($P<0.05$) when compared to low anxiety conditions.

Performance was lower in both low and high anxiety conditions in the novice players when compared to the expert players.

Appendix 2a

Amended Downs and Black (1998) checklist for measuring study quality

For each scoring, Yes = 1, No = 0

1 Is the hypothesis/aim/objective of the study clearly described?
2 Are the main outcomes to be measured clearly described in the Introduction or Methods section?
3 Are the characteristics of the patients included in the study clearly described?
4 Are the interventions of interest clearly described?
5 Are the distributions of principal confounders in each group of subjects to be compared clearly described?
6 Are the main findings of the study clearly described?
7 Does the study provide estimates of the random variability in the data for the main outcomes?
8 Have all important adverse events that may be a consequence of the intervention been reported?
9 Have the characteristics of patients lost to follow-up been described?
10 Have actual probability values been reported (e.g. 0.035 rather than <0.05) for the main outcomes except where the probability value is less than 0.001?

External validity

11 Were the subjects asked to participate in the study representative of the entire population from which they were recruited?
12 Were those subjects who were prepared to participate representative of the entire population from which they were recruited?
13 Were the staff, places and facilities where the patients were treated, representative of the treatment the majority of patients receive?

Internal validity – bias

14 Was an attempt made to blind study subjects to the intervention they have received?
15 Was an attempt made to blind those measuring the main outcomes of the intervention?
16 If any of the results of the study were based on 'data dredging', was this made clear?
17 In trials and cohort studies, do the analyses adjust for different lengths of follow-up of patients, or in case-control studies, is the time period between the intervention and outcome the same for cases and control?
18 Were the statistical tests used to assess the main outcomes appropriate?
19 Was compliance with the intervention/s reliable?
20 Were the main outcome measures used accurate (valid and reliable)?

Internal validity – confounding (selection bias)

21 Were the patients in different intervention groups (trials and cohort studies) or were the cases and controls (case-control studies) recruited from the same population?
22 Were study subjects in different intervention groups (trials and cohort studies) or were the cases and controls (case-control studies) recruited over the same period of time?
23 Were study subjects randomised to intervention groups?
24 Was the randomised intervention assignment concealed from both patients and healthcare staff until recruitment was complete and irrevocable?
25 Was there adequate adjustment for confounding the analyses from which the main findings were drawn?
26 Were losses of patients to follow-up taken into account?

Power

27 Did the study have sufficient power to detect a clinically important effect where the probability value for a difference being due to chance is less than 5%?

Appendix 2b

Kmet et al. (2015) checklist for assessing the quality of quantitative studies

	Yes (2)	Partial (1)	No (0)
1 Question/objective sufficiently described?			
2 Study design evident and appropriate?			
3 Method of subject/comparison group selection or source of information/input variables described and appropriate?			
4 Subject (and comparison group, if applicable) characteristics sufficiently described?			
5 If interventional and random allocation was possible, was it described?			
6 If interventional and blinding of investigators was possible, was it reported?			
7 If interventional and blinding of subjects was possible, was it reported?			
8 Outcome and (if applicable) exposure measure(s) well defined and robust to measurement/misclassification bias? Means of assessment reported?			
9 Sample size appropriate?			
10 Analytic methods described/justified and appropriate?			
11 Some estimate of variance is reported for the main results?			
12 Controlled for confounding?			
13 Results reported in sufficient detail?			
14 Conclusions supported by the results?			
Total			

Appendix 2c

Kmet et al. (2015) checklist for assessing the quality of qualitative studies

	Yes (2)	Partial (1)	No (0)
1 Question/objective sufficiently described?			
2 Study design evident and appropriate?			
3 Context for the study clear?			
4 Connection to a theoretical framework/ wider body of knowledge?			
5 Sampling strategy described, relevant and justified?			
6 Data collection methods clearly described and systematic?			
7 Data analysis clearly described and systematic?			
8 Use of verification procedure(s) to establish credibility?			
9 Conclusions supported by the results?			
10 Reflexivity of the account?			
Total			

Appendix 3

Procedure for formatting $\dot{V}$ in Microsoft Word

---

1 From the 'Insert' menu click on 'Object' (or hold down the 'ALT key and 'I' together and then the 'O' key on its own).
2 Scroll down the options and click on 'Microsoft equation 3.0'. Here an 'equation' tool bar will be shown. If you hover your mouse arrow over the bar options you will see the options: relational symbols, spaces and ellipses, embellishments, etc.
3 First, type in 'V' (or whatever letter is required) in the text box provided.
4 Then click on 'embellishments' and choose the embellishment required (i.e. a dot over the centre of the character [represented by the grey box], third line down). The line spacing will be disrupted a little, but this can be overcome by using the line spacing option in format paragraph options.

Appendix 4a

Typical figures for a range of experimental designs for Exercise 4.1 – answers

Data set	*Potential figure*
Relationship between personality score and performance anxiety	Scatter plot
Differences between centre of gravity at heel strike during running in elite and novice runners	Block graph
Difference in peak power during a Wingate anaerobic test in a group of cyclists before and after 8 weeks of sprint training	Block graph
Maximal oxygen uptake in a group of runners during two different exercise protocols	Block graph for means Scatter plot for relationship between them
Motivation to train in international male rowers, national-level female rowers and club-level rowers	Block graph
Blood pH at rest and during interval training	Time-based figure (line or scatter plot with straight lines between)
Core temperature at rest and during prolonged exercise on two occasions, one where participants could drink and one where they could not	Time-based figure (line or scatter plot with straight lines between)

Appendix 4d

Answer to Exercise 4.6. Normality outputs for each of the three typical lab classes

Lab class 1. $\dot{V}O_{2max}$

Tests of Normality

	Kolmogorov–Smirnov[a]			Shapiro–Wilk		
	Statistic	df	Sig.	Statistic	df	Sig.
TM	.226	10	.159	.903	10	.238
CE	.232	10	.137	.896	10	.197
ACE	.181	10	.200*	.962	10	.808

* This is a lower bound of the true significance.
[a] Lilliefors Significance Correction

Lab class 2. Anxiety

Tests of Normality

	Kolmogorov–Smirnov[a]			Shapiro–Wilk		
	Statistic	df	Sig.	Statistic	df	Sig.
NOV_LO	.142	10	.200*	.931	10	.454
NOV_HI	.152	10	.200*	.946	10	.622
EXP_LO	.262	10	.051	.872	10	.106
EXP_HI	.165	10	.200*	.940	10	.548

[a] Lilliefors Significance Correction
* This is a lower bound of the true significance.

Lab class 3. Ground reaction forces

Tests of Normality

	Kolmogorov–Smirnov[a]			Shapiro–Wilk		
	Statistic	df	Sig.	Statistic	df	Sig.
Walk	.131	8	.200*	.970	8	.899
Jog	.182	8	.200*	.911	8	.360
Run	.163	8	.200*	.948	8	.694

* This is a lower bound of the true significance.
[a] Lilliefors Significance Correction.

Appendix 4e

Answer to Exercise 4.8. Correlation matrices for key variables from each of the three typical lab classes

Lab class 1: correlation matrix for $\dot{V}O_{2max}$ for each mode of exercise (Excel above, SPSS below)

	TM	CE	ACE
TM	1		
CE	0.980182	1	
ACE	0.621234	0.622205	1

Correlations

		TM	CE	ACE
TM	Pearson correlation	1	.980**	.621
	Sig. (2-tailed)		.000	.055
	N	10	10	10
CE	Pearson correlation	.980**	1	.622
	Sig. (2-tailed)	.000		.055
	N	10	10	10
ACE	Pearson correlation	.621	.622	1
	Sig. (2-tailed)	.055	.055	
	N	10	10	10

** Correlation is significant at the 0.01 level (2-tailed).

Summary

	TM vs. CE	TM vs. ACE	CE vs. ACE
P =	P<0.05	0.055	0.055
r =	0.980	0.621	0.622
r^2 =	0.960	0.386	0.387

Lab class 2: correlation matric for heart rate between high and low conditions for novice and expert performers (Excel above, SPSS below)

Novice players Expert players

	Low anxiety	*High anxiety*			*Low anxiety*	*High anxiety*
Low anxiety	1			Low anxiety	1	
High anxiety	0.665766347	1		High anxiety	0.509118884	1

Correlations (Novice)

		NOV_LO	NOV_HI
NOV_LO	Pearson correlation	1	.666*
	Sig. (2-tailed)		.036
	N	10	10
NOV_HI	Pearson correlation	.666*	1
	Sig. (2-tailed)	.036	
	N	10	10

* Correlation is significant at the 0.05 level (2-tailed).

Correlations (Expert)

		EXP_LO	EXP_HI
EXP_LO	Pearson correlation	1	.509
	Sig. (2-tailed)		.133
	N	10	10
EXP_HI	Pearson correlation	.509	1
	Sig. (2-tailed)	.133	
	N	10	10

Summary

Novice	Expert
P = 0.036	P = 0.133
r = 0.666	r = 0.509
r^2 = 0.444	r^2 = 0.280

Lab class 3: correlation matrix for ground reaction forces between walking, jogging and running (Excel above, SPSS below)

	Walk	*Jog*	*Run*
Walk	1		
Jog	0.767004	1	
Run	−0.3269	−0.26184	1

Correlations

		Walk	*Jog*	*Run*
Walk	Pearson correlation	1	.777*	−.328
	Sig. (2-tailed)		.023	.428
	N	8	8	8
Jog	Pearson correlation	.777*	1	−.262
	Sig. (2-tailed)	.023		.531
	N	8	8	8
Run	Pearson correlation	−.328	−.262	1
	Sig. (2-tailed)	.428	.531	
	N	8	8	8

* Correlation is significant at the 0.05 level (2-tailed).

Summary

Walk vs. Jog	Walk vs. Run	Jog vs. Run
P = 0.023	0.428	0.531
r = 0.767	0.327	−0.262
r^2 = 0.588	0.107	0.067

Appendix 4f

Data for motivation to train in elite and non-elite athletes (hypothetical data).

	Elite	Non-elite
1	21	15
2	20	13
3	19	10
4	16	19
5	18	8
6	22	11
7	24	9
8	23	16
9	19	11
10	20	9

Lab class 3: ground reaction force during walking and running = paired t-test (i.e. same participants did both trials). SPSS output below (=P<0.05)

Paired samples test

Paired differences

		Mean	Std. deviation	Std. error mean	95% Confidence interval of the difference Lower	Upper	t	df	Sig. (2-tailed)
Pair 1	Walk–Run	-2.17750	.23669	.08368	-2.37538	-1.97962	-26.021	7	.000

Appendix 4h

Answer to Exercise 4.13. What statistical test?

1   $\dot{V}O_{2max}$ in arm crank ergometry, cycle ergometry and treadmill running
    = one-way ANOVA repeated measures (i.e. all participants undertake all trials)
2   Heart rate in high anxiety conditions in novice, intermediate and expert players
    = one-way ANOVA independent groups (i.e. different participants undertake each trial)
3   Ground reaction force during walking, jogging and running
    = one-way ANOVA repeated measures (i.e. all participants undertake all trials)

Appendix 4i

Answer to Exercise 4.18. What statistical test?

1   $\dot{V}O_{2max}$ in arm crank ergometry, cycle ergometry and treadmill running in males and females
    = two-way (factorial) ANOVA repeated measures on one factor (exercise mode) and independent on the other (i.e. sex)
2   Heart rate in novice, intermediate and expert players in high and low anxiety conditions
    = two-way (factorial) ANOVA repeated measures on one factor (anxiety condition) and independent on the other (i.e. playing standard)
3   Ground reaction force during walking, jogging and running when wearing shoes and barefoot (in the same participants)
    = two-way (factorial) ANOVA repeated measures on both factors (all participant undertake each speed and both conditions)

Appendix 5a

Statistical outputs for Excel

Lab report 1. Maximal oxygen uptake

Maximal/Peak oxygen consumption
ANOVA: single factor

SUMMARY

Groups	Count	Sum	Average	Variance
Treadmill	10	585	58.5	37.36889
Cycling	10	533.4	53.34	29.81156
Arm cranking	10	387	38.7	40.74222

ANOVA

Source of variation	SS	df	MS	F	P-value	F crit
Between groups	2109.984	2	1054.992	29.32633	1.7E-07	3.354131
Within groups	971.304	27	35.97422			
Total	3081.288	29				

Maximal/Peak heart rate
ANOVA: single factor

SUMMARY

Groups	Count	Sum	Average	Variance
Treadmill	10	1936	193.6	25.15556
Cycling	10	1863	186.3	28.45556
Arm cranking	10	1794	179.4	40.93333

ANOVA

Source of variation	SS	df	MS	F	P-value	F crit
Between groups	1008.467	2	504.2333	15.99988	2.61E-05	3.354131
Within groups	850.9	27	31.51481			
Total	1859.367	29				

References

Akoglu H (2018). User's guide to correlation coefficients. *Turkish Journal of Emergency Medicine*, 18(3): 91–3.

Alexandrov AV (2004). How to write a research paper. *Cerebrovascular Diseases*, 18: 135–8.

Alexandrov AV, Hennerici MG (2007). Writing good abstracts. *Cerebrovascular Diseases*, 23(4): 256–9.

Altinörs N (2002). The structure of a neurosurgical manuscript. *Acta Neurochirurgica. Supplement*, 83: 115–20.

Andreacci JL, LeMura LM, Cohen SL, Urbansky EA, Chelland SA, Von Duvillard SP (2002). The effects of frequency of encouragement on performance during maximal exercise testing. *Journal of Sports Science*, 20(4): 345–52.

Annesley TM (2010). Bring your best to the table. *Clinical Chemistry*, 56(10): 1528–34.

Artioli GG, Gualano B, Coelho DF, Benatti FB, Gailey AW, Lancha AH Jr (2007). Does sodium-bicarbonate ingestion improve simulated judo performance? *International Journal of Sport Nutrition and Exercise Metabolism*, 17(2): 206–17.

Astorino TA, Tam PA, Rietschel JC, Johnson SM, Freedman TP (2004). Changes in physical fitness parameters during a competitive field hockey season. *Journal of Strength and Conditioning Research*, 18(4): 850–4.

Atkinson G, Reilly T (1996). Circadian variation in sports performance. *Sports Medicine*, 21(4): 292–312.

Azevedo LF, Canário-Almeida F, Almeida Fonseca J, Costa-Pereira A, Winck JC, Hespanhol V (2011). How to write a scientific paper: Writing the methods section. *Revista Portuguesa de Pneumologia*, 17(5): 232–8.

Baltzopoulos V (2004). The reviewing process. *Journal of Sports Sciences*, 22(2): 147–8.

Bartlett R (2001). Writing for the *Journal of Sports Sciences*. *Journal of Sports Sciences*, 19(7): 467–8.

Baumgart JK, Berit B, Øyvind S (2020). Comparison of peak oxygen uptake between upper-body exercise modes: A systematic literature review and meta-analysis. *Frontiers in Physiology*, 11: 412. https://doi.org/10.3389/fphys.2020.00412

Beel J, Gipp J, Wilde E (2010). Academic Search Engine Optimization (ASEO). *Journal of Scholarly Publishing*, 41(2): 176–90.

Bem D (1995). Writing a review article for *Psychological Bulletin*. *Psychological Bulletin*, 118(2): 172–7.

Bhandari RS, Bansal A (2018). Impact of search engine optimization as a marketing tool. *Jindal Journal of Business Research*, 7(1): 23–36. https://doi.org/10.1177/2278682117754016

Bland JM, Altman DG (1986). Statistical methods for assessing agreement between two methods of clinical measurement. *Lancet*, 1(8476): 307–10.

Bland JM, Altman DG (1995). Comparing two methods of clinical measurement: A personal history. *International Journal of Epidemiology*, 24(Suppl 1): S7–14.

Bleakley C, MacAuley D (2002). The quality of research in sports journals. *British Journal of Sports Medicine*, 36(2): 124–5.

Borg GA (1973). Perceived exertion: A note on "history" and methods. *Medicine and Science in Sports*, 5: 90–3.

Bougault V, Lonsdorfer-Wolf E, Charloux A, Richard R, Geny B, Oswald-Mammosser M (2005). Does thoracic bioimpedance accurately determine cardiac output in COPD patients during maximal or intermittent exercise? *Chest*, 127(4): 1122–31.

Branson RD (2004). Anatomy of a research paper. *Respiratory Care*, 49(10): 1222–8.

Brink Y, Louw QA (2012). Clinical instruments: Reliability and validity critical appraisal. *Journal of Evaluation in Clinical Practice*, 18(6): 1126–32. https://doi.org/10.1111/j.1365-2753.2011.01707.x

British Medical Journal (1996). Declaration of Helsinki (1964). *BMJ*, 313: 1448.2. https://doi.org/10.1136/bmj.313.7070.1448a

Brozek J, Grande F, Anderson JT, Keys A (1963). Densitometric analysis of body composition: Revision of some quantitative assumptions. *Annals of the New York Academy of Sciences*, 110: 113–40.

Burrows M (2007). Circadian rhythms. In EM Winter, AM Jones, RCR Davidson, PD Bromley, TH Mercer (Eds.), *Sport and Exercise Physiology Testing Guidelines* (347–57). London: Routledge.

Burrows M, Bird S (2000). The physiology of the highly trained female endurance runner. *Sports Medicine*, 30(4): 281–300.

Campbell SC, Moffatt RJ, Kushnick MR (2011). Continuous and intermittent walking alters HDL(2)-C and LCATa. *Atherosclerosis*, 218(2): 524–9.

Charkoudian N, Joyner MJ (2004). Physiologic considerations for exercise performance in women. *Clinics in Chest Medicine*, 25(2): 247–55.

Christmass MA, Dawson B, Passeretto P, Arthur PG (1999). A comparison of skeletal muscle oxygenation and fuel use in sustained continuous and intermittent exercise. *European Journal of Applied Physiology and Occupational Physiology*, 80(5): 423–35.

Clarke M, Alderson P, Chalmers I (2002). Discussion sections in reports of controlled. Trials published in *General Medical Journals*. *JAMA*, 287: 2799–801.

Clarke M, Chalmers I (1998). Discussion sections in reports of controlled trials published in general medical journals islands in search of continents? *JAMA*, 280: 280–2.

Cohen J (1988). *Statistical Power Analysis for the Behavioral Sciences* (2nd ed.). Hillsdale, NJ: Lawrence Erlbaum.

Collins Shorter Thesaurus (1994) Harper Collins Publishers, UK.

Conover WJ, Guerrero-Serrano AJ, Tercero-Gómez VG (2018). An update on 'a comparative study of tests for homogeneity of variance'. *Journal of Statistical Computation and Simulation*, 88(8): 1454–69. https://doi.org/10.1080/00949655.2018.1438437

Conover WJ, Johnson ME, Johnson MM (1981). A comparative study of tests for homogeneity of variances, with applications to the outer continental shelf bidding data. *Technometrics*, 23(4): 351–61.

Constantini NW, Dubnov G, Lebrun CM (2005). The menstrual cycle and sport performance. *Clinic in Sports Medicine*, 24(2): e51–82, xiii–xiv.

Corbett J, Barwood MJ, Parkhouse K (2009). Effect of task familiarisation on distribution of energy during a 2000 m cycling time trial. *British Journal of Sports Medicine*, 43: 770–4.

Correll J, Mellinger C, McClelland GH, Judd CM (2020). Avoid Cohen's 'small', 'medium', and 'large' for power analysis. *Trends in Cognitive Sciences*, 24(3): 200–7.

Coughlan M, Cronin P, Ryan F (2007). Step-by-step guide to critiquing research. Part 1: Quantitative research. *British Journal of Nursing*, 16(11): 658–63.

Creme P, Lea MR (2006). *Writing at University: A Guide for Students* (2nd ed.). Maidenhead: Open University Press.

Crowe M, Sheppard L (2011). A review of critical appraisal tools show they lack rigor: Alternative tool structure is proposed. *Journal of Clinical Epidemiology*, 64(1): 79–89.

Crowe M, Sheppard L, Campbell A (2011). Comparison of the effects of using the Crowe Critical Appraisal Tool verses informal appraisal in assessing health research: A randomised trial. *International Journal of Evidence-Based Healthcare*, 9(4): 444–9.

Crowe M, Sheppard L, Campbell A (2012). Reliability analysis for a proposed critical appraisal tool demonstrated value for diverse research designs. *Journal of Clinical Epidemiology*, 65: 357–83.

Cushman M (2018). Search engine optimization: What is it and why should we care? *Research and Practice in Thrombosis and Haemostasis*, 2: 180–1. https://doi.org/10.1002/rth2.12098

Damavandi M, Dixon PC, Pearsall DJ (2012). Ground reaction force adaptations during cross-slope walking and running. *Human Movement Science*, 31(1): 182–9.

Day RA (1998). *How to Write & Publish a Scientific Paper*. Cambridge: Cambridge University Press/Phoenix, AZ: Oryx Press.

Deane M (2010). *Academic Research, Writing & Referencing: Inside Track*. Harlow: Pearson Education.

Domholdt E, Flaherty JL, Phiilips JM (1994). Critical appraisal of research literature by expert and inexperienced physical therapy researchers. *Physical Therapy*, 74(9): 853–60.

Downs SH, Black N (1998). The feasibility of creating a checklist for the assessment of the methodological quality both of randomised and non-randomised studies of health care interventions. *Journal of Epidemiology and Community Health*, 52: 377–84.

Drust B, Reilly T, Cable NT (2000). Physiological responses to laboratory-based soccer-specific intermittent and continuous exercise. *Journal of Sports Science*, 18(11): 885–92.

Durnin JV, Womersley J (1974). Body fat assessed from total body density and its estimation from skinfold thickness: Measurements on 481 men and women aged from 16 to 72 years. *British Journal of Nutrition*, 32(1): 77–97.

Elmer SJ, Durocher JJ (2020). Moving student research forward during the COVID-19 pandemic. *Advances in Physiology Education*, 44(4): 741–3.

Siri WE (1961). Body composition from fluid space and density. In J Brozek, A Hanschel (Eds.), *Techniques for Measuring Body Composition* (223–44). Washington, DC: National Academy of Science.

Skelton J (1994). Analysis of the structure of original research papers: An aid to writing original papers for Publication. *British Journal of General Practice*, 44: 455–9.

Skelton JR, Edwards (2000). The function of the discussion section in academic medical writing. *BMJ*, 320: 1269–70.

Smith PM, Doherty M, Drake D, Price MJ (2004). The influence of step and ramp type protocols on the attainment of peak physiological responses during arm crank ergometry. *International Journal of Sports Medicine*, 25(8): 616–21.

Smith PM, Price, MJ (2007). Upper-body exercise. In EM Winter, AM Jones, RCR Davidson, PD Bromley, TH Mercer (Eds.), *Sport and Exercise Physiology Testing Guidelines* (138–44). London: Routledge.

Speed HD, Andersen MB (2000). What exercise and sport scientists don't understand. *Journal of Science and Medicine in Sport*, 3(1): 84–92.

Spencer M, Fitzsimons M, Dawson B, Bishop D, Goodman C (2006). Reliability of a repeated-sprint test for field-hockey. *Journal of Science and Medicine in Sport*, 9: 181–4.

Squires BP (1990). Structured abstracts of original research and review articles. *Canadian Medical Association Journal*, 143(7): 619–22.

Stone J, Gurunathan U, Glass K, Munn Z, Tugwell P, Doi SAR (2019). Stratification by quality induced selection bias in a meta-analysis of clinical trials. *Journal of Clinical Epidemiology*, 107: 51–9. https://doi.org/10.1016/j.jclinepi.2018.11.015

Sunderland C, Nevill M (2003). Effect of the menstrual cycle on performance of intermittent, high-intensity shuttle running in a hot environment. *European Journal of Applied Physiology*, 88(4–5): 345–52.

Sunderland C, Nevill ME (2005). High-intensity intermittent running and field hockey skill performance in the heat. *Journal of Sports Science*, 23(5): 531–40.

Suriano R, Edge J, Bishop D (2010). Effects of cycle strategy and fibre composition on muscle glycogen depletion pattern and subsequent running economy. *British Journal of Sports Medicine*, 44(6): 443–8.

Svedenhag J, Sjödin B (1985). Maximal and submaximal oxygen uptakes and blood lactate levels in elite male middle- and long-distance runners. *International Journal of Sports Medicine*, 5(5): 255–61.

Tabachnick BG, Fidell LS (1996). *Using Multivariate Statistics* (3rd ed.). New York: Harper Collins.

Taylor and Francis (2021). *Search Engine Optimisation for Journal Articles*. https://authorservices.taylorandfrancis.com/research-impact/search-engine-optimization-for-academic-articles/

Teo W, Newton MJ, McGuigan MR (2011). Circadian rhythms in exercise performance: Implications for hormonal and muscular adaptation. *Journal of Sports Science & Medicine*, 10(4): 600–6.

Thompson B (1999) Statistical significance tests, effect size reporting and the vain pursuit of pseudo-objectivity. *Theory and Psychology*, 9(2): 191–6.

Thomas JR, Nelson JK (2001). *Research Methods in Physical Activity* (4th ed.). Champaign IL: Human Kinetics.

Thompson A, Taylor BN (2008). *The International System of Units*. NIST Special Publication 330. Gaithersburg, MD: National Institute of Science and Technology.

Thun E, Bjorvatn B, Flo E, Harris A, Pallesen S (2015). Sleep, circadian rhythms, and athletic performance. *Sleep Medicine Reviews*, 23: 1–9. https://doi.org/10.1016/j.smrv.2014.11.003

Turk C, Kirkman J (1989). *Effective Writing: Improving Scientific Technical and Business Communication*. London: Spon.

Tyler C, Sunderland C (2009). The effect of ambient temperature on the reliability of a preloaded treadmill time-trial. *International Journal of Sports Medicine*, 29: 812–16.

Vincent WJ (1999). *Statistics in Kinesiology* (2nd ed.). Champaign IL: Human Kinetics.

Vrbik I, Sporiš G, Štefan L, Madić D, Trajković N, Valantine I, Milanović Z (2017). The influence of familiarization on physical fitness test results in primary school-aged children. *Pediatric Exercise Science*, 29(2): 278–84. https://doi.org/10.1123/pes.2016-0091

Wells WA (2006). Unpleasant surprises: How the Introduction has wandered into the discussion. *The Journal of Cell Biology*, 174(6): 741.

Westfall PH (2014). Kurtosis as peakedness, 1905–2014. R.I.P. *American Statistician*, 68(3): 191–5. https://doi.org/10.1080/00031305.2014.917055.

Wieseler B, McGauran N (2010). Reporting a systematic review. *Chest*, 137(5): 1240–6.

Wilson JM (2003). Gantt charts: A centenary appreciation. *European Journal of Operational Research*, 149(2), 430–7.

Winter E (2005). Writing: Bartlett revisited. *Journal of Sports Science*, 23(8): 773.

Winter E, Eston RG, Lamb KL (2001). Statistical analyses in the physiology of exercise and kinanthropometry. *Journal of Sports Sciences*, 19(10): 761–75. https://doi.org/10.1080/026404101317015429

Winter EM, Maughan RJ (2009). Requirements for ethics approvals. *Journal of Sports Science*, 27(10): 985.

Yap BW, Sim CH (2011). Comparisons of various types of normality tests. *Journal of Statistical Computation and Simulation*, 81(12): 2141–55. https://doi.org/10.1080/00949655.2010.520163

Young AJ, Sawka MN, Epstein Y, Decristofano B, Pandolf KB (1987). Cooling different body surfaces during upper and lower body exercise. *Journal of Applied Physiology*, 63: 1218–23.

Young JM, Solomon MJ (2009). How to critically appraise an article. *Nature Clinical Practice Gastroenterology & Hepatology*, 6: 82–91 https://doi.org/10.1038/ncpgasthep1331

Zeng X, Zhang Y, Kwong JS, Zhang C, Li S, Sun F, Niu Y, Du L (2015). The methodological quality assessment tools for preclinical and clinical studies, systematic review and meta-analysis, and clinical practice guideline: A systematic review. *Journal of Evidence-based Medicine*, 8(1): 2–10. https://doi.org/10.1111/jebm.12141

Index

Page numbers in italics refer to figures. Page numbers in bold refer to tables.